John Marston of the Middle Temple

John Marston

An Elizabethan Dramatist in His Social Setting

of the Middle Temple

Philip J. Finkelpearl

Harvard University Press
Cambridge, Massachusetts
1969

© Copyright 1969 by the President and Fellows of Harvard College
Distributed in Great Britain by Oxford University Press, London

Publication of this book has been aided by a grant from the
Hyder Edward Rollins Fund

Library of Congress Catalog Card Number 69-12722
Printed in the United States of America

To Bernard F. Huppé

Preface

Primarily this book is a detailed examination of the Elizabethan poet and dramatist John Marston (1576–1634), but it is also a study of the milieu in which he lived and worked. During most of his career as a writer Marston resided at one of the Inns of Court, the Middle Temple. As I shall try to demonstrate, a consideration of the interaction between his sensibility and the particular environment of the Inns provides a valuable way of assessing Marston's purposes and of defining his achievements.

For nearly one hundred fifty years a significant segment of England's gentry came to the Inns to study law or to live in London, or both. An astonishing number of important writers had this experience. The fact that the Inns, with their concentration of wealth, cultural interests, and learning, constituted a cohesive and influential milieu in London, that they were, as Ben Jonson said, the "Noblest Nurseries of Humanity and Liberty in the Kingdom," is very widely recognized and has been the subject of much investigation by political and cultural historians. In a general way, literary historians have also discussed the importance of the Inns, but no one has made a detailed effort to define their literary traditions or to describe the nature of the Inns as a home for writers. In the first part of this book, I have tried to supply this need, to provide the context for a deeper comprehension of Ben Jonson's description.

In attempting some kind of reconstruction of the prevailing ethos and atmosphere at the Inns in the late Elizabethan and early Jacobean period, I discuss the development and formal operation of the Inns as institutions, but I make no attempt to go beyond an elementary treatment of these matters. My prime interest is in the sociological makeup and in the manners, morals, politics, and tastes of this restricted world. As a means of discovering shared interests and assumptions, I study carefully some of the Inns' Christmas revels. Here again I must stress that although I use some of the same materials as does A. Wigfall Green in his book *The Inns of Court and Early English Drama* and although I present some new material about the history and production of these entertainments, my interest is not in the relationship of the revels to the institutional history of the Inns. The focus is always on what such material can reveal about the assumptions and characteristics of the Inns' writers and writing.

With this background I proceed in the second part of the book to make a thorough study of the works of John Marston.

T. S. Eliot's essay in 1932 accurately summarized Marston's place among Elizabethan dramatists: "Marston has enjoyed less attention, from either scholars or critics, than any of his contemporaries of equal or greater rank; and for both scholars and critics he remains a territory of unexplored riches and risks. The position of most of his contemporaries is pretty well settled; one cannot go very far wrong in one's estimate of the dramatists with whom Marston worked; but about Marston a wide divergency of opinion is still possible. His greater defects are such as anyone can see; his merits are still a matter for controversy."

Recently, a modest interest in Marston has been developing. We now have an excellent edition of the poems, a complete edition of the plays is being prepared by Gerald Smith of the State University of New York, and editions of individual plays have been published in the Regents Renaissance Drama Series. There has been one book on Marston in English as well as several from the Continent, articles are appearing, and dissertations are under way. Nonetheless Eliot's estimate of the difficulty in writing about Marston still holds, except that even his "greater defects" are also a matter for controversy. Where there is no *consensus gentium,* there is no rapid way of defining one's positions and there is no substitute for pedestrian methods.

What distinguishes my study from previous ones is the attempt to show how Marston's works are related to his residence at the Inns of Court. Thus the relationship of the second part of the book to the first is one of loose, even intermittent, but necessary dependence. Inevitably, the effect of a milieu varies from one work to the next. At times, Marston's plays verge on intramural entertainment for his colleagues at the Inns; at times, notably in *The Malcontent,* the relationship to a specific setting is only tangential. But, as I try to demonstrate, its effect is at all times discernible, and, I would claim, an awareness of its existence is crucial for a comprehension of Marston's work as a whole. I should mention that I did not conceive this approach a priori; it grew out of a sense of dissatisfaction with my doctoral dissertation (Harvard University, 1954), in which I described Marston's works without much concern for his precise relationship to the world in which he lived. Once I was able to define the missing element with some precision, I found that I could account for many puzzling aspects of his work and became aware of elements which had been ignored completely. Specifically, I have found Marston more concerned with topical, personal, and political matters and less of a rebel in morals and language than previous scholars have claimed.

In addition to what my study says about Marston, it also suggests an alternative way of looking at some of the material which Alfred Harbage handled in his learned and influential study *Shakespeare and the Rival Traditions.* He, too, devotes much attention to Marston, treating him as the prime example of a "private theater" dramatist. I admire Harbage's attempt to deal with the shaping force of the audience and his insistence on the differences between two theatrical traditions. But when it comes to an interpretation of Marston's work and, hence, of his audience, I can only say that my disagreement could scarcely be greater. He finds tasteless and harmful what I find witty or justifiable dramatically. "About Marston a wide divergency of opinion is still possible."

I must add an explanatory note about my quotations from Marston's plays. I have used H. Harvey Wood's edition, *The Plays of John Marston* (3 vols.; Edinburgh, 1934–1939). Because this text has no line numbers, I have been forced to locate quotations solely by reference to page numbers in the appropriate volume. I should also mention that I have not felt it necessary to include a bibliography of the Inns of Court material consulted in view of the appearance of D. S. Bland's excellent "Checklist of Drama at the Inns of Court," *Research Opportunities in Renaissance Drama,* 9 (1966), 47–61.

For advice and encouragement at various stages in the composition of this work, I would like to thank Professors Harry T. Levin, Max Bluestone, Dean T. Mace, and especially Professor Herschel Baker who, amid his many tasks and responsibilities, gave the manuscript a characteristically painstaking inspection. I also wish to make grateful acknowledgment to Vassar College for the Faculty Fellowship which enabled me to complete this work.

P. J. F.

Poughkeepsie, New York
June 1968

Acknowledgments

My thanks are due to the following publishers whose generous permissions have made it possible for me to quote from copyrighted materials:

The Clarendon Press, Oxford, for quotations from E. K. Chambers, *The Elizabethan Stage* (1923); *The Works of Ben Jonson*, ed. C. H. Herford, Percy and Evelyn Simpson (1925–1952); C. S. Lewis, *English Literature in the Sixteenth Century* (1954).

Oliver and Boyd Ltd., Edinburgh, for quotations from *The Plays of John Marston*, ed. H. Harvey Wood (1934–1939).

Liverpool University Press for quotations from *The Poems of John Marston*, ed. Arnold Davenport (1961), Liverpool English Texts and Studies, General Editor Kenneth Muir.

Contents

One

The Milieu of the Inns of Court

I The Inns of Court
in the Late Sixteenth Century

The origin of the four law schools in London, the so-called Inns of Court,[1] is shrouded in uncertainty and legend. There were students of the common, as well as of the canon, law in London in the twelfth century, and by the fourteenth century common law students had banded into groups for formal study and domicile. By the fifteenth century something like the modern organization of the four Inns of Court and their affiliated

[1] According to Sir John Fortescue, they were called Inns of Court "because the Students in them, did there, not only study the Laws, but use such other exercises as might make them the more serviceable to the King's Court." Quoted by William Dugdale, *Origines Juridiciales* (London, 1671), p. 141.

Inns of Chancery had taken shape. Each Inn was a separate institution; but their similarity of purpose and organization, their physical proximity, and their common supervision by the legal authorities of the government gave the appearance of four colleges in the "Third University of England," as Sir George Buck named the City of London in 1615.[2]

Two of the Inns, the Inner Temple and the Middle Temple, occupied an area and some of the buildings originally constructed by the Knights Templar; hence their names. Though they shared the Temple Church and its "Master," they were in every other respect totally distinct bodies and apparently always had been. A third, Gray's Inn, had originally been the residence of the Lords Gray of Wilton. The fourth, Lincoln's Inn, was built upon the ruins of the Blackfriars and given to the legal society by the Earl of Lincoln.

Each of the Inns had jurisdiction over certain Inns of Chancery, so-called because the clerks of the Chancery had resided there: Thavie's (or Davy's) and Furnivall's Inns attached to Lincoln's Inn; Clifford's, Clement's, and Lyon's Inns attached to the Inner Temple; New and Strand Inns attached to the Middle Temple; Staple and Barnard's Inns attached to Gray's Inn. At one time, apparently, these Inns of Chancery were of equal importance with the Inns of Court, but by the sixteenth century (perhaps earlier) they had become preparatory institutions for younger law students and residences for attorneys and law clerks.

In Sir John Fortescue's fifteenth-century description, the Inns stood "between *Westminster* and the city of *London,* which, as to all necessaries and conveniences of life is the best supplied of any city or town in the kingdom: the place of study is not in the heart of the city itself, where the great confluence and multitude of the inhabitants might disturb them in their studies; but in a private place, separate and distinct by itself, in the suburbs, near to the Courts of Justice aforesaid, that the students, at their leisure, may daily and duly attend, with the greatest ease and convenience." [3] This ideal isolation no longer existed in the late sixteenth century. London had reached out and surrounded the Inns. Across the river was Southwark with its playhouses and stews, readily accessible by boat from the Temple stairs. Next door to the Temple was the old Blackfriars liberty occupied by debtors, cony catchers, and sometimes private theaters. Another immediate neighbor during the 1590's was the Earl of Essex's establishment, where on one occasion, at least, the Templars could watch real history and tragedy unfold. In short, the Inns of Court were located in the heart of Elizabethan London.

In the last decades of the sixteenth century, the Inns of Court were filled to capacity and expanding yearly. In 1574 they had seven hundred sixty-nine members and had admitted seven hundred thirty new members over the past five years — roughly the same total Fortescue had estimated one hundred years earlier.[4] By the end of the century, there were said to be 1,040 men in residence (1,703 including those in the Inns of Chancery),[5] and the total of admissions for the last five years of the century (a corroborating index, as I have found) was 1,096 men: a thirty percent increase in attendance that was achieved only by extensive building and renovation. In a city whose population has been variously estimated between 100,000 and 200,-000,[6] this is not a large number. Nevertheless it was the largest single group of literate and cultured men in London. The only other comparable group, those who lived at the Court, must have been much smaller. Cheyney says that Elizabeth's entire Royal Household from Queen to scullery maid consisted of 1,500 people.[7]

Ideally, the makeup of the student body of the Inns conformed to Fortescue's description written in the fifteenth century: "In these greater inns a student cannot well be maintained under *eight and twenty pounds* a year: and, if he have a servant to wait on him (as for the most part they have) the expence is proportionably more: for this reason, the students are sons to persons of quality; those of an inferior rank not being able to bear the expences of maintaining and educating their children in this way. As to the merchants, they seldom care to lessen their stock in trade by being at such large yearly expences. So that there is scarce to be found, throughout the kingdom, an eminent lawyer, who is not a gentleman by birth and fortune; *consequently they have a greater regard for their*

---

[4] F. A. Inderwick, ed., *Calendar of the Inner Temple Records* (London, n.d.), I, 468–469. The figure for the five-year period is my calculation.

[5] Henry B. Wheatley, *London, Past and Present* (London, 1891), II, 261, and Hugh H. L. Bellot, *The Temple* (London, 1922), p. 28.

[6] Alfred Harbage, *Shakespeare's Audience* (New York, 1961), p. 41, estimates that the population was 160,000 around 1605.

[7] Edward P. Cheyney, *History of England from the Defeat of the Armada to the Death of Elizabeth* (New York, 1926), I, 17.

character and honour than those bred in another way." [8]
Whatever the truth at the time Fortescue was writing, the sociological and economic background of Inns of Court men at
the end of the sixteenth century was not quite so homogeneous.
We can find many admissions in the 1590's like that to the
Middle Temple of John Borlas in 1595, "son and heir of Edmund, citizen and mercer of London," and of Edmund Double-
day in 1598, "son and heir of Henry of London, merchant." [9]
William Harrison was nearer the truth, although also exaggerat-
ing, in claiming that the yeoman class had become so wealthy
that "many of them are able and do buy the lands of unthrifty
gentlemen, and often sending their sons to the schools, to the
universities, and the inns of court, or otherwise leaving them
sufficient lands whereupon they may live without labour, do
make them by these means to become gentlemen." [10] As late as
the time of King James an effort was made to limit admission
at the Inns to those who could demonstrate a pedigree for at
least three generations, but Elizabethan society was much too
fluid for such a requirement to be workable.

Nevertheless it remains roughly accurate to say that the Inns
of Court were largely populated by the sons of the landed
gentry. According to Lawrence Stone, "The Inns were at all
times more frequented by the gentry than both the universities
put together." [11] To a much smaller and diminishing extent
the nobility sent its sons there.[12] The average age at admission
was about seventeen, and about seventy percent of the membership ranged from seventeen to thirty. At the same time,
there was a wide range of ages among the residents, from the
youngest "puisnes" to the "ancients" who occupied the same
room during term time throughout their lives. It was not unusual for a lawyer-father to have as his chambermate his own
son: such was the case with John Marston, the dramatist, whose
father was one of the Benchers of the Middle Temple.

The educational background of the students admitted to the
Inns was by no means uniform. During a period I have studied
closely, 1587 to 1603, the records of the Middle Temple mention 1,070 names, of whom forty-three percent definitely spent
some time at Oxford or Cambridge. Allowing for defects in the
admissions records, particularly those of Oxford, it seems fair

---

[8] *De Laudibus*, p. 183.
[9] *Middle Temple Records*, ed. Charles H. Hopwood (London, 1904), I, 355, 384.
[10] Quoted by John B. Black, *Reign of Elizabeth* (Oxford, 1959), p. 216.
[11] *The Crisis of the Aristocracy* (Oxford, 1965), p. 690.
[12] Ibid., Appendix XXXV, p. 793.

to say that about half the students at the Middle Temple at the end of the sixteenth century had first spent some time at one of the universities. About ten percent of those who came from a university also enrolled at an Inn of Chancery. John Donne followed such a course, entering Thavie's Inn before going to Lincoln's Inn. Of those who did not go to a college first, about ten percent prepared themselves at one of the Inns of Chancery. I suspect that students would have been considered too young to enter one of the Inns of Court directly from a grammar school, but there is no way of determining this with certainty.

Scrutiny of the admissions to all of the Inns over a twenty-five year period reveals another significant pattern in the makeup of the student body. As in the colleges, students tended to cluster at one Inn or another on the basis of geographical origin. Thus the largest, Gray's Inn, had a very high percentage, twenty-three percent, of students from the six northern counties; no other Inn had more than nine percent. Of such concentrations, the most extreme occurred in the Middle Temple: forty-seven percent of its students from 1574 to 1599 came from ten counties in the south and southwest. It was also the favorite Inn for Warwickshire: thirty-one admitted between 1587 and 1603, while the three other Inns admitted a total of twenty.[13] Family and neighborhood traditions account for this practice. We find son following father, neighbor going up along with neighbor, nephew following uncle, as young William Ashcomb did: "A.D. 1607. I went to London and was admitted into the Innes of Courte, the Middle Temple, where I remember the tresurer, a grave man, for my uncle William Ayshcombe's sake abated me 20 l. in my admittance, saying — We must nourishe the line of good studentes."[14] As a result, each Inn must have had some sort of individual character and a tendency, inherent in all collegiate life, toward clannishness.

From 1550 until 1700 (at least), a period of residence at one of the Inns of Court was a normal stage in the education of the sons of the gentry and would-be gentry. The reasons for this custom are various and interlocking. With the triumph of the common law and the vast increase in litigation during the Tudor Reformation, the legal profession became one of

[13] All of these calculations are my own. For a list of Middle Templars from Warwickshire at this period, see Leslie Hotson, *Shakespeare's Sonnets Dated and Other Essays* (New York, 1949), pp. 45–46. See also Christopher Whitfield, "Some of Shakespeare's Contemporaries in the Middle Temple," *Notes and Queries*, 211 (1966), 122–125, 283–287, 363–369, 443–448.

[14] *Historical Manuscript Commission Report 10*, Appendix, Part 6, p. 83.

the surest paths to wealth. The law student John Manningham recorded a truism when he said, "The posterity of lawyers hath more flourished then that either of the clergy or citisens." [15] Even if one did not intend a legal career, it was practical for anyone with property to have some acquaintance with the law. As one contemporary said, the gentry did not feel "their sons duly educated till they have passed some time in some of the houses of Law, tho they never design them to practice it, as seems to be evident from the many who comence Students and never are, and probably never design'd to be, Called to the Barr, and many others who take upon them the degree of an Utter Barrister, without any design to practice the law." [16]

For the study of the law, the Inns contained no professional teachers, nor was there any group corresponding exactly to the fellows of a college. The Inns, it should be understood, were societies; their members were either apprentices or qualified, active practitioners who used their chambers as law offices during term time. One of the duties of those already admitted to the bar was the tuition of the younger members of the society. Thus it would be fairly accurate to place the Inns of Court as an institution somewhere between the craft guilds and the universities. With their commons, chapel, and residential living, they resembled the universities physically. At the same time, they were like any other guild in which apprentices were introduced by their masters to the mysteries of a craft.

The organization of the Inns, all nearly identical, was rigidly hierarchical. At the bottom was the Inner Barrister, who had to submit to traditional "freshman" rituals: among these, a long gown and round, flat cap worn to church and to the dining hall where he ate at special tables named "Clerks' Commons." After two years he could proceed to "Masters' Commons," which was divided into places for Inner Barristers, Outer (or "Utter") Barristers, and Benchers. If the Inner Barrister dutifully performed the required exercises, he could be admitted after seven years as an Utter Barrister, that is, a qualified member of the bar. From these ranks were chosen the governing members of the Inn, the Benchers, who held so-called Parliaments at which students were admitted, expelled, fined,

[15] *Diary of John Manningham*, ed. John Bruce, Camden Society Publication 99 (London, 1868), p. 43.

[16] William Downing, *Observations on the Constitution, Customs, and Usuage of the Honourable Society of the Middle Temple . . . for the Use of Charles Worsley* (London, 1896), p. 43.

and the other business of the Inn was conducted.[17] From these ranks also were chosen the Readers, whose task it was (in Dugdale's words) "to *reade,* expound, and declare some Estatute openly unto all the Company of the House, in one of the two principal times of their learning, which they call the *Grand Vacations.*" [18] (These learning periods of about three weeks each were called vacations because they occurred during the Easter and summer intervals between legal terms.) After the Reader expounded his statute, the youngest Utter Barrister among his auditors argued one of the questions, followed in order of seniority by the rest of the Utter Barristers and Benchers, after which the Reader replied.

Another type of formal instruction was the mock disputation or moot, conducted every night during Grand Vacation and twice a week in term. The "young Lerners" pleaded in "homely Law-French" [19] on some doubtful question in the law before three Benchers. Afterwards two Utter Barristers took up the point and argued on opposite sides, also in Law-French. Then the Benchers declared their opinions in English. A variant of this, done every day of the year according to Dugdale, took place after dinner and supper. Inner Barristers and Utter Barristers sat three and three opposite one another, and one of them put questions to the others. This was called "bolting." In term, students supplemented this training by attending the Court at Westminster and the Guildhall, where they sat in a special section reserved for their use, called in Law-French "le cribbe." Moreover students could read certain law texts in Latin and the classic compilations of cases made by Brooke, Perkins, Plowden, Littleton, and Dyer. There were no examinations at the Inns. Apparently the major consideration in promotion to the Utter Bar was the quantity of moots in which the student had engaged. Thus mere diligence, "plodding" as some called it, could gain one admission to the bar.

Dugdale also asserts that students studied not only the laws, "but use such other exercises as might make them the more serviceable to the King's Court." [20] In Fortescue's day the students learned "to dance, to sing, to play on Instruments on the ferial days; and to study Divinity on the Festival." [21] By the

---

[17] I am generalizing from the separate accounts of the various Inns in Dugdale's *Origines.*
[18] Dugdale, p. 194.
[19] Ibid.
[20] Ibid., p. 141.
[21] Ibid.

late sixteenth century tuition in these skills was no longer formally conducted at the Inns, but such exercises were pursued on a less formal basis through academies and tutors.[22] The ideal persisted of producing not merely a well-trained lawyer but a True Gentleman.

The version I have just given of education at the Inns of Court was the official one, formulated by Fortescue and perpetuated by Dugdale. But Dugdale does make a candid concession, although it rather tarnishes his idealized picture of smooth-running, well-regulated law schools, the perfect training ground for future courtiers and governors: "There is none there, that be compelled to learn, and they that are learners, for the most part, have their Studies and places of learning so sett, that they are much troubled with the noise of walking and communication of them that be no learners: and in the Terme time they are so unquieted by Clyents and servants of Clyents, that resort to such as are Attorneys and Practisers, that the Students may as quietly study in the open streets, as in their Studies." [23] This does not sound like an atmosphere for serious study, and serious study was far from the minds of many of the young gentlemen. In fact, during the last thirty years of the sixteenth century, only fifteen percent of those admitted to the Inns of Court pursued their studies far enough to be admitted to the bar.[24]

Of course, as with any school, many students entered the Inns only to discover that they were interested in something else. Passing through the Middle Temple at the end of the sixteenth century were such figures as William Lower, the astronomer; Peter Maunsell, Gresham Professor of Physics from 1607 to 1615; and Bartholomew Gosnell, the explorer. Among such, Herbert Croft is a notable example. After years of orthodox pursuits (M.P., 1588; admitted to the Middle Temple, 1594; knighted, 1603), he became a Catholic convert at the age of fifty-two and died at Douay, having written some Catholic apologetics. On the other hand, the learned anti-Catholic Puritan, Humfrey Lynd, was also a member, admitted in 1601. For a more bizarre deviation from the law we may note the lives of

---

[22] See Walter Houghton, *The Formation of Thomas Fuller's Holy and Profane States* (Cambridge, Eng., 1938), pp. 120–121.

[23] Dugdale, p. 195.

[24] My calculation. It should not be inferred that this produced a shortage of lawyers. During the period from 1574 to 1602 the Middle Temple admitted 241 and the Inner Temple, 175 members to the Bar. The Middle Temple Parliament constantly complained that too many were being admitted and that standards were not being maintained.

Robert and Thomas Winter. Both at the Middle Temple from 1590 to 1592, they devoted their lives almost wholly to Catholic plotting, and both were executed in 1606 for their deep complicity in the Gunpowder Plot.

But the main pursuits of most of the young men were not serious, treasonous, or scholastic. For a few, admission to an Inn was merely a convenient solution to London's severe housing shortage.[25] For many, probably the majority, the Inns were a finishing school: a place to mingle with the "creame o'th kingdome," [26] to sample the glories of the great capital city, and perhaps incidentally to acquire some useful knowledge, including the law. It is difficult to ascertain exactly when such a use of the Inns arose, although it was essentially a product of Elizabeth's reign. The Middle Temple's Parliament expressed concern about the tendency as early as 1574: "None hereafter admitted shall enjoy any Chamber or be in Commons unless he doth Exercise moots, and other Exercises for learning within three years after his admission, and be allowed a Student or Inner Barrister by the Bench." [27] Forty years later the Privy Council issued an edict which sheds much light on conditions at the Inns: "For that the institution of these Societies was ordained chiefly for the profession of the law and in the second degree for the Education of the sons and youth of riper years of the Nobility and Gentry of this Realm, and in no sort for the lodging or abode of the Gentlemen of the Country, which if it should be suffered were to disparage the said Societies, and to turn them from hospitia to diversoria, It is Ordered that no Knight or Gentleman foreigners, or discontinuers shall be admitted or allowed to lodge in any of the Societies aforesaid, or be in Commons, except he be an allowed Utter Barrister." [28] This was as unsuccessful as the earlier order. At least through the eighteenth century, the Inns of Court were, for many, "diversoria" rather than "hospitia."

[25] Henry Wotton, the famous ambassador and Provost of Eton, was admitted to the Middle Temple at the special request of the Reader in August, 1595. Shortly thereafter, he was living in Essex House as a secretary to the Earl. Admission by the Reader in this instance appears to have been a matter of obliging a neighbor while his house was temporarily overcrowded. See also Milton's plan in 1637 "of migrating into some Inn of the Lawyers, wherever there is a pleasant and shady walk, because there I shall have a more convenient habitation among some companions, if I wish to remain at home, and more suitable head-quarters if I choose to make excursions elsewhere." (*Life Records of John Milton*, ed. J. Milton French [New Brunswick, N.J.], I [1949], 349.)

[26] Francis Lenton, *Innes of Court Anagrammatist* (London, 1634), sig. A2r.

[27] Downing, *Observations*, p. 34.

[28] Ibid., p. 36.

A large element of wealthy young men with time on their hands inevitably drew the attention of the satirists. A stereotype of the "Inns-a-Court" man emerged, of which the following portrait is a fair sample:

> Publius student at the common law,
> Oft leaves his bookes, and for his recreation,
> To parish garden doth himselfe withdraw,
> Where he is ravisht with such delectation,
> As downe amongst the dogges and beares he goes,
> Where whiles he skipping cries to head to head,
> His sattin doublet and his velvet hose,
> Are all with spittle from above bespread.
> Then is he like his fathers country Hall,
> Stinking with dogges, and muted all with hawkes,
> And rightly too, on him this filth doth fall,
> Which for such filthy sports his bookes forsake,
>   Leaving old Ployden, Diar, and Brooke alone,
>   To see old Harry Hunkes and Sakersone.[29]

This epigram written by John Davies while a member of the Middle Temple is full of firsthand observations and reliable details. Publius is dressed in violation of the Middle Temple Parliament's prohibitions against elaborate clothing; the names of the authors and the bears are accurate; and his origins in a country hall are related to his tastes in recreation. Publius is a comic figure partly because his father does have a hall in the country. Although he ignores old Ployden, he will return to the hall, serve as a J.P., and lie to his cronies about "the feats he hath done about Turnbull St." [30] in his youthful days at the Inns.

But a young man alone in London and without adequate financial resources could easily be ruined, as the satirists and moralists frequently pointed out. Such is the burden of a long moral poem by Francis Lenton, written in 1629, called "The Young Gallants Whirligigg." [31] It deserves some attention because Lenton managed to include in one connected sequence a very accurate picture of the mores of a segment of the young men as well as many of the adverse attitudes toward them.

---

[29] *Poems of Sir John Davies*, ed. Clare Howard (New York, 1941), pp. 55–56.
[30] Shakespeare, *2 Henry IV*, III,ii,329–330. Falstaff is referring to Robert Shallow of Clement's Inn.
[31] F[rancis] L[enton], *The Young Gallants Whirligigg: or Youths Reakes* (London, 1629). Page references in the text are to this edition.

Lenton tells his story by inventing a case history which he begins in his hero's earliest days in grammar school,

> Where in processe of time he grew to bee
> A pretty Scholler; after tooke degree
> I'th *Universitie,* as it was fit,
> Whose Tutor said hee had a ready wit,
> And well could argue by old *Ramus* layes,
> And in the thirteene Fallacies had praise. (p. 3)

Under the strict regimen of collegiate life he makes a promising start:

> His tutor was the man that kept him in,
> That hee ran not into excesse of Sinne.
> His literature fill'd his Parents hearts
> With joy, and comfort, hoping his deserts
> Might purchase credit and a good report,
> And therefore send him to the *Innes of Court,*
> To study Lawes, and never to surcease,
> Till he be made a Justice for the peace. (p. 3)

But we must remember, as C. S. Lewis has stated, that "in respect of the students' ages, the life lived, the temptations, and the intellectual stimulus, the inn of court was to them very much what the university is to their successors: the university was more like one's public school." [32] The Inns, Lenton points out, were situated in the very nursery of sin:

> For when the Country cannot finde out sinnes
> To fit his humour, *London* doth invent
> Millions of vices, that are incident
> To his aspiring minde. (pp. 3–4)

The gallant begins his decline in a classic way: he abandons the study of law and becomes addicted to literature:

> No, no, good man, hee reades not *Littleton,*
> But *Don Quix Zot,* or els *The Knight o' th Sun*:
> And if you chance unto him put a Case,
> Hee'll say perhaps you offer him disgrace. . . .
> Instead of *Perkins* pedlers French, he sayes
> He better loves Ben: Johnsons booke of Playes,

[32] *English Literature in the Sixteenth Century* (Oxford, 1954), p. 61.

> But that therein of wit he findes such plenty,
> That hee scarce understands a Jest of twenty. (p. 4)

The next inevitable step in his path downward is women, and he woos them in the formulaic language of quasi-Petrarchan love poetry:

> Hee now courts every thing hee heares or sees,
> With more delight then Lawyers take their fees.
> And when he is farre distant from his Faire,
> (Through ardencie) he complements with ayre,
> Wishing (Camelion-like) that hee might live
> Inclos'd within the breath which she doth give:
> All amorous conceits he now commends,
> And for the same his mony vainly spends:
> He now scornes Prose, and on his Mistress Name
> Writes an Acrostique, or some Anagramme,
> To shew his wit. (pp. 6–7)

Like most Inns of Court men,

> Your Theaters hee daily doth frequent
> (Except the intermitted time of Lent)
> Treasuring up within his memory
> The amorous toyes of every Comedy
> With deepe delight. (p. 7)

Inns of Court men were always reputed to be among the figures who sat conspicuously on the stage:

> The Cockpit heretofore would serve his wit,
> But now upon the Fryers stage hee'll sit,
> It must be so, though this expensive foole
> Should pay an angell for a paltry stoole. (p. 13)

Part of the reason for sitting on the stage was to display his fancy clothes, for which Inns' men were said to be always in debt to their tailors:

> His silken garments, and his sattin robe
> That hath so often visited the Globe,
> And all his spangled rare perfum'd attires
> Which once so glistred in the Torchy Fryers,
> Must to the Broakers to compound his debt. (p. 16)

Finally, utterly ruined, he looks back regretfully on all his "pampered daies," which included

> His Oysters, Lobstars, Caviare, and Crabs,
> With which he feasted his contagious drabs;
> Oringoes, Hartichoakes, Potatoe pies,
> Provocatives unto their luxuries. (p. 19)

Down to the last aphrodisiac Lenton has catalogued the vices of Inns-a-Court men as they were described in numberless plays, satires, prose invectives, and characters.

Although in part conventional, Lenton's account is generally confirmed by the great and sober historian Clarendon, who gives a very similar description of life at the Middle Temple: "great license [was] used of all kinds, in clothes, in diet, in gambling; and all kinds of expenses equally carried on, by men who had fortunes of their own to support it, and by others, who, having nothing of their own, cared not what they spent, whilst they could find credit; so that there was never an age, in which, in so short a time, so many young gentlemen, who had not experience in the world, or some good tutelar angel to protect them, were insensibly and suddenly overwhelmed in that sea of wine, and women, and quarrels, and gaming, which almost overspread the whole kingdom, and the nobility and gentry thereof." [33]

Life at the Inns may have had pitfalls, but there were also rich opportunities and rewards. Clarendon describes three circles of friends he cultivated while still a young student at the Middle Temple. First, there were business associates, all lawyers from the Middle Temple, many of them distinguished. His roommate and a lifelong friend was the son of John Bramston, Chief Justice of the King's Bench. [34] A second circle included older men who lived in London, many of whom were or had been at one of the Inns: John Selden, Thomas May, Thomas Carew, Charles Cotton, and Ben Jonson. A third group were contemporaries who lived in the country and whom he visited between terms: Sir Lucius Carey, Sir Francis Wenman, Sidney Godolphin, and Edward Waller, among them. Apparently Clarendon missed the path to ruin; so doubtless did many

---

[33] *Life of Edward, Earl of Clarendon . . . Written by Himself* (Oxford, 1827), I, 76.

[34] Another intermittent roommate was William Davenant, the playwright, who lived in Clarendon's rooms although he was not really a member of the Inn. See Alfred Harbage, *William Davenant* (Philadelphia, 1935), p. 36.

others. Otherwise it is scarcely credible that the gentry would have continued to enroll their sons in such abundance.

Naturally many members followed an orthodox course and for this received high rewards. There is no need to list all the future judges, high government officials, and successful barristers who were receiving their training at the Middle Temple at this time, but the career of John Bramston (1577–1654) may serve as an illustration of the pattern which fathers would hold up to their reveling sons. The son of a lawyer who was still a member of the Middle Temple when he was admitted, Bramston took a degree at Jesus College, Cambridge, before coming to the Middle Temple in 1593. He participated in the social life of his Inn, but applied himself to his studies, and in due course became an Utter Barrister. Then the clients and the honors began to arrive. He was counsel to the University of Cambridge in 1607, was appointed Reader at the Middle Temple in 1623–24 (his topic being the statute of limitations of 32 Henry VIII, his Reader's Feast costing no less than £500), promoted to Serjeant at Law in 1634, became a knight the same year, and finally Chief Justice of the King's Bench in 1635. But all was not smooth in Bramston's career; this was a period when one had to choose sides. At first he seemed to be in opposition to the King. He was an advocate in 1627 for Darnel and Heveningham when they were sent to the Fleet for refusing to contribute to a forced loan. In 1629 he was one of the counsel for some M.P.'s indicted for seditious speeches in Parliament. But offices and honors turned him into the King's man. This appears most clearly in 1636–37, when as Chief Justice he ruled that it was lawful to levy ship money. However, in fairness, Bramston always tried to steer a middle course, as Cromwell acknowledged by requesting him to serve as Chief Justice in the Commonwealth. Bramston begged off by pleading ill health and died in the same year, 1654.[35]

We have further testimony that in the midst of all the chaos at the Inns it was possible to lead a sober, respectable life and to gain an education in the law. John Manningham of the Middle Temple kept a diary for about thirteen months during 1602–03 which has fortunately survived.[36] Although it is not sufficiently connected or personal to be a true diary, it is the only document of the period which reveals something of the day-by-day life of the Inns. Obviously the product of a relatively stolid, diligent young man with his eye on a successful career,

[35] Dictionary of National Biography.
[36] Diary of Iohn Manningham (see n. 15 for full reference).

much of it might have been written by a law student at any time. Manningham notes the good marriages contracted by indigent contemporaries and the incomes of those in high places. He collects memorable sayings and jokes and summarizes sermons in great detail. He engages in moots, discusses legal quiddities at supper, and attends the law courts. It is true that his Victorian editor felt the need to censor the text, apparently omitting some coarse expressions and lewd jokes. Nonetheless it is clear that Manningham led a serious and responsible life.

We have similar evidence from a young man much higher on the social scale, George Manners of the family of the Earls of Rutland. Writing to his father, John Manners of Haddon, in 1586 "from his study in the Inner Temple Garden," he re-assures him that he is following "those precepts . . . I have received from you": "Your chefest precepts were these, vide, to applie my booke, to use good company and flie the contrary, to wright, and to give myselfe to honest and lawfull exercises for my boodie. For the firs I hope yt shall be found when as occasion shall be ministred; for the second I appeale to the socitie wherin I live iff I have not acquaynted and used the company of Barristers, those of 7 or 8 years standing, the best for calling, as my Lord of Buckhurst soons [the sons of the co-author of *Gorboduc*], Mr. Rose and such like; and for ill company, truly I know not any, but here and there some odd person which noboodie will kepe company with at all; and for Mr. Blackwall I have cleane abandoned him from mee; for he commeth not to me nor I to him. For wrighting, my papers in my studdie ar a sufficient —— ; and for exercises which ar last of all, I use the dancing scole, tennise, runing, and leapinge and such like in the felds." [37]

This is the sort of letter a son writes from school for his father's consumption, but it does show that the goals of an Inns of Court education were roughly the same at the end of the sixteenth century as they had been in Fortescue's day. Whether the number of young men like Davies' Publius and Lenton's gallant had increased is impossible to determine, although the proportion of residents who were admitted to the bar remained fairly constant during the last half of Elizabeth's reign. During this period the Inns produced Bacon and Coke, two of the greatest lawyers in English history, housed during some of his most productive years at least one great poet, Donne, and contained the best educated and liveliest society in London.

---

[37] *Manuscripts of the Duke of Rutland,* Historical Manuscripts Commission (London, 1888), I, 195–196.

Damnation was possible there, but so also was a rich and multifarious education.[38]

[38] This general estimate is not, I think, materially altered by the recent claims of Kenneth Charlton, "Liberal Education and the Inns of Court in the Sixteenth Century," *British Journal of Education*, 9 (1960), 25–38, and Wilfrid Prest, "Legal Education of the Gentry at the Inns of Court, 1560–1640," *Past and Present*, 38 (1967), 20–39. Charlton says that the educational function of the Inns was in a state of serious decay in the sixteenth century, and Prest makes the important point that "it would be very rash to assume that the mere record of an individual's admission to an Inn of Court is sufficient evidence that he received there a legal education of any kind" (p. 38). But whatever the state of the Inns as schools of law in the sixteenth century, they did produce many competent and great lawyers, and their social and cultural centrality is undeniable.

II Literary Life at the Inns of Court in the Latter Half of the Sixteenth Century

According to tradition, both Chaucer and Gower were members of the Inns of Court. This is not absolutely substantiated, but certainly in the sixteenth and seventeenth centuries an astonishing number of important writers lived there for some length of time: More, Ascham, Turbervile, Googe, Gascoigne, Sackville and Norton, North, Lodge, Fraunce, Raleigh, Harington, Campion, Donne, Bacon, Davies, Marston, Ford, Beaumont, Shirley, Davenant,[1] William Browne, Wither, Denham, Quarles, Carew, Suckling, and Congreve, among others.[2] The

[1] See Chapter I, n. 34.
[2] I conclude the list at this point because it would distort matters to list the many famous writers who rented rooms at the Inns in the eighteenth and nineteenth centuries without being part of a legal society.

impact of the experience obviously varied from one writer to another. Some of them studied the law seriously and became writers later. Some wrote worthless juvenilia, while a few thrived in the atmosphere and did some of their most important work there.

During part of this period something like a literary movement occurred at the Inns of Court. From 1558 to 1572, the Inns had a group which, as Carey Conley put it in *First English Translators of the Classics,* constituted "a compact, self-conscious renaissance movement." He found that "of the fifty-four known translators of the classics working between the years 1558 and 1572, inclusive, twenty-three or twenty-five were actually members of the inns of court and certainly two, possibly four, others, had some status there, to say nothing of five about whom there is little or no information. Three other members produced their classical translations too late to be counted among the first fifty-four, and four had been pre-Elizabethan translators." [3]

Jasper Heywood's preface to his translation of Seneca's *Thyestes* makes it clear that this was felt to be a group movement:

> But yf thy will be rather bent,
>   a yong mans witt to prove,
> And thinkst that elder lerned men
>   perhaps it shall behove,
> In woorks of waight to spende theyr tyme,
>   goe where Minervaes men,
> And finest witts doe swarme: whome she
>   hath taught to passe with pen.
> In Lyncolnes Inne and Temples twayne,
>   Grayes Inne and other mo,
> Thou shalt them fynde whose paynfull pen
>   thy verse shall florishe so,
> That Melpomen thou wouldst well weene
>   had taught them for to wright,
> And all their woorks with stately style,
>   and goodly grace t'endight.
> There shalt thou se the selfe same Northe,
>   whose woorke his witte displayes,
> And Dyall dothe of Princes paynte,
>   and preache abroade his prayse.
> There Sackvyldes Sonetts sweetely sauste
>   and featly fyned bee,

[3] (New Haven, 1927), pp. 26–27.

There Nortons ditties do delight,
   there Yelvertons doo flee
Well pewrde with pen: suche yong men three,
   as weene thou mightst agayne,
To be begotte as Pallas was,
   of myghtie Jove his brayne.
There heare thou shalt a great reporte,
   of Baldwyns worthie name,
Whose Myrrour dothe of Magistrates,
   proclayme eternall fame.
And there the gentle Blundville is
   by name and eke by kynde,
Of whome we learne by Plutarches lore,
   what frute by Foes to fynde,
There Bavande bydes, that turnde his toyle
   a Common welthe to frame,
And greater grace in Englyshe geves,
   to woorthy authors name.
There Googe a gratefull gaynes hath gotte,
   reporte that runneth ryfe,
Who crooked Compasse dothe describe,
   and Zodiake of lyfe.
And yet great nombre more, whose names
   yf I shoulde now resight,
A ten tymes greater woorke then thine,
   I should be forste to wright.
A pryncely place in Parnasse hill,
   for these there is preparde,
Where crowne of glittryng glorie hangs,
   for them a ryght rewarde.[4]

Here we find all the basic ingredients for a literary movement: a large number of young men engaged in a common pursuit; a high regard for each other's work; and, perhaps most important, the best of all entrenched establishments, "elder lerned men," in this case the scholars at the universities who opposed translating the classics. Conley has shown that there was a profound and widespread battle in which "the translators and the liberal party were aligned against the medieval reactionaries . . . [who were] enemies to Protestantism; university men, adept in scholastic philosophy; medieval stylists; readers of the ancient authors that were in vogue during the middle ages,

[4] *The Seconde Tragedie of Seneca entitled Thyestes* (London, 1560), sigs. *viir–*viiir.

Aristotle and Vergil, but not of the renaissance favorites, Plato and Cicero." [5]

Conley also ascribed political motives to the translators. They, along with their patrons, the new nobility, aimed to improve and enlighten the nation. Through direct access to certain useful classics — especially books on warfare like Caesar's *Commentaries* and books to discourage sedition like Lucan's *Pharsalia* — it was hoped that "goode gouvernemente" could be "throughlie executed and discharged" (as William Bavande of the Middle Temple put it).[6] Although they did not completely achieve their aims, the translators left a lasting impression on English literature, not merely by the production of one indubitable masterpiece, North's Plutarch, and the lesser achievements of Newton's collection of translations of Seneca's plays and Golding's of Ovid,[7] but by making a large number of ancient writers accessible to English readers for the first time.

A political impulse also motivated another, equally important literary project which had some connection with the Inns. The collection of poems known as *A Mirror for Magistrates* was originally supervised by William Baldwin, admitted to the Middle Temple in 1557 and connected with the Inn by Heywood in the long extract quoted above. It is not a coincidence that many of the authors of the *Mirror* were members of Inns and became lawyers. Despite differences in emphasis these tales are unified not merely by their subject matter, the fall of princes, but by their purpose. As Baldwin says in directing the book to "the nobilitye/and all other in office": "For here as in a loking glas, you shall see (if any vice be in you) howe the like hath bene punished in other heretofore, whereby admonished, I trust it will be a good occasion to move you to the soner amendment. This is the chiefest ende, whye it [this book] is set furth." [8] It seems to have been a natural function — it was at any rate their self-appointed task in the sixteenth and seventeenth centuries — for the lawyers of the Inns of Court to "instruct" their governors on their proper duties and responsibilities.

The tales in the *Mirror* were utterly orthodox in their loyalty to the will of the monarch and their horror of sedition, but they did imply some limits to obedience. One repentant rebel,

[5] *First English Translators*, pp. 86–88.

[6] Quoted by Conley, ibid., p. 37.

[7] Golding had many intimate connections at the Inns. See ibid., p. 144.

[8] *The Mirror for Magistrates*, ed. Lily B. Campbell (Cambridge, Eng., 1938), pp. 64, 65–66.

the Cornish blacksmith, goes so far as to say, "A christen subject should with honour due,/Obey his soveraygne though he were a Jue." On the other hand, Edmund, Duke of Somerset, can conclude after having obeyed immoral commands from his king: "let none such office take,/Save he that can for right his prince forsake." [9] This is a characteristically Tudor reservation, one which King James could never understand.

The same impulse to advise magistrates lies behind the most famous dramatic production at the Inns during this period, the Inner Temple's *Gorboduc* of 1562.[10] The desire of the young gentlemen to warn their sovereign in person of the dangers threatening a state which lacks a definite successor may strike us as impertinent, but clearly it did not affect Queen Elizabeth that way. After the first production of the play in the Inner Temple Hall, it was repeated for the Queen a few weeks later at Whitehall Palace; and one of its authors, Sackville, was an especially fortunate recipient of her favor throughout his long career. At the same time that the authors of *Gorboduc* were exercising the Inns' function of advice with or without consent, they also developed a new form for tragedy. Tillyard's view of their inventiveness is an outstanding piece of historical reconstruction: "Once more the novelty of *Gorboduc* must be insisted on. The rigid decorum of the play with its choruses, its long sententious speeches, its avoidance of all violence on the stage, its unity of action, and the blank verse now first used in the drama must have had for the young intellectuals of the time something of the glamour of *Poems and Ballads* in 1866 or the *Waste Land* in 1922. Behind it were the recent formulations of Italianate neo-classicism corresponding to the poetical novelties of Baudelaire and Laforgue behind Swinburne and Eliot respectively. Only by realizing a certain awe which this novelty must have created in the audience can we estimate the effect that the play's content must have produced." [11]

Tillyard's view is a useful adjunct to Alfred Harbage's iconoclastic but valid observation that *Gorboduc* and the other early academic plays had very little to do with the development of the main, Shakespearian line of Elizabethan drama: "*Ralph Roister Doister* and *Gorboduc*, traditionally designated the first 'regular' comedy and tragedy, are as exceptional in respect

[9] Ibid., pp. 412, 202.

[10] If R. J. Schoeck's speculation in "Satire of Wolsey in Heywood's 'Play of Love,'" *Notes and Queries*, 196 (1951), 112–114, is correct, the use of drama as a political weapon by the Inns can be seen as early as 1520.

[11] E. M. W. Tillyard, *Shakespeare's History Plays* (New York, 1962), p. 112.

to the bulk of the plays that followed as of those that preceded them, and may be considered epoch-making only if we exclude from the epoch the drama we value most. Nearly twenty years after its birth *Gorboduc* was cited by Sidney as the swallow that had failed to make a spring, plays generally having remained coarsely irregular." [12] *Gorboduc* did not produce significant progeny, but its purpose reflects the independent spirit of the Inns and its form reveals what was probably a prevailing taste among the educated for classical drama. This is a taste which died hard. As Harbage mentioned, Sidney regretted that it had not inaugurated a dramatic reformation; Greville and Daniel in the 1600's tried variations on its form in closet dramas; and even a professional man of the theater like John Webster could regret as late as 1612 that his audience would not accept a play like *Gorboduc*.[13]

Heywood's list of writers at the Inns includes the poet Barnabe Googe, who in addition to his translations wrote a volume of verse modeled on Tottel's *Miscellany*. His poems influenced George Turbervile, one of the most popular poets of the period, who resided intermittently from 1562 at one of the Inns — it is unclear which — and did most of his writing there. George Gascoigne also spent a significant amount of time at Gray's Inn in the 1550's and 1560's studying "learned Littleton," although "in the end, he proved but a dawe/For lawe was darke and he had quickly done." [14] While there, he composed two plays for the revels of 1566, *Supposes,* often called the first vernacular prose comedy, and the tragedy *Jocasta*. His many efforts, often as an innovator, in prose fiction, literary criticism, and poetry, as well as in the drama, place him as the leading man of letters in his period.

I mention these well-known facts because, taken together, they show that during the period between Wyatt and Surrey and the appearance of Spenser and Sidney all the poets, in fact almost all writers of any value, were connected with the Inns of Court. For a brief space of time — roughly from 1550 to 1575 — they were the literary center of England. The importance of the poets — especially Googe, Turbervile, and Gascoigne — has been emphasized by Yvor Winters, among others. He suggests that they perpetuated a reasonable, logical, moral, and unrhetorical tradition of poetry (as opposed to the Petrarchan),

[12] *Shakespeare and the Rival Traditions* (New York, 1952), pp. 58–59.

[13] See below, Chapter XIV.

[14] "Gascoignes Woodmanship," *The Posies,* ed. John W. Cunliffe (Cambridge, Eng., 1907), p. 348.

one which provided an important element in the style of Jonson, Shakespeare, and Donne.[15] Whether or not one accepts so high an estimate of poets whom C. S. Lewis labels "drab," it is no exaggeration to say that through their activity the translators, playwrights, and poets at the Inns of Court kept writing alive under unpropitious circumstances. When the greater writers appeared, they did not have to create an audience or to invent new forms. They merely had to do better what had already been attempted by an interconnected group of serious men intent on making the Reformation in England humanistic and its government secure and humane. Their collective effort established the Inns as an intellectual center with a special character: critical, independent, aesthetically innovative, and politically concerned.

After the advent of Spenser and Sidney, when English literature moved into its period of greatest glory, the writers at the Inns were no longer the sole custodians of serious writing. Yet interest in literature was as lively as ever there. An earnest student of the law like Manningham was as fascinated as Lenton's Inns-a-Court prodigal by poetry and drama. Intermixed with his legal and personal concerns and with his expert condensations of sermons, Manningham quotes epigrams, paradoxes, and witticisms by fellow students, notes down gossip about Jonson, Donne, and Shakespeare, commends the characterization of Malvolio in the play given the previous night in the Middle Temple Hall, suggests an Italian source for it, and copies a long extract from a dull poem in the style of *The Mirror for Magistrates* on Mary, Queen of Scots. Satires on Inns-a-Court men emphasize that opinions on literature were a social necessity in their world, as we hear in another epigram by John Davies:

> The fine youth Ciprius is more tierse and neate,
> Then the new garden of the old temple is,
> And still the newest fashion he doth get,
> And with the time doth change from that to this, . . .
> Yet this new-fangled youth made for these times,
> Doth above all prayse old Gascoins rimes.[16]

Davies' point is that Ciprius is more à la mode in clothes than in the more important fashions, but it is noteworthy that a

---

[15] "The Sixteenth Century Lyric in England," *Poetry*, 53 (1939), 258–272, 320–335; 54 (1939), 35–51.

[16] *Poems of Sir John Davies,* ed. Clare Howard (New York, 1941), p. 43.

foolish clotheshorse did have a favorite poet, albeit a hopelessly old-fashioned one.

One of the clearest facts about late Elizabethan literary life is that the men at the Inns were the prime consumers of serious literature. Bartholomew Griffin in 1596 expresses a realistic attitude toward the "Gentleman of the Innes of Court" when he asks them to accept his poem "Fidessa, more chaste then kinde": "Sweete Gentlemen, censure mildlie, as protectors of a poore stranger, judge the best, as incouragers of a young beginner." [17] William Goddard makes virtually the same request for his volume of satires, *A Mastiff Whelp*:

> Renoewned flattcapps (worthy sprighted men)
> Accept (but doo't with thanks) fruites of my penn.
> Protect with tongues (for tongues are Lawyers helpes).[18]

There were bookstalls within the precincts of the Temple and many ready buyers. Of course, much of the interest in literature was suspect, as one satirist implies by depicting an "Innes-of-Court Man in his Gowne" browsing among the new books at a stall. The student cries

> *Mew,* what *Hackneys* brought this wit to towne.
> But soone again my gallant Youth is gon,
> Minding the *Kitchin* more then Littleton.[19]

Since literary interest was in part a fashion, it seems inevitable that Francis Meres should have dedicated that stock market report on the newest writers, *Palladis Tamia* (1598), to a member of the Inns, Thomas Elliot of the Middle Temple. Franklin Williams' *Index of Dedications and Commendatory Verses in English Books before 1641* [20] shows clearly what had long been suspected, that the lawyers and law students were, next to

---

[17] (London, 1596), sig. A4r.

[18] (London, 1599), sig. A1v. Contrary to the Dictionary of National Biography, I can find no evidence that William Goddard was a member of the Middle Temple.

[19] Henry Parrot, *The Mastive or Young Whelpe of the Olde Dogge, Epigrams and Satires* (London, 1615), sig. H4v.

[20] (London, 1962). The number of Inns' members is much larger than Williams suggests — to give such totals was not his purpose — because he often designates a patron by a title or mark of identification for which he became important only after the book was published. Thus the above mentioned Thomas Elliot is described in the *Index* as Sir Thomas of Newland Hall although he was not knighted until 1603 and is described on the title page as "of the Middle Temple."

courtiers, the most important patrons and benefactors of contemporary writing.

They also provided a significant part of the audience at playhouses, both public and private. William Prynne's notorious *Histriomastix* (1633) suggests that the men at the Inns and the actors were mutually dependent: "That Innes of Court men were undone but for Players; that they are their chiefest guests and imployment, and the sole busines that makes them afternoons men: that this is one of the first things they learne as soone as they are admitted, to see Stage-playes." [21]

Alfred Harbage corroborates Prynne's view. Speaking of the public theaters, he says, "Two groups are mentioned again and again in contemporary allusions to the theatres — the students of the Inns of Court and the apprentices of London . . . What the [Inns'] group lacked in total numbers was counterbalanced by the large proportion of those numbers possessing the money, leisure, and inclination for playgoing. A student at the Inns of Court was a well-born, affluent, university-educated young man in his earlier twenties. He lived in a society devoted to intellectual pursuits and well disposed towards belles-lettres. He must have made a good spectator." [22] Because of higher admission prices and other factors that Harbage has analyzed in detail, the proportion of Inns' men in the audience at the private theaters would have been much greater. The small size of these theaters, their close proximity to the Inns, their infrequent performances (usually only one a week), and the avidity of Inns' men for the theater — all these factors suggest that the Inns provided by far the largest and most influential element in the audience. Occasionally, as in the two private theater plays by Edward Sharpham of the Middle Temple and *The Fawne* by John Marston, also of the Middle Temple, the references to intramural matters at the Inns are so frequent or recherché that the playwrights seem to have directed their plays almost exclusively to the Inns' element in the audience.

Many of the same readers, patrons, and playgoers also did some writing themselves, as Manningham's diary and various commonplace books indicate. Ideally, it was as much a part of a gentleman's accomplishments to write passable verse as it was to dance well. The young men at the Inns scribbled quantities

[21] Fol. 3v.
[22] *Shakespeare's Audience* (New York, 1961), p. 80. For a highly rhetorical version of the same estimate, see G. M. Young, "Shakespeare and the Termers," *Proceedings of the British Academy*, 33 (1947).

of verse, or claimed to, or imitated others, or, as the recurrent gibe had it, hired professionals to write for them. John Donne of Lincoln's Inn had little respect for this sort of activity:

> they who write, because all write, have still
> That excuse for writing, and for writing ill;
> But hee is worst, who (beggarly) doth chaw
> Others wits fruits, and in his ravenous maw
> Rankly digested, doth those things out-spue,
> As his owne things.[23]

When it comes to a consideration of serious writing in the 1590's, we find that a large proportion of the best literature was now being published by professional writers. There are great differences in social class, education, and economic resources in a list which includes Peele, Greene, Marlowe, Nashe, Daniel, Drayton, Chapman, Jonson, and Shakespeare, but they all made more or less of a living directly or indirectly from their writing. These are the writers who occupy most of the space in the histories of the period, while, with a few exceptions, writing at the Inns appears to be in eclipse. In fact, it was not. Many important writers lived at the Inns during this period, as reference to Appendix A will show, and their work reflects continuity with, as well as development from, their predecessors. What was changed in the writers' situation was that publication had become increasingly associated with the desire for money and social advancement. Inns' writers responded by adopting the fashion of the Court, affecting the role of disengaged amateurs, and circulating their work in manuscript among friends. This was not a new development; it had been widely practiced since the time of Wyatt and Surrey.[24] But during the period under discussion, 1550 to 1575, the writers had to forgo this courtly custom in order to cooperate in what were essentially political or religious projects — the translations and the *Mirror* poems. When someone like Barnabe Googe did publish a volume of his own poetry, *Eclogues, Epitaphs, and Sonnets* (1563), he felt the need to offer a most elaborate and circumstantial explanation for its public appearance. In his dedication to the Reader of Gray's Inn, he made the familiar excuse that he had always felt his poems to be trifles, but that they had been sent to a printer in his ab-

---

[23] *The Poems of John Donne*, ed. Herbert J. C. Grierson (Oxford, 1912), I, 150, ll. 23–28.

[24] See J. W. Saunders, "The Stigma of Print," *Essays in Criticism*, 1 (1951), 139–164.

sence and without his knowledge. Because "it could not without great hindrance of the poor printer be now revoked," he could do nothing but cooperate with the scheme.[25] Something similar appears in the preface to *Gorboduc*. But on the whole, both Courtly and Inns of Court writers avoided publication throughout the Tudor and early Stuart period.

Thus the relative silence of the Inns in the 1590's does not reflect any change or diminution in literary productivity. Writing was never a public activity; rather, it was a matter of pleasing a small, select audience. The case of John Donne is the best illustration. It is probably a piece of luck that we have very much of his poetry. He wrote a large part of his work before 1600 but published none of it; during his lifetime he published only three poems, all under special circumstances and with great reluctance. John Hoskins' son lent someone his father's "booke of poemes, neatly written by one of his clerkes, bigger then Dr. Donne's poemes," [26] but it was never returned. Fortunately, Dr. Donne's son was more careful. Of course, we would still have many of his poems from manuscript collections, but even these date from the 1620's, rather late in his life. None of Donne's poems appeared in any of the poetical miscellanies during his lifetime. What is even more surprising, there are very few published indications that the general reader was aware of the existence of his poetry until the second decade of the seventeenth century.

Nevertheless, Sir Richard Baker's familiar description of Donne in the 1590's shows him as anything but a recluse. He "lived at the *Inns of Court* not dissolute, but very neat, a great visiter of Ladies, a great frequenter of Playes, a great writer of conceited verses." [27] He and some of his friends made a practice of writing to each other in verse. Clearly he showed them his other poems. Indeed, the earliest surviving sign that someone knew Donne's poetry appears in a volume of verse satires by Everard Guilpin of Gray's Inn, a friend to whom Donne wrote a verse epistle. In the fifth satire of *Skialetheia* (1598) he imitates a portion of Donne's first satire.[28]

The poetry which Donne wrote during the 1590's — the epi-

---

[25] Quoted in *Poetry of the English Renaissance*, ed. J. William Hebel and Hoyt H. Hudson (New York, 1944), p. 72.

[26] John Aubrey, *Aubrey's Brief Lives*, ed. Oliver Lawson Dick (London, 1949), p. 170.

[27] Sir Richard Baker, *A Chronicle of the Kings of England* (London, 1696), p. 450.

[28] In "Donne and Everard Guilpin," *Review of English Studies*, 14 (1963), 164–167, I demonstrated that three alleged allusions in Hall's *Virgidemiarum* do not in fact refer to Donne.

grams, satires, elegies, many of the *Songs and Sonets* — was highly original, virtually revolutionary: "every worke, of thy most earely wit,/Came forth example, and remaines so, yet," as Ben Jonson said.[29] Yet he was far from being an Elizabethan Gerard Manley Hopkins, producing his work for the uncomprehending or for the next generation. In his verse epistles occur many instances of his recondite learning and startling wit, but the tone is always that of an easy intimacy, of someone speaking to an audience of equals; often he appears to be improvising entertainment for their amusement. In fact, Donne in the 1590's was part of a loosely connected circle of wits, lawyers, and poets, all of whom, with the exception of Ben Jonson, were members of the Inns.[30] Donne's precise role within this web of connections is unclear, but it is at least possible that even before 1600 he was, as Carew said in his elegy, "King, that rul'd as hee thought fit/The universall Monarchy of wit." [31] In his satires, Donne's friend Guilpin castigates "this sinne leapered age" when "folles doe sit/More honored then the *Prester John* of wit." [32] It is difficult to imagine any other "John" to whom Guilpin, especially, would have applied this epithet. Jonson makes a very similar appraisal by saying that approval by Donne would be the highest praise since he "so alone canst judge, so alone dost make." [33]

Donne's was merely the most important of several intellectual groups at the Inns of Court in the 1590's. Thomas Campion at Gray's Inn from 1586 to 1595 [34] and Sir John Davies at the

[29] *Ben Jonson*, ed. C. H. Herford and Percy and Evelyn Simpson (Oxford, 1947), VIII, 34.

[30] See A. Alvarez, *The School of Donne* (New York, 1967), Appendix I, pp. 143–148.

[31] Thomas Carew, "An Elegie upon the Death of the Deane of Pauls, Dr. John Donne," *Metaphysical Lyrics and Poems of the Seventeenth Century*, ed. Herbert J. C. Grierson (Oxford, 1921), p. 180, ll. 95–96.

[32] Everard Guilpin, *Skialetheia or A Shadowe of Truth, in certain Epigrams and Satyres* (London, 1598), sig. C2v.

[33] *Ben Jonson*, VIII, 62.

[34] Campion was active in the social life of Gray's Inn, having participated in the revels of 1587–88 and 1594–95. His considerable circle of friends at Gray's is listed by Percival Vivian, ed., *Campion's Work* (Oxford, 1909), p. xxviii. Among these was Thomas Michelborne, through whom he met his brother Edward Michelborne, a Latin epigrammatist at Oxford of great influence. (See Leicester Bradner, *Musae Anglicanae* [New York, 1940], pp. 77–90). Campion knew John Davies and his epigrams, as appears in his Latin epigram to Davies (*Works*, p. 345). Campion's connection with the larger circle of London wits is shown by his contribution to the collection of poems prefaced to Coryat's *Crudities* (1611). It is possible that Campion was a crucial figure in the vogue for elegies and epigrams that swept through Inns' circles in the 1590's, and his style may have exerted some influence. His role as innovator and his influence depend on the original date of his *Observations*, published in 1602, which contains

Middle Temple from 1588 to 1598 were also writing some of their most important poetry while living in other circles of wits and poets; all of them overlapped and interconnected.

What we are dealing with, therefore, is a sealed-off, loosely organized confederation of monarchies, possibly presided over by Prester John. It would be fascinating and extremely valuable to know more about the laws and life of such a powerful government. Such knowledge would help us to comprehend more precisely the nature of the poems and plays which came from these circles. In particular, it would help us to assess the degree to which this work was rooted in its milieu, how far it was designed for an audience with special or parochial concerns. This is particularly important in dealing with the drama, that most social of literary forms, where, without the response of the audience and the voices of the actors, we are constantly in danger of misinterpreting tone and meaning.

From their works we may reconstruct a group with certain shared assumptions and something like a prevailing ethos. But such a procedure is obviously circular, defining the milieu from the work and the work from the milieu. Unfortunately, almost no external evidence about this world in the form of diaries and letters has survived. But from the texts of certain public entertainments at the Inns, the so-called "revels" which took place at Gray's Inn and the Middle Temple in the 1590's, we can gain some valuable, if partial insights. Although these have often been discussed generally, they have never been subjected to close scrutiny. As descriptions of traditional and communal activities, they can tell us something of the form and pressure of the intellectual and literary milieu of the Inns of Court in the 1590's.

---

many English epigrams in experimental meters and one elegy. They may have been written as early as 1591. (See J. V. Cunningham, "Lyric Style in the 1590's" in *The Problem of Style* [New York, 1966], pp. 159–173 and esp. p. 167.)

III Revels at the
Inns of Court

Ad Graios
Graii, sive magis iuvat vetustum
Nomen, Purpulii, decus Britannum,
Sic Astraea gregem beare vestrum,
Sic Pallas velit; ut favere nugis
Disiuncti socii velitis ipsi,
Tetrae si neque sint, nec infacetae,
Sed quales merito exhibere plausu
Vosmet, ludere cum lubet, soletis.

Thomas Campion, *Epigrammatum*[1]

[1] *Campion's Works,* ed. Percival Vivian (Oxford, 1909), pp. 304–305.

"Revels" were an integral part of the life of the Inns, but it is often difficult to determine what contemporaries meant by this term. At one extreme, it refers to licentious and immoral actions, as in a letter from Francis Bacon's mother: "I trust they will not mum nor mask nor sinfully revel at Gray's Inn." [2] Fortescue's use in the fifteenth century is very general as he describes the opportunity at the Inns to learn "singing, and all kinds of music, dancing, and such other accomplishments and diversions (which are called *Revels*) as are suitable to their quality, and such as are usually practised at Court." [3] This is similar to Sir George Buck's usage in the seventeenth century when he says that the "Art of Revels . . . requireth knowledge in Grammar, Rhetorike, Logicke, Philosophie, Historie, Musick, Mathematikes, and in other Arts (and all more then I understand I confess)." [4] Apparently the term was applied to virtually every pleasurable form of human activity.

Members of the Inns seem to have made a deep, if unconscious, connection between reveling and the study of the law. This is discernible even in a serious student like the future Chief Justice, John Bramston, as we see in one of Manningham's anecdotes. Manningham and Bramston were sitting in the Middle Temple dining hall after supper discussing a law case with Thomas Fleetwood, a barrister and son of the late Recorder of London, in accordance with the methods of learning described in Chapter I: "Mr. Fleetwood, after he was gone from supper, remembered a case to the purpose he was talking of before he went, and came againe to tell us of it, which Mr. Bramston said was as yf a reveller, when he had made a legg at the end of his galliard, should come againe to shewe a tricke which he had forgotten." [5] The comparison is especially fitting if we consider that the hall was the location for reveling as well as for legal disputation. Campion's epigram, quoted as the epigraph to this chapter, also demonstrates the tendency of members to think of revels as an inseparable aspect of the Inns. The same association with reveling was made by outsiders as well, as in this remark by a satirist:

[2] *The Works of Francis Bacon*, ed. James Spedding, Robert Ellis, and Douglas Heath (London, 1862), VIII, 326.

[3] Sir John Fortescue, *De Laudibus Legum Angliae*, trans. A. Amos (Cambridge, Eng., 1825), pp. 183–184.

[4] "The Third University," Appendix in John Stow, *Chronicle of England* (London, 1615), p. 988.

[5] *Diary of John Manningham*, ed. John Bruce, Camden Society Publication 99 (London, 1868), p. 42.

> You kept such revell with your carelesse pen,
> As made me thinke you of the Innes of Court:
> For they use Revels more then any men.[6]

It was an accurate observation. The Inns were constantly the scene of banquets, lavish masques, plays, dancing, musical entertainments, and other types of revels.

Of these, the grandest and most formal were the banquets given by the Readers at their installation. They consisted of sumptuous feasting at which many courtiers assisted in the conspicuous consumption and of certain specified rituals, which differed at the various Inns. A detailed description of these banquets, available in Dugdale's *Origines Juridiciales,* is not relevant here,[7] but it is instructive to note their general tone. Each Inn appointed a Master of its revels. At the Reader's Feast it was his task to call the Reader to lead the "measures," a slow stately dance which all members were obliged to perform in order of precedence. The dancing was accompanied by the enactment of an elaborate tissue of arbitrary rituals, particularly during a special ceremony when wafers and hippocras were distributed. This was reveling as the Ancients engaged in it, and the young men seem to have disliked it. A series of fines had to be devised at the Middle Temple to enforce participation; and at Lincoln's Inn on February 6, 1610, more drastic action was required: "It appears that the *Under Baristers* were by Decimation put out of Commons, for examples sake, because the whole Bar offended by not dancing on *Candlemas* day preceeding, according to the *antient Order* of this Society, when the Judges were present: with this, that if the like fault were committed afterwards, they should be fined or disbarred." [8]

Dugdale follows his description of the Reader's Feasts by touching on the sort of revels the young gentlemen preferred: "Besides these *solemn Revels* or Measures aforesaid, they [that is, the Inns] had wont to be entertained with *Post Revels,* performed by the better sort of young Gentlemen of the Society with Galliards, Corrantoes, and other Dances; or else with Stageplayes: the first of these Feasts being at the beginning, and the

---

[6] "W. I.," *The Whipping of the Satyre* (London, 1601), sig. E4v.

[7] William Dugdale, *Origines Juridiciales* (London, 1671), pp. 203–205. See also A. Wigfall Green, *The Inns of Court and Early English Drama* (New Haven, 1931), pp. 40–52.

[8] *Records of the Honourable Society of Lincoln's Inn* (London, 1897–1902), II, 131.

other at the later end of Christmas." [9] An order by the Middle
Temple Parliament in 1631 supplements Dugdale's description
by defining its Christmas entertainments to include "Revels
[that is, dancing], barriers, arraignments, and other manly and
ingenious exercises tending to the grace of the actors and the
honour of the Society." [10]

For the small amount we can learn about the Christmas
entertainments, we must combine a variety of documents.[11]
They indicate that all the Inns seem to have followed roughly
the same pattern for these ceremonies; it is as though they
derived from some common source. Moreover, basic elements
in the format must have been arranged quite early. By the
year 1500 the records of the Inns' Parliaments designate the
assignment of some offices or roles in the revels which the
students assumed as late as the Restoration.[12]

Generalizing from the various accounts, we find that the
revels usually began just before Christmas with the selection
of a suitable leader, or Prince, called by a unique name at each
Inn: Prince of Purpoole at Gray's Inn, Prince de la Grange at
Lincoln's Inn, Prince of Sophie at the Inner Temple, and
Prince d'Amour at the Middle Temple. The Prince and a
court selected by him were installed at the first Grand Night
and apparently held a certain power for the duration of the
festivities. As the young gentlemen of the Inner Temple put

[9] *Origines*, p. 205. For a discussion of "Post Revels" see D. S. Bland, "Inns of
Court Nomenclature," *Notes and Queries*, 202 (1957), 49.

[10] *Middle Temple Records*, ed. Charles H. Hopwood (London, 1904), II, 787–
788.

[11] The major documents are Dugdale's account of the Inner Temple's revels
(*Origines*, pp. 153–157), the texts of the revels at Gray's Inn in 1594–95 and
1617–18, and the Middle Temple's "Prince d'Amour" revels of 1597–98 (for all
of which full citations are given below). As far as I know, all other extant documents are small scraps from revels. For example, Mark Eccles reprinted a speech
by Francis Beaumont delivered at the Inner Temple not long after 1600:
"Francis Beaumont's *Grammar Lecture*," *Review of English Studies*, 16 (1940),
402–414. Also, Leslie Hotson in *Shakespeare's Sonnets Dated and Other Essays*
(New York, 1949), pp. 239–243, printed some edicts from a Middle Temple revel
of ca. 1635. There are some additional negligible scraps, but I feel that I must
have missed other important documents.

[12] D. S. Bland, "Interludes in Fifteenth-Century Revels at Furnivall's Inn,"
Review of English Studies, 3 (1952), 263–268, has shown that there were revels
at one of the Inns of Chancery, Furnivall's Inn, in the fifteenth century. No
one has investigated the possibility that the Inns' revels of the sixteenth century
were influenced by the highly developed ceremonies of the law clerks in France
known as the "Basoches." Certainly the similarities are striking: the formation
of a mock court, fictitious arraignments, concentration on sexual jokes, the
formulation of satiric laws and regulations for their kingdom. See Howard G.
Harvey, *The Theatre of the Basoche* (Cambridge, Mass., 1941).

it in a remonstrance to the Privy Council drawn up to regain their ancient privileges, "the benchers have usually governed in term time, the barristers in vacation, and the gentlemen in the Christmas." [13] Over the next few weeks a succession of ceremonies took place: an elaborate emblazoning of the Prince's titles, a detailed description of the responsibilities of court officers, a conferring of "knighthoods," a declaration of laws and edicts for the Prince's realm, an arraignment of a criminal with his incarceration in "the tower" (that is, the stocks), and many long orations on a variety of subjects. These entertainments were supplemented by the presentation of one or more plays and masques, sometimes acted by students, sometimes by professional groups. Often some portion of the revels was presented at Court. Finally the Prince "died" and the Christmas revels ended, usually with a banquet on Candlemas Night, February 2. On at least one occasion, however, the revels persisted intermittently until Lent.

Although the general picture is clear, much uncertainty exists about important matters, even about so fundamental a problem as whether the revels occurred annually at each Inn. The Middle Temple's Parliament mentions both "grand" and "solemn" Christmas celebrations, but the distinction is unclear. The revels were elaborate there in 1597–98, but that Christmas was decreed as "solemn," not "grand." A "solemn" Christmas may have involved a shorter period of revelry or an unwillingness by the Benchers to allot money out of the Inn's treasury for elaborate entertainment. Some sort of revelry, at least some dicing and dancing, went on every year when the plague did not interfere, but it would seem that the degree of elaboration within the basic framework depended on the enthusiasm and financial resources of the students who happened to be resident. There is some evidence that revels on the elaborate scale I am going to describe were very infrequent.[14]

It is equally difficult to decide how much of the ceremony was traditional and how much was original from year to year. One would expect the general form of the ceremonies to remain fixed, but I have noticed that even some rather obvious jokes in the Middle Temple's revels of 1597–98 were repeated verbatim in 1610. In the absence of other data, one might suppose that the revels of 1610, about which we know very little,

[13] *State Papers Domestic, Charles I*, 1639–1640, p. 304.

[14] Since the Prince of Purpoole in the Gray's Inn revels of 1617–18 was called "Henry II," it seems likely that there had been no large-scale revelry since 1594–95, when "Henry I" ruled.

were merely refurbishing an older entertainment, but the 1597–98 revels also contain various topical jokes which make obsolete references.[15] I conclude that the revels were a mixture of old and new materials incorporated into a traditional format.

But the most important uncertainty about the revels concerns their tone. The Inns of Court Christmas Prince was evidently similar to a "Lord of Misrule," and his reign was often characterized by disorderly conduct, abuse of authority, and a general atmosphere of "solemn foolery" (to use Evelyn's term for one such revel).[16] Yet it is not clear that Christmas revels always had such a tone or that it was ever purely a time for satiric or disorderly conduct. In the earliest detailed description of such an event, Gerard Legh portrays the revels at the Inner Temple in 1560–61 as a highly serious occasion: "The Prince so served with tender meates, sweet frutes and deinte delicates, confeccioned with curious Cookerie: as it semed wonder, a world to serve the provision. And at every course, the Trompetts blew the couragious blast of deadly warre with noise of drome and fyffe, with ye swete Armony of violetts, shakbutts, recorders, & cornetts, with other instruments of musicke, as it semed Apollos harpe had tewned ther strock. Thus ye hall was served after most ancient order of the Iland, in commendacion wherof I saye: I have also sene, the service of great princes, in solempne seasons and times of triumphe, yet thorder herof was not inferior to any . . . I assure you I languish for lack of conning ripelie to utter. That I sawe so orderlie handeled apperteinyng to service." After several solemn speeches, "knighthoods" were conferred: "This done Palaphilos obeyng his princes commaundement departed. And after a whyle retourned accompanid wyth xxiiii valiaunte Knightes all appareled in longe whyte vestures, with eche man a Scarfe of Pallas colours and them presented with there names to the Prince. who allowed well his choise, and commaunded him to do his office. who after hys dutie to the Prince, Bowed towardes these worthie personages, Standyng everie man in his aunciente. As he had borne Armes in the fielde. And began to showe hys Princes pleasure with thonour of thorder." [17]

In assessing this often quoted description (only a small portion of which I have reproduced), it is relevant to know that

[15] Edward Pudsey's commonplace book (Bodleian MS. Eng. Poet. d. 3) of about 1610 records several jokes from "MT Christ." revels on fol. 87r which also appear in the revels of 1597–98, while these earlier revels refer to the playhouse of the Children of Paul's, closed since ca. 1590.

[16] Quoted by A. Wigfall Green, *The Inns of Court*, p .89.

[17] *Accedens of Armory* (London, 1562), fol. 213r–v; 214v–215r.

its author, Legh, was very ponderous and unimaginative. Since Henry Machyn described the same "noble prince" in his *Diary* as a "lord of mysrull," [18] it is possible that Legh was distorting the true nature of the proceedings in order to depict the Inns of Court as some kind of bastion of true "generosity." Yet it was pedagogical policy at the Inns that the officers of the Christmas revels were to be the same as those "in the King's highness house and other noblemen and this is done onely to the intent that they [that is, the students] should in time to come know how to use themselves." [19] We will probably come close to the true tone of the revels if we see them as a mixture of disorderly conduct, mock solemnity, and a serious miming of dignified roles. As least in their later phase, the revels were a kind of drama, the actors in which were serious even though they frequently mocked themselves and others.

The famous revels at Gray's Inn in 1594–95 provide a good illustration of this mixture. These must have been the most elaborate of the period. Among the events was a masque by Francis Davison, at least one poem in which was written by Thomas Campion; a group of speeches by Francis Bacon; and (apparently) Shakespeare's *Comedy of Errors*. It is not surprising that the text of so important a revel has survived. Titled *Gesta Grayorum, or the History of the High and Mighty Prince Henry, Prince of Purpoole . . . Who Reigned and Died, A.D. 1594. Together with a Masque as it was presented . . . for the Entertainment of Q. Elizabeth . . .* , it was first published in 1688, almost one hundred years after its presentation; other partial versions have survived in manuscript.[20]

Gray's Inn was the largest of the Inns and, according to the figures from the 1586 census of the Inns, would have had approximately one hundred fifty-five Inner Barristers in residence during the Christmas vacation. The text of the *Gesta Grayorum* lists the names of about ninety participants and designates parts for at least forty others. The "cast" also requires many "extras," especially one large group called "The Family, and Followers." It is easy to see that these revels were not merely

[18] *Diary*, ed. J. G. Nichols (London, 1848), pp. 273–274.

[19] Quoted by A. Wigfall Green, *The Inns of Court*, p. 57.

[20] Reprinted as *Gesta Grayorum 1688*, ed. W. W. Greg, Malone Society Reprints (Oxford, 1914). Page numbers in the text refer to this edition. The text is not strictly an account of what occurred; in part, it is what the young men had planned to present. Unfortunately, the Benchers felt that the revels could not continue after Candlemas, when the legal term resumed. Thus they decreed that the scaffold in the Hall be removed and that the plans for two extra Grand Nights be abandoned (see p. 53). But the Prince's formal reign was extremely long, extending to March 4.

entertainment for a small coterie. Whether by decree or choice, almost every available member of the Inn participated.

We learn from the text that for several years preceding 1594, Gray's Inn had had no Christmas revels, mainly because the plague had interfered. To keep up the Inn's good name, a group of members decided to select a Prince and embark on a season of revels. On December 12, 1594, they chose as "Prince of Purpoole" Henry Helmes, "a *Norfolk*-Gentlemen, who was thought to be accomplished with all good Parts, fit for so great a Dignity; and was also a very proper Man of Personage, and very active in Dancing and Revelling" (p. 2). Then followed the selection of his entire court, as well as his place of lodging and the provision of a treasury "for the Support of his State and Dignity." The initiators raised a large sum through requests to old members and friends of the Inn, among whom William Cecil, the Lord Treasurer, contributed "10 1. and a Purse of fine rich Needlework" (p. 4). But the revels were so long and elaborate that in May the Inn had to assess each member a fixed sum according to his rank and also to disburse money from its treasury. (A masque for the Queen was an unexpected and large expense.) Another regular part of the preliminaries involved a courtly invitation by Gray's to its old friend, the Inner Temple, to participate in the planning. On a similar occasion, the Middle Temple invited its ally, Lincoln's Inn.

The first of the Great Nights was December 20, 1594:

> The Prince, with all his Train in Order . . . marched from his Lodging, to the great Hall; and there took his place in his Throne, under a rich Cloth of State: His Counsellors and great Lords were placed about him, and before him; below the Half-pace, at a Table, sate his learned Council and Lawyers; the rest of the Officers and Attendants took their proper Places, as belonged to their Condition.
>
> Then the Trumpets were commanded to sound thrice; which being done, the King at Arms, in his rich surcoat of Arms, stood forth before the Prince, and proclaimed his Style as followeth.
>
> *By the sacred Laws of Arms, and authorized Ceremonies of the same (maugre the Conceit of any Malecontent) I do pronounce my Sovereign Liege Lord, Sir Henry, rightfully to be the high and mighty Prince of Purpoole, Arch-Duke of Stapulia and Bernardia, Duke of the high and Nether Holborn, Marquis of St. Giles's and Totten-*

> ham, *Count Palatine of* Bloomsbury *and* Clerkenwell,
> *Great Lord of the Cantons of* Islington, &c. *Knight of*
> *the most honourable Order of the* Helmet, *and Sover-*
> *eign of the same.* (p. 9)

From the beginning it is apparent that we are dealing with an ambiguous ceremonial. The rhetoric of chivalry at court entertainments like the "barriers" was a fiction agreed upon by the audience and participants, a pretense that the world of Palmerin of England still existed. The Inns of Court revels, while different, were not mock-heroic. The young men were expensively, royally dressed, but this was not wholly "play" inasmuch as they were endowed with some of the power which their clothing symbolized. Occasionally they exploited the quasi-real aspect of their roles, as we can see in the order by the Parliament of the Middle Temple in 1589: "The order set down in the buttery book by the Christmas lord and Utter Barristers then in commons for removing Henry Poole, the Steward, from his office for ill provision of victual and other abuses, is revoked, as the makers of the order had no sufficient authority, but his misdemeanours and evil usage of the Butlers and other officers is referred to the Treasurer and two others of the Bench." [21]

When "Sir Henry" was titled Prince of Purpoole (that is, the parish of Portpool in which Gray's Inn was situated) and Arch-Duke of Stapulia and Bernardia (that is, the Inns of Chancery, Staple's and Barnard's, over which Gray's had jurisdiction), the audience must have felt the justification for his traditional exercise of power as well as the obvious fiction. At times one has the impression that all of London, including the Queen, was taking part in the Gray's Inn revels: "The Prince and his company continued their Course, until they came to the Tower; where, by her Majesty's Commandment, he was welcomed with a Volley of great Ordnance, by the Lieutenant of the *Tower.* At the *Tower-hill* there waited for the Prince's Landing, Men attending with Horses, very gallantly Appointed, for all the Company, to the number of one hundred; the most of them being great Horses, and the rest very choice Geldings; and all very bravely furnished with all things necessary. So the Prince being mounted, and his Company in Order, as before set down, every Man according to his Office, with the Ensign thereof, they rode very gallantly through *Tower-street, Fen-church-street, Grace-church-street, Corn-hill, Cheap-side,* and so

[21] *Middle Temple Records,* I, 303–304.

through St. *Paul's Church-yard;* where, at St. *Paul's* School, His Highness was entertained with an Oration, made by one of the Scholars of that School" (p. 55). It is a unique mixture of make-believe and reality, not really parallel to our various "governor-for-a-day" rites since the fiction lasted for so long and was agreed to by so many. Frequently Inns writers and lawyers acted as though they lived in a separate kingdom. It is a habit of mind in which they had had training.

In addition to ceremonies, a large part of the revels consisted of speeches filled with hyperbolic courtly language, metaphoric clichés, Ciceronian periods, and rhetorical flourishes, but there is nothing to suggest that these stylistic features were being satirized. Apparently they were meant to be exercises in the high-flown, traditional rhetoric which the dramatic situation suggested. Nor is there any consistently parodic purpose behind the speeches ascribed to Bacon. Instead, his fertile lawyer's wit is employed in producing six well argued, contradictory sugges-tions to the Prince on how best to occupy his time. The first counsellor advocates "the Exercise of War":

> if you embrace the Wars, your Trophies and Triumphs will be as continual Coronations, that will not suffer your Glory and Contentment to fade and wither. Then when you have enlarged your Territories, ennobled your Country, distributed Fortunes, good or bad, at your pleasure, not only to Particulars, but to Cities and Na-tions; marked the Computations of Times with your Expeditions and Voyages, and the Memory of Places by your Exploits and Victories, in your later years you shall find a sweet Respect into the Adventures of your Youth, you shall enjoy your Reputation, you shall record your Travels, and after your own time, you shall Eternize your Name, and leave deep Foot-steps of your Power in the World. (p. 33)

I find no ironic excess, no hint that the author disapproves of the argument here or in the subsequent speeches urging the pursuit of philosophy, building, and so forth. It is difficult to argue with Spedding's conclusion that the speeches "carry his [Bacon's] signature in every sentence . . . All these councillors speak with Bacon's tongue and out of Bacon's brain; but the second and fifth speak out of his heart and judgment also. The propositions of the latter contain an enumeration of those very reforms in state and government which throughout his life he was most anxious to see realized." [22]

However, the Gray's Inn's revels were far from being totally serious. They contained a great deal of mockery of legal forms, as in the very long general pardon of all offenders and its numerous exceptions. "*Except,* All such Persons as by any Slander, Libel, Word, or Note, bewray, betray, defame, or suffer to be defamed any Woman, Wife, Widow, or Maid, in whose Affairs, Secrets, Suits, Services, Causes, Actions, or other Occupations, he hath been at any time conversant, employed, or trained in, or admitted unto, contrary to his plighted Promise, Duty and Allegiance; and to the utter Disparagement of others hereafter to be received, retained, embraced, or liked in like Services, Performances, or Advancements" (p. 17). This is but the fifth of twenty such exceptions, the total effect of which is to negate the pardon. It is a gigantic, self-defeating "amplificatio," a parody of the attempt of legal documents to embrace all categories and possibilities. Similarly, a mock-arraignment was conducted to determine the cause of the mix-ups on the night when *The Comedy of Errors* was offered: "the Prisoner was freed and pardoned, the Attorney, Sollicitor, Master of the Requests, and those that were aequainted with the Draught of the Petition, were all of them commanded to the Tower; so the Lieutenant took charge of them. And this was the End of our Law-sports, concerning the Night of Errors" (p. 24).

"Law-sports" at the Inns always contained jokes about sex, as the fifth exception in the mock-pardon illustrates. The convention was to assume a society of merry devils whose main occupation was frequenting the stews. It would be almost impossible to discover a Christmas celebration at a men's college where this theme was not prominent. It appears more explicitly, although always more or less veiled in metaphors, in a "letter" from the Lord Admiral to the Prince: "on the 9th Day of *January,* in the straits of the Gulf of *Clerkenwell,* there was an hot Skirmish between a Merchant of St. Giles's, called *Amarpso,* and the Admiral of the *Amazons,* called the *Rowseflower;* wherein the Merchant having gained the Wind, came up with her in such close manner, that he brake his Boltsprite in her hinder Quarter: Yet notwithstanding, the Fight continued fiercely, on either part, two long Hours, and more; in which time, our Gunner, being a very expert Soldier, shot her four or five times under Water: Then the Merchant perceiving his Powder to be spent, was inforced to grapple; and so, with great Resolution, laid her a-board

[22] *Works of Francis Bacon,* VIII, 342.

on the Waste, which he found stoutly defended by the *French*; yet, at length, being driven from their close Fight, they were constrained to keep under Hatches, where one of the Soldiers entring, spied Fire in the Gun-room" (pp. 49–50). The joke about venereal disease which begins at this point continues at some length. The only standard element that is missing from the narrative is a catalogue of aphrodisiacs. Jokes at the law and at sex, legal joking about sex, sexual jokes about the law: these always appeared in the Inns of Court revels.

The milieu is further defined by the articles to which the "knights" had to subscribe during their induction into the "Order of the Helmet," so called because of Prince Henry Helmes's name. They indicate the kind of admiration for verbal fluency and wit which we would expect of such a group. Warned that they must apply themselves to some "vertuous Quality or Ability of Learning, Honour and Arms," that "good Apparel" and proficiency in gaming are not enough to gain admission to the Prince's presence, the knights are enjoined to "endeavour to add Conference and Experience by Reading" (p. 29). On the recommended list are *"Plutarch, the Arcadia,* and the Neoterical Writers" (pp. 29–30), among others. The knights are also required to frequent the theater and the better sort of taverns "whereby they may not only become accomplished with Civil Conversations, and able to govern a Table with Discourse; but also sufficient, if need be, to make Epigrams, Emblems, and other Devices appertaining to His Honour's learned Revels" (p. 30). Also among the articles are a few satiric touches against Inns' gallants, but this theme is not stressed.

The element of spectacle through pageantry and masque was also important in the *Gesta Grayorum.* In order to celebrate the friendship of Gray's Inn with the Inner Temple, a pageant was offered for the entertainment of a dazzling audience, worth listing if only to show the intimate connections between the Court and the Inns: "there was a most honourable Presence of Great and Noble Personages, that came as invited to our Prince; as namely, the Right Honourable the Lord Keeper, the Earls of *Shrewsbury, Cumberland, Northumberland, Southampton,* and *Essex,* the Lords *Buckhurst, Windsor, Mountjoy, Sheffield, Compton, Rich, Burleygh, Mounteagle,* and the Lord *Thomas Howard;* Sir Thomas *Henneage,* Sir *Robert Cecill;* with a great number of Knights, Ladies, and very worshipful Personages" (p. 25). At one side of the hall an altar was erected to the Goddess of Amity. Amidst music, fairies, and incense, a parade of mythical friends entered arm in arm: Theseus and Perithous, Achilles and Patroclus, and others. Last came "Graius" and "Templarius," who pledged perpetual friendship and amity.

A masque presented at the Court as part of these revels was far more important artistically. According to the historian of the court masque, Enid Welsford, the Gray's Inn endeavor was "a turning-point in the history of the masque. It is the first piece that we know of which gives the norm of the masque as composed by Ben Jonson and his fellow-poets. Later masques were more elaborate, but with the exception of the antimasque all the elements are here." [23] The speeches in the masque were written by Francis Davison, son of William Davison, at one time the Queen's Secretary of State. The whole constitutes an elaborate compliment to the Queen who is shown to be a "Power/Which in attractive Vertue" surpasses the "Adamantine Rocks/Which forceth Iron [that is, the magnetic pole]" (p. 63). Introduced by a lovely lyric by Campion, the masque is in the purest vein of Elizabethan pastoral idealism. The hero who wins the rock through his faith in the Queen's superior power is none other than the Prince of Purpoole. Set free from the rock by Proteus' trident, Henry Helmes and seven of his knights concluded the masque by dancing several "new devised measures" (p. 66) for the Queen.

It was not a long trip from the make-believe court of Purpoole to "Neptune's empire"; and the brothels in the "straits of the gulf of Clerkenwell" were equally close. The students at the Inns loved pastoral poetry like that in the masque at the same time that they admired the vicious realism of Juvenal and Martial. Professing to be rakes and whoremongers, they read (and wrote) Petrarchan love sonnets. The atmosphere in these revels is a mixture, not a compound, of youthful idealism and cynical sophistication, and the two attitudes seem to coexist comfortably. The same things can be said about the Middle Temple's revels, but differences in emphasis provide a valuable contrast between two very similar entertainments.

[23] *The Court Masque* (Cambridge, Eng., 1927), pp. 163–164.

IV The Middle Temple's
"Prince D'Amour" Revels of 1597–98

During the period from 1590 to 1610, the Middle Temple housed about two hundred men in its one hundred thirty-eight chambers.[1] Ten were Benchers who through seniority and the performance of a "reading" had become officers and administrators of the Inn. One of them, selected by the others, was the chief officer of the Middle Temple with the title of Treasurer. About forty other men in residence were fully qualified barristers, members of the Outer (or Utter) Bar. The

[1] These are round numbers based on the Inns' census of 1586 (Hugh H. L. Bellot, *The Temple* [London, 1922], p. 28) and the normal ratio of students to Utter Barristers and Benchers.

remaining one hundred fifty gentlemen composed a spectrum which ranged from serious "plodderly" students of the law to satin-clad revelers. Some of the most interesting students fitted into both these extreme categories, perhaps by burning the candle at both ends. I refer specifically to a group of students who arrived at the Middle Temple in the late 1580's and early 1590's.[2] As Appendix A shows, it was at Winchester School that some of them first met. They were part of a literary group which contained John Owen, the Latin epigrammatist; John Hoskins, lawyer, poet, rhetorician, and parliamentarian; Henry Wotton, ambassador, educator, poet; Thomas Bastard, clergy-man and epigrammatist; and the best known literary figure, John Davies, poet, lawyer, and judge. From Winchester four of them proceeded to William of Wykeham's other educational foundation, New College, Oxford, while Davies went to Queen's College. Perhaps it was at Oxford that some of them met Richard Martin of Broadgates Hall, the man who seems to have been the social leader of this group at the Middle Temple as well as a generally admired wit and Recorder of London. Also at Oxford was another future friend, Benjamin Rudyerd, poet and parliamentarian. Thomas Bastard did not go up to London, having to live a penurious existence as a country parson, and John Owen chose to go to the Inner Temple, but both of them remained in close contact with the others who proceeded to the Middle Temple. Henry Wotton's residence there seems to have been quite brief,[3] but he, too, continued to be friendly with some of his schoolmates for the rest of his life. At the Temple, Charles Best, a lawyer who published a few poems, became attached to the circle. Later, with inevitable losses but with the addition of other members of the Middle Temple who fused with Donne's and Jonson's circles, this group evolved into, or possibly formed the nucleus of, the one that congregated at the Mermaid Tavern. Recent scholarship has shown that the alleged "wit combats" at the Mermaid between Shakespeare and Jonson are an amiable fiction.[4] Nonetheless a group that contained Donne, Jonson, and Hoskins was formidable enough.

To a remarkable degree, these Middle Temple wits came from the same background, pursued the same course in life,

[2] This group has been discussed frequently, especially by Louise B. Osborn, *The Life, Letters and Writings of John Hoskyns* (New Haven, 1937).

[3] See Chapter I, n. 25.

[4] I. A. Shapiro, "The 'Mermaid Club,'" *Modern Language Review*, 45 (1950), 6–17.

shared the same tastes and preferences, and often tended to act
in very similar ways. First we should note, as Appendix A indicates, that they all became lawyers, most of them highly distinguished ones. None of them had much money; consequently
they had to acquire a profession. I mention this as an antidote
to Lenton's picture. They may have been revelers, but they had
to be serious students as well. Second, most of them were trou-
blemakers, more or less serious disciplinary problems, and not
merely as youths. Hoskins was forced to resign his fellowship
and to leave Oxford for giving "a bitterly satyricall" formal address at his commencement. It must have been satiric indeed
because in his assigned role as "terrae filius" he was empowered
to speak freely.[5] Perhaps it was also his loose tongue that em-
broiled him in a duel with another member of the group,
Benjamin Rudyerd. It certainly caused his detention in the
Tower in 1614 (as I shall later show).

Richard Martin and John Davies conducted themselves similarly on several occasions, as the minutes of the Middle Temple
Parliament attest. In 1591, "Messrs. Lower, Fletwood, Martyn,
Ameridyth, Thornhill, Swetnam, Davys, and Jacob . . . broke
the ordinance by making outcries, forcibly breaking open
chambers in the night and levying money as the Lord of Misrule's rent, and contemptuously refused to declare the names of
others; and Mr. Lower abused Mr. Johnson, a Master of the
Bench." [6] Along with Martin and Davies were William Lower,
the future astronomer, and William Fleetwood, brother of the
lawyer mentioned in Chapter II and son of the eminent Recorder of London. Clearly Martin and Davies were among the
ringleaders, for we find them under censure for precisely the
same misdemeanor at the next (1592) Candlemas Night disorders. This time Martin was expelled and Davies temporarily
denied admission to commons.[7] These escapades cannot be dismissed as the pecadilloes of spirited youth because both persisted in this kind of activity. Davies had been a member of the
Bar for two years and was twenty-nine years old when he committed his notorious assault on Martin (to be discussed below).
As for Martin, it was bruited about London in 1614 that he had

[5] Osborn, p. 19.

[6] *Middle Temple Records*, ed. Charles H. Hopwood (London, 1904), I, 318. A
Christmas Lord of Misrule at the Temple in 1627 exacted 5 s. "rent" from
residents of Ram Alley and Fleet Street until City authorities put a stop to it.
See B. H. C., "The Templars and Their Christmas Revels in 1627," *Notes and
Queries*, 3rd. ser, 3 (1863), 24.

[7] *Middle Temple Records*, I, 326–327.

killed a fellow Templar, although nothing came of it because of his own death soon afterward.[8]

Hoskins' suffering for his self-destructive wit had its parallels in the careers of Henry Wotton and Thomas Bastard. According to Anthony Wood, Bastard was deprived of his fellowship at New College for writing a libel about the sexual activities of certain prominent members of the academic community.[9] And Wotton's jesting definition of an ambassador as "an honest man, sent to lie abroad for the good of his country" cost him many years of advancement because it unexpectedly embarrassed King James. Any explanation of this group tendency toward physical violence and untimely exhibition of wit would be mere conjecture, but such a concentration of these traits within a small circle must be considered unusual even among uninhibited Elizabethans.

It is these men who were largely responsible for the revels at the Middle Temple in 1597–98. Thus special interest attaches to these revels: they express something of the taste of an important group of wits in the 1590's about whom we have a great deal of additional information. One of them, Benjamin Rudyerd, collected some of the speeches and ceremonials and appended a chronological narrative of all the festivities. He composed it from the point of view of a participant, even to the extent of expressing personal animosity toward one of the revelers. Rudyerd's text, published in 1660 as *Le Prince d'Amour or the Prince of Love,* appears to be a helter-skelter assemblage of unconnected material,[10] but the relation between its parts becomes clear once the appended chronological summary is studied carefully.[11] The text of the revels is far from complete. In

---

[8] See *Historical Manuscript Commission Report 10,* Appendix, Part 6, p. 84.

[9] *Athenae Oxoniensis,* ed. Philip Bliss (London, 1815), II, 227. In a poem, Bastard disclaimed authorship of this libel. See J. L. Sanderson, "Thomas Bastard's Disclaimer of an Oxford Libel," *The Library,* 5th ser., 17 (1962), 145–149.

[10] Rudyerd, *Prince d'Amour,* p. 77, says that it was "transcribed from scattered papers." Page references in the text refer to the edition of the *Prince d'Amour* of 1660. The attribution of *Le Prince d'Amour* (London, 1660) to Rudyerd is based on the fact that the account of the revels is signed "B. R." on p. 90 and that the account is nearly identical with that which J. A. Manning printed from a MS by Rudyerd in *Memories of Sir Benjamin Rudyerd* (London, 1841), pp. 9–18. The date 1597–98 for the revels is arrived at by internal evidence, for which see Hoyt H. Hudson, ed., *Directions for Speech and Style by John Hoskins* (Princeton, 1935), p. 109, n. 2. I have shown that a letter from the Middle Temple to the Earl of Shrewsbury (discussed below) corroborates the accuracy of this date. See *N & Q,* 209 (1964), 37.

[11] Hudson, *Directions,* pp. 109–110, gives instructions on how to make sense out of Rudyerd's account.

fact, it is clear both from external evidence and from the marked similarity of most of his selections that Rudyerd tended to include only what he and his friends wrote or, at least, what he felt was most interesting in the festivities.

The account of the early stages of preparation is valuable because it indicates how casually a season of elaborate revels could be initiated. At an entertainment at Lincoln's Inn some guests from the Middle Temple suggested that their hosts set up a Christmas Prince. The suggestion was thrown back to the Templars, who then agreed that they should hold the revels since their hall was larger. The next step was to select a leader to organize the endeavor. One of the Templars, called "Stradilax" in the account, was eager to serve, but the majority wanted "Seignor Martino" to fill the post. He was reluctant since "he rather now desired to settle his name then to spread it" (p. 80), but finally he was prevailed upon to accept.[12] After some initial difficulties, the instigators began, like Gray's Inn, by sending out "Privy Seals directed to all within these Dominions towards the charge of this undertaking, but slowly returned" (p. 80). One of these, not mentioned in Rudyerd's account, did bear fruit. A letter sent to Gilbert Talbot, Earl of Shrewsbury, signed "Middle Temple," has survived. It asks the Earl "to lend us such a some of money as to your Ho. shall seem convenient, in favour of our pretended extraordinarye designes." The letter is endorsed: "This Privy Seale beynge brought unto me at X'temas 1597, in respect of the Prince d'Amore's kepinge his Revells in yt In of Courte, I sent him, by the hands of Mr. Davyes of that house £30. Gilb. Shrewsbury." [13]

Money having been obtained through the agency of John Davies and others, the revels were able to proceed. The organizers must have done a prodigious amount of work. Over a period of three weeks they managed to offer two comedies, three banquets, four masques, two encounters at the barriers, and six evenings at least partially devoted to "law

[12] Perhaps his reluctance to serve sprang from an unwillingness to spend the large amount of money which the office sometimes required. According to E. K. Chambers, *Medieval Stage* (Oxford, 1903), I, 417, Francis Vivian spent £2000 as Prince in 1635. He was knighted soon after his reign ended. In the revels of 1597–98, it is more likely that the Prince, Richard Martin, was interested in expunging his reputation as a reveler, which, as we saw above, began with his punishments for disorders in 1591 and 1592.

[13] Printed in Edmund Lodge, *Illustrations of British History, Biography, and Manners* (London, 1791), III, 91. The letter is also printed in J. Nichols, *The Progresses and Public Processions of Queen Elizabeth* (London, 1823), III, 423.

sports."[14] I have reconstructed a day-by-day schedule in order to illustrate the variety of events and the pace of activity. An asterisk marks those speeches or events for which Rudyerd supplied the text.

Schedule of the Prince d'Amour's Revels

Saturday, Dec. 24, 1597. Prince d'Amour publicly elected. Orations of congratulation and answer by the Prince.

Sunday, Dec. 25 (Christmas). "Private meditations."

Monday, Dec. 26. Inauguration and Coronation of the Prince. Proclamation of his title*; justification by a champion*. Challenge by a stranger knight on behalf of Queen Elizabeth*. Strangers come to give allegiance and to beg the Prince's mediation in quarrels with foreign princes.

Tuesday, Dec. 27. Councilors argue against the Prince's hazarding his throne on the outcome of one combat*. A Templar given the name "Stradilax" is publicly satirized*.

Wednesday, Dec. 28. A comedy presented. The duties of the Prince's Officers are read*.

Thursday, Dec. 29. A Prognostication which "foretold things past"*. The "Orator" gives a "Tufftaffeta Oration" to which the Clerk of Council, "importuned by the Prince and Sir Walter Raleigh," gives a "Fustian answer"*.

Friday, Dec. 30. Fast day to prepare for "sacrifice of love."

Saturday, Dec. 31. Ceremony called the Sacrifice of Love. Banquet. Masque by eight gentlemen. Ceremony for the creation of six "knights of the Quiver"*. Stradilax recites three "confessions."

Sunday, Jan. 1, 1598. Nothing.

Monday, Jan. 2. A comedy. Dancing and a banquet.

Tuesday, Jan. 3. A commendation of woman's inconstancy, scheduled but not delivered.[15]

Wednesday, Jan. 4 and Thursday, Jan. 5. Preparations for entertainment at Court.

Friday, Jan. 6 (Twelfth Night). A procession through the streets on the way to Court: "there went to the Court 11.

---

[14] It is scarcely credible that all of this could have been done without hiring a professional acting company to supply the plays, as Gray's Inn did in 1594–95 and as the Middle Temple did when the Chamberlain's Men presented *Twelfth Night* on Candlemas night, Feb. 2, 1602. E. K. Chambers, *The Elizabethan Stage* (Oxford, 1923), I, 222, makes a similar point. It is possible that the masque on Dec. 31 was repeated on Jan. 13 and that the one at Court on Jan. 6 was repeated at the Middle Temple on Jan. 7.

[15] Such a speech was delivered at a later Middle Temple revel, as Edward Pudsey recorded in his commonplace book (Bodleian MS. Eng. Poet. d.3), fol. 87r. He did not realize that it was Donne's first paradox.

Knights and 11. Esquires, 9. Maskers, 9. Torchbearers. Their setting forth was with a peal of Ordnance, a noise of Trumpets always sounding before them, the Herald next, and after two Esquires and two Knights" (p. 86). (Everyone, including the horses, was dressed sumptuously; there were a hundred torches carried by servants.) "The Knights broke every man a Lance & two swords . . . The nine Maskers like Passions issued out of a Heart" (p. 86).

Saturday, Jan. 7. A "solemn Barriers" by two knights. A masque.

Sunday, Jan. 8. Prince sups with a royal gentleman. "Stradilax" recites a "comparison of pork"—apparently an obscene poem.

Monday, Jan. 9. Prince goes to the Lord Mayor's in great state.

Tuesday, Jan. 10. Nothing noteworthy.

Wednesday, Jan. 11. The Prince inspects the chambers of his subjects, apparently causing disorder in his capacity as Lord of Misrule.

Thursday, Jan. 12. Lincoln's Inn pays a visit to the Prince's court, but there is too much uproar to receive them "worthily." "Stradilax" tries to stir enmity between the Prince and the Lincolnians.

Friday, Jan. 13. Lincoln's Inn comes with an ambassador. A masque by eight gentlemen. Arraignment of a discontented and a jealous lover*.

Saturday, Jan. 14. Banquet for Lincoln's Inn during which their league is renewed. This is the last consecutive day of reveling.

Thursday, Feb. 2 (Candlemas Night). The Prince resigns after hearing advice from his councilors: "One advised him to follow the Sea; another to Land travel; a third to marry a rich widow; and a fourth to study the Common Law. He chose the last, and refused not the third if she stood in his way" (p. 89).

N. B. To complete the picture, we must remember that the Middle Temple Hall was also the site of dicing and other forms of gambling during lulls in the proceedings.

Even in summary, the resemblance to the Gray's Inn revels is evident. These entertainments may have changed in the course of the sixteenth century, but it is clear from the variety and type of material presented that the Inns had adhered to Fortescue's ideal. For those students who availed themselves of the opportunity, such exercises provided unparalleled training for the well-rounded gentleman and would-be courtier as well as the prospective lawyer. What is more, by entertaining high court officials and frequently the Queen herself, many a young man gained attention for his wit, his forensic power, or, in one famous episode, that of Christopher Hatton in 1561, his dancing ability.

Although the audience would have included many distinguished visitors,[16] a large amount of the humor was inevitably based on intramural jokes and local personalities. Its existence at revels will alert us to its presence in certain Inns of Court writers who wrote for a larger but similarly closed circle. To discover what was happening, we must first know precisely who took part in the festivities. Unlike the anonymous compiler of the *Gesta Grayorum,* Rudyerd does not supply a list of participants and the parts they played, but it is not difficult to identify several of the most important revelers. The Prince d'Amour, "Seignor Martino," was certainly Richard Martin, who served in that office whenever there was need for the rest of his life.[17] We know that John Hoskins acted as the "Clerk of Council" because it is the Clerk who gives a "fustian" speech which Hoskins acknowledges as his own in his book of rhetoric, *Directions for Speech and Style;*[18] this book also includes other material which Rudyerd assigns to the Clerk. The "Prince's Orator" is called "Carolus Asinius Bestia" in Rudyerd's account. This would be Charles Best, identified in Appendix A. Rudyerd himself must have played some role, although it is not clear which one.

One of the important figures who appears frequently in Rudyerd's account is left unidentified, the person called "Stradilax." We learn that he had tried unsuccessfully to become the Prince; that he constantly gave senseless advice which went unheeded; that he wore a "Marmelad-Colour-Taffata-Gown . . . never seen after [hence rented]" (p. 82) at one evening of the revels; and that a libel against him was posted in prominent spots around London. On several occasions he took an important part in the festivities, reciting three "confessions" on December 31, and on January 8 giving "his old comparison of Pork, to the dispraise of noble Women there

---

[16] Bartholomew Young, in the dedication to Lady Rich of his translation of Montemayor's *Diana* (London, 1598), mentions his apprehensiveness at playing the part of a French orator "in a publike shewe at the Middle Temple, where your Honorable presence with many noble Lordes and fine Ladies graced and beautified those sportes" (sig. a2r).

[17] *Middle Temple Records,* II, 610 and 612, indicate that he was taking part in Inns' entertainments, as was Hoskins, as late as 1616.

[18] See Hudson, *Directions,* pp. 108–113.

present" (p. 87). Apparently he also gave a "soldier's speech" but disclaimed it, "because it wanted Applause" (p. 84). On the other hand, he "usurped upon the commendation of all tolerable speeches" (p. 84). He served as the Commissioner in the arraignment of the discontented lover on January 13, and called himself "Erophilus, in sawcy imitation of the great Earle of the time" (p. 89) (that is, the Earl of Essex). Plainly, Stradilax was personally distasteful to Rudyerd.

Rudyerd's account of the events on the night of December 27 helps to identify "Stradilax" with a high degree of certainty: "This night *Stradilax,* in great pompe, with a left handed Truncheon Marshalled himself a Lord, no man gainsaying it, or crying God save thy Lordship, but Poet *Matagonius,* who presented him a Sheild wherein was drawn the Monster *Sphinx;* the word was *Davus sum, non Oedipus,* and saluted him by the name of *Stradilax,* to the Tune of the Tanner and the King" (p. 83). I suggest that "Davus" is a bilingual pun which identifies "Stradilax" as John Davies (often spelled and still pronounced in England as though it were "Davis"). As we have seen, he was one of the organizers of these revels. The choice of tune continues the gibe, for his father was reputed to be a wealthy tanner.[19] The tag from Terence suggests that Davies is a "davus" (the name of a slave), not an Oedipus; a tanner, not a king. In addition, Rudyerd says that Stradilax recited three "Confessions; for a Souldier, a Traveller, and a Country Gentleman." The poems in Davies' *Twelve Wonders of the World* might well be called confessions; the third is spoken by a soldier and the seventh by a country gentleman. They are sufficiently poor in their heavy irony to justify Rudyerd's adverse judgment — "so bad, that the meanest Wit would not undertake to bring them in" (p. 84). It may be noted that the name "Stradilax" was attached to him by "Matagonius" as part of the satire. I suggest that the name refers to Davies' waddling gait,[20] which Manningham describes so coarsely and vividly in his diary: "Jo. Davys goes wadling with his arse out behinde as though he were about to make every one that he meetes a wall to pisse against." [21]

[19] See Anthony Wood, *Athenae,* II, 400. Alexander Grosart, *Poems of John Davies* (London, 1876), I, xv–xvi, says that Wood was mistaken, but that Davies' brother was a tanner.

[20] The relevant *NED* definition of "straddle" is to "spread the legs wide apart in walking."

[21] I am indebted to Professor Robert Sorlien of the University of Rhode Island, who is preparing a new edition of Manningham, for this transcription from MS. Harl. 5353, fol. 127v.

Why, one wonders, did his friends turn on the amiable-sounding author of *Orchestra*? If we ignore the evidence of Rudyerd's account, the only apparent motives are resentment of his ambition and jealousy of his success. In 1598 Davies was the only one of his circle who had already become a barrister (1595); he had made very important connections at Court; and he was a published poet. Perhaps his friends felt that he was a little too pushy and opportunistic. This would seem to be the burden of an epigram recently ascribed to Rudyerd and alleged to be about Davies:

> Mathon hath got the barr and many graces
> by studdyinge, noble men, newes, and faces.[22]

Whatever the causes, if the identification of Davies with Stradilax be accepted, we can say that he was libeled, ridiculed in a public ceremony, and generally made the butt of the revelers. It may have been his treatment at the revels which goaded Davies into his notorious, half-insane attack on Richard Martin; or perhaps it was the collusion of his "deerest friend" (as he calls Martin in *Orchestra*) with the other revelers which caused Davies to single him out. But one week after Martin resigned as Prince d'Amour, on February 9, 1598, the incident occurred which, however well-known, must be included in any account of life at the Middle Temple in the 1590's: "While the Masters of the Bench and other fellows were quietly dining publicly in the Hall, John Davyes, one of the Masters of the Bar, in cap and gown, and girt with a dagger, his servant and another with him being armed with swords, came into the Hall. The servant and the other person stayed at the bottom of the Hall, while he walked up to the fireplace and then to the lower part of the second table for Masters of the Bar, where Richard Martyn was quietly dining. Taking from under his gown a stick,

---

[22] *The Dr. Farmer Chetham MS.*, ed. Alexander Grosart (Manchester, 1873), I, 101. For the identification of Matho as Davies, see James L. Sanderson, "Epigrames P[er] B[enjamin] R[udyerd] and Some More 'Stolen Feathers' of Henry Parrot," *Review of English Studies*, n.s., 17 (1966), 241–255. This view of Davies is re-enforced by another anecdote. As part of Lord Hunsdon's entourage, Davies went to Scotland to make the official announcement to James of his accession. The King asked him "whether he were 'Nosce Teipsum'" and learning that he was, "embraced him and conceived a considerable liking for him" (*Athenae*, II, 401). Flushed by his prospects, Davies returned to the Temple and, according to Manningham (*Diary of John Manningham*, ed. John Bruce, Camden Society Publication 99 [London, 1868], p. 168), crowed about his good fortune: "Jo. Davis reports that he is sworne the Kings Man, that the King shewed him great favors." Manningham, never an admirer of Davies, adds sourly: "*Inepte.* (He slaunders while he prayses.)"

which is commonly called 'a Bastianado,' he struck Martyn on the head with it till it broke, and then running to the bottom of the Hall he took his servant's sword out of his hand, shook it over his own head, and ran down to the watersteps and jumped into a boat. He is expelled, never to return." [23]

Three years of rustication, a volume of poems to Queen Elizabeth (*Astraea*), the publication of another poem of high repute (*Nosce Teipsum*), and the intercession of some of the most powerful lawyers and judges in the land were required before Davies was restored to membership in the Middle Temple — although not again to friendship with Martin. Personal satire is endemic to intramural entertainment. The gentlemen at Gray's Inn indulged in the same sort of byplay, as we can see in some recently discovered "libels" written about participants in the revels of 1594–95.[24] What would seem to be the special mark of these Middle Templars — I shall describe some further examples in the next chapter — is that they went too far, lost control, and ended with violence.

In other ways as well Rudyerd's document suggests the tastes and interests of the participants. In addition to the account of the proceedings, the *Prince d'Amour* contains six separate blocks of material of varying lengths: (1) the installation of the Prince, including an encomium of the Queen and debates about whether the Prince should engage in single combat (twenty-two pages); (2) a description of each court officer's duties (nine pages); (3) a "Prognostication" (six pages); (4) the "fustian" speech (three pages); (5) the installation of knights in the "Order of the Quiver" (seven pages); and (6) the arraignment of a discontented lover (twenty-eight pages). In all but the first and fourth of these items, the text consists mainly of a succession of relatively disconnected, brief jokes and displays of wit. They are cast in the form of laws or stipulations or requirements, and their nearest kin among literary genres is the epigram, a form which most of the prominent participants practiced. There are nineteen "charges to officers," twenty-nine "articles" for members of the Order, thirty "offences inquirable by the grand jury" and thirty by the Petty Jury: in sum, one hundred eight separate items plus an indeterminate amount of similar material in the Prognostication. In contrast, the *Gesta Grayorum*

[23] *Middle Temple Records*, I, 381. The account by Lord Stowell in *Archaeologia*, 21 (1827), 107–112, is the most satisfactory and complete because it contains the original Latin text of Davies' expulsion. This makes it clear, as the translation quoted above does not, that the attack occurred on Feb. 9, 1597/8.
[24] James L. Sanderson, "An Elizabethan Libel against Some Gray's Inn Gentlemen," *Notes and Queries*, n.s., 10 (1963), 298–300.

lists only eighteen "laws." Thus, for Rudyerd at least, the most important part of the revels was a series of short sallies of satiric wit directed at the manners and morals of the inhabitants of the Inns.

Much of the wit was consonant with the fiction of a "Prince d'Amour" presiding over a kingdom of lovers, in this again offering a somewhat different emphasis from the Gray's Inn revels. In almost all the texts which Rudyerd collected — the description of the officer's duties, the installation of the "Knights of the Quiver," and the arraignments of the discontented and jealous lovers — the subject is love, or more precisely, sex. The *Gesta Grayorum* was not silent on this subject, but it was not the raison d'etre of the Prince of Purpoole.

The sexual mores that pervade the Prince d'Amour's kingdom are nearly identical with those we find in Donne's libertine elegies and in some Jacobean private theater comedy; it is a world of amoral women, cuckolds, aphrodisiacs, whores, and venereal disease, a world where the right true end of love is the maximum number of female conquests. Thus it is the task of the Prince's Archflamen "to give absolution or dissolution for false Protestations, affectionate Oathes, &c. To enjoyn Penance to Lovers impotent in performance, that they fast upon dry Alegant, cold Lobsters, Oysters, and Hartichokes, and such like tamers of the flesh . . . that it shall be lawful for them, with the Favors and Gifts which they receive from Ill-favoured, to purchase fair Mistresses; and that he may allow Pluralities in Love to them which have extraordinary parts" (p. 23). The Lord Chamberlain must "keep all Roomes voide of Spies, sweetly perfumed, the Couches made all for advantage, that the Windows admit but twilight, to cover Blemishes, and discover perfections, to accommodate Ladies in Chambers to their content" (p. 25). Or more grossly, the Lord Admiral "shall, in passing the narrow Seas, be continually sounding least he run his Ship aground so that he cannot soundly get it off again; neither shall he come to an Anchor in foul ground" (p. 27).

The Middle Temple's revels are permeated with such jokes, yet in this setting few would call them offensive. They were, as Campion says in the epigram prefixed to Chapter III, "nugae," trifles uttered in a holiday mood. His audience would not have regarded the jokes I have just quoted as "tetrae" or "infacetae." We recognize the vein well enough and take it for what it is: the bravado of young men trying to pass as devil-may-care rakes. In the revels' atmosphere of licensed rebellion, it was the sons' responsibility to shock their fathers; they fulfilled it to every-one's satisfaction.

But there is another note intermixed with this "wanton" joking which is far more critical and mature: "Item, That he have the wit to mislike the fashion of his clothes before he pawn them; and that he be alwayes furnished with reasons for the convenience of every fashion" (p. 45). Another item requires "That no Knight shall entertain his Mistris with talking of other men" (p. 43). And another, that "he learn no speeches out of Playes to entertain the time" (p. 45). The difference in tone from the quasi-worldly material around these items is startling. They sound peremptory, born of impatience with time-wasting "young masters of the Temple," as Hoskins sarcas-tically calls them in his *Directions*.[25] Some of these items also reveal an observant satiric vision which could produce comedy of manners or verse satire; it is easy to imagine Jonson or Marston creating comic characters out of such material. In fact, one item prefigures, and possibly even inspired, scenes in Marston's *The Fawne* and *Antonio and Mellida*: "That no Knight shew a Ladies name in the bottom of a Letter, that is either of his own making, or else was written by the Lady to some other . . . That he letting fall some Tailors Bill, snatch it not up in haste, and say he had hazarded the discovery of the Love of some great nameless Lady" (pp. 44–45).[26]

A note of literary sophistication sounds clearly in a set of "laws" which simultaneously mock legal language and satirize fashions in lovemaking, in particular the tendency to act like Petrarchan lovers. There is a prescription that "if any man kissing his hand superstitiously hath taken his Mistresses dog by the tail, swearing her breath hath perfumed the same; he is to be punished for the first part as an Idolater, and for the second as a blasphemer" (p. 62). Again, "if any man kiss the seat of his Mistresses saddle, or the stool whereon she hath sitten, he shall be taken as a vain worshipper of Idols" (p. 62). Manners and language are frequently seen as aspects of each other; hence the satire attacks the trite, secondhand language of Petrarchan lovers: "If any man deprave the books of *Ovid de Arte amandi; Euphues* and his *England, Petite Pallace,* or other laudable discourses of Love; this is loss of his Mistris favor for half a year" (p. 57).

[25] Hudson, *Directions,* p. 3.
[26] Cf. *The Plays of John Marston,* ed. H. Harvey Wood (3 vols., Edinburgh, 1934–1939), II, 195, and I, 37, respectively.

Such satire was part of a larger linguistic concern that, as one of the decrees went, "once in three dayes . . . [a man] speak with some spice of Wit, and to the purpose twice every night if it be possible" (p. 43). This concern for proper language sometimes produced very detailed prohibitions like that against the use of "perfumed terms, as spirit, apprehension, resolution, accommodate, humors, complement, possessed, respective, etc." (p. 43). This is but one of several pieces of evidence that John Hoskins composed the precepts and satiric material in the revels respecting language, for nearly the same list appears in his *Directions for Speech and Style*.[27]

In this brief book of rhetoric composed by Hoskins for a young member of the Middle Temple, the author occasionally alludes to his contributions to these revels and clarifies his purposes. For example, he says about the "fustian" answer he delivered at the importunity of Sir Walter Raleigh to the "tufftaffeta" address by the Prince's Orator on December 29: "If you will read over that speech, you shall find most of the figures of rhetoric there, meaning neither harm nor good, but as idle as yourself when you are most at leisure" (p. 50). But it is more than a jeu d'esprit: "This figure cannot be out of season, but of purpose, as was in the fustian speech" (p. 50). And again, "Use this, or any other point, unseasonably, it is as ridiculous as it was in the fustian oration . . . But let discretion be the greatest and general figure of figures" (p. 15). The fustian speech is a piece of conscious indiscretion, as its first words reveal: "Then (Mr. Orator) I am sorry that for your Tufftaffeta Speech, you shall receive but a Fustian Answer. For alas! what am I (whose ears have been pasted with the Tenacity of your Speeches, and whose nose hath been perfumed with the Aromaticity of your sentences) that I should answer your Oration, both Voluminous and Topical, with a Replication concise and curtal? For you are able in Troops of Tropes, and Centuries of Sentences to muster your meaning: Nay, you have such Wood-piles of words, that unto you Cooper is but a Carpenter, and Rider himself deserves not a Reader" (*Prince*, p. 37, and *Directions*, p. 111). Through this reductio ad absurdum of the art of rhetoric, Hoskins demonstrates that restraint and taste are necessary adjuncts to artificial rules. It is not enough merely to muster troops of tropes and centuries of sentences.

Hoskins' *Directions* is a learned compendium of the work of

---

[27] Page 7. Page numbers in the text refer to Hudson's edition of *Directions*.

many rhetoricians, unified by a personal and original point of view. At a moment when the fashion for metaphysical conceits was incubating, he warns against metaphor that is "too bold or far-fetched" (p. 8). He suggests that his pupil "avoid too great swelling without substance in the figure comparison" (p. 22). At a time when amplification was practiced by multiplying synonyms, he cautions that such misuse "will sooner yield a conjecture of superfluity of words than of sufficienty of matter" (p. 24). Yet he was not so anti-Ciceronian as to fall into the other trap of Senecan sententiousness: "It is very true that sentence is a pearl in a discourse; but is it a good discourse that is all pearl? It is like an eye in the body; but is it not monstrous to be all eyes? I take Cyclops to be as handsome a man as Argus . . . in my judgment *sententia* is better for the bench than the bar. Then of all others, why would the writers of these days imprison themselves in the straitness of these maxims? It makes their style like *arena sine calce*" (pp. 39–40).

Hoskins opposes stylishness in writing, the tendency of even the "bravest wits" (p. 39) to imitate each other. A "learned man," he feels, should avoid this "as seeming to come more of the general humor than the private judgment" (p. 17). His own writing is a good example of the plain style, which (following Lipsius) he prefers for epistolary writing: "Both in method and word to use, as ladies use in their attire, a kind of diligent negligence" (p. 7). This last phrase encapsulates the essential attitude toward language of the *Directions*. But behind this casual formulation — "diligent negligence" — lies an exalted view of the proper use of language: "The shame of speaking unskilfully were small if the tongue were only disgraced by it. But as the image of the king in a seal of wax, ill represented, is not so much a blemish to the wax or the signet that sealeth it as to the king whom it resembleth, so disordered speech is not so much injury to the lips which give it forth or the thoughts which put it forth as to the right proportion and coherence of things in themselves" (p. 2).

I do not want to give a distorted picture of the Prince d'Amour's revels by implying that they were totally dominated by the point of view of Hoskins and his friends. As the summary of events indicates, these revels contained many traditional elements. There is the inevitable expression of devotion to the Queen: "She remaines the onely Divine Pattern of all creatures to imitate . . . Her kingdom seated in the midst of the Waters, gives the Windes free liberty to spread her glorious fame every where" (pp. 10–11). Establishing the machinery of a court in-

volved the traditional exercises in stately, ceremonious elocution
for the training of the young men. We can assess their relative
adherence to Fortescue's ideals by contrasting them with the
revels of 1617–18 at Gray's Inn. The text we have contains many
of the revels' standard elements in addition to a masque.[28] This
masque, sometimes known as "The Mountebank's Masque" and
at one time ascribed to Marston on the basis of a forgery by
Collier, contains obscene recipes and songs and a very long
series of one-sentence paradoxical jokes on sexual topics delivered by a character named "Paradox." The revels may very
well have been entertaining in their day: at least four manuscripts have survived, part of the masque was reprinted, and
the Lord Chancellor, Bacon, attended the festivities on Candlemas Night. But what is striking to a modern reader is the total
concentration on bawdy jokes in legal language. Aside from
one lovely lyric in the masque, the unending succession of brief
quips, nearly all on one topic and with nothing to counter-
balance them, conveys a sense of obsession which serves as a
measure of the broader and more mature range of interests in
the earlier revels.

Surprisingly enough, the ostensible aim in establishing the
Prince d'Amour's court, as announced in the opening speech,
was to revive a more chivalrous attitude toward love: "For
who of late hath taken the honorable course of Love, or so
much as set foot on the pathway to Chivalry? Easie and low-
prized Venery hath been basely pursued, whilst desires illuminated by the Celestial flame of Beauty, have been accounted
either Fictions or Frensies" (p. 7). A simultaneous admiration
for the code of courtly love and for the morals of an Aretino
is everywhere apparent in the *Prince d'Amour,* as it was in the
Gesta Grayorum. In the largest block of material, the arraignment of the discontented lover, the attitude toward licentious
conduct is radically confused. The arraignment aims to root
out "the male-contented, way-ward, false, jealous, leud, wanton,
dissembling and disdainful persons making Love, an outward
shew and shadow, and a deceitful practice, which should be
indeed inward compunction and passion of the heart" (pp. 48–
49). This sounds serious and thoughtful enough to counteract
the libertine joking by the discontented lover. He is arraigned
for bragging that he shifted his mistresses "as often as he shifts
his clothes" (p. 69), for twisting words into bawdy puns, and
for writing three poems, the texts of which are given in full,
of which the following excerpt is a fair sample:

[28] Printed in Nichols, *Progresses . . . of Queen Elizabeth,* III, 320–348.

Live still, I cannot miss thee,
I must enjoy thee one day,
Dear sweet come home & kiss me
Where I did sit on Sunday. (p. 72)

About half of the laws read for the juries are in this ribald
vein, but half of them, while humorous, are quite severe toward
such attitudes: "If any of the Princes subjects hath abused the
Favor of his Mistris by the Act of dissimulation, or the Mystery
of double dealing, he shall be punished by dismembring"
(p. 63).

Thus the revels help us to reconstruct an inbred milieu of
young men, mostly wealthy, whose orthodox ideals and ambitions mingled easily with licentious conduct (or the pretense
of it) and whose fashions in clothes and literature were picked
up and discarded overnight. It is a world ripe for satire. What
gives the Middle Temple's revels their special character — only
partially visible in our text — is the superimposition onto a
set of traditional institutional complacencies of the attitudes
and actions of a group of satirists, rhetoricians, and disorderly
wits. I do not refer only to the way their personal feuds imparted a special flavor to these revels. Within the old framework they managed to inject satire of the wealthy idlers, rakes,
clotheshorses, and fools among whom they lived. "True judging eyes, quick sighted censurers," as Marston called such
wits,[29] they were not above overt didacticism to improve their
time-wasting colleagues. They inconspicuously shifted the emphasis in many parts of the revels so that the satire was often
about the audience rather than the outside world. Ben Jonson
was accused in *Satiromastix* of "bumbasting out a new Play,
with the olde lynings of Jests, stolne from the Temples Revels." [30] The accusation was as just as most of the invective in
the War of the Theaters, but the material was clearly there to
be plucked. In the audience were many prime Jonsonian
humors characters (for example, Master Matthew in *Every Man
in His Humor*), from the stage in the great hall emanated the
jests, and when the play had been bumbasted out by a comic
genius, from the Temple would troop a horde of gallants to
see themselves receive a verbal bastinado.

[29] *Poems of John Marston*, ed. Arnold Davenport (Liverpool, 1961), p. 99, l. 87.
[30] *Dramatic Works of Thomas Dekker*, ed. Fredson Bowers (Cambridge, Eng.,
1953), I, 382, ll. 295–296.

V The Political Climate
at the Inns of Court (1590–1615)

We get another brief but revealing glimpse into the atmosphere of the Temple at this time through a famous theological controversy that took place at the Temple Church. Upon the illness in 1585 of the Master of the Temple — this was the title of the minister who presided over the church held in common by the two Temples — the well-known Calvinist Walter Travers was appointed to fill the preaching functions. However, on the death of the incumbent, Richard Alvey, Richard Hooker was appointed Master while Travers retained his subordinate position. Thus the famous encounter occurred: "Here the pulpit spake pure Canterbury in the morning, and Geneva in the afternoon." [1] The grounds of their disagreement were doctrinal niceties, but no argument could have been more timely, no two antagonists better fitted to represent their positions. The response at the Temple was enthusiastic; it was a situation to their taste, not unlike a moot. Fuller says, "Here might one on Sundays have seen almost as many writers as hearers. Not only young students, but even the gravest benchers (such as sir Edward Coke and sir James Altham then were,) were not more exact in taking instructions from their clients, than in writing notes from the mouths of their ministers." [2]

It made the Archbishop of Canterbury, Whitgift, nervous to contemplate so persuasive a man as Travers reaching such an important audience, particularly when he seemed to be having the better of it: "Some say the congregation in the Temple ebbed in the forenoon and flowed in the afternoon and that the auditory of Mr. Travers was far the more numerous." [3] As Fuller put it, Travers' influence was such that it was "in effect to retain half the lawyers of England to be of counsel against the ecclesiastical government thereof." [4] Therefore the Archbishop counseled the Queen against Travers' continuation at the Temple: "The living is not great, yet doth it require a learned, discreet, and wise man, in respect of the company there: who being well directed and taught may do much good elsewhere in the commonwealth, as otherwise also they may do much harm." [5] Though Travers was ultimately ejected from the Temple and though Hooker generously acknowledged the value to his thinking of Travers' challenge, Hooker found the Mastership of the Temple an uncongenial position, as he said in a letter to Whitgift in 1591: "I am weary of the noise and oppositions of this place, and indeed God and nature did not intend me for contentions, but for study and quietness." [6]

It is difficult to ascertain the proportion of Puritans in the Inns of Court at this time. In fact, the Middle Temple has been accused of an opposite tendency toward Papism. Out of two hundred sixty members in Commons in 1609, only one hundred twenty had received Communion.[7] But an Inns of Court man

[1] Thomas Fuller, *History of the Worthies of England*, ed. P. Austin Nuttall (London, 1840), I, 423.

[2] *The Church History of Britain*, ed. James Nichols (London, 1840), III, 128.

[3] Ibid.

[4] Ibid., p. 131.

[5] *The Works of Richard Hooker*, ed. John Keble (Oxford, 1845), I, 29.

[6] Ibid., p. 67.

[7] A. L. Rowse, *The England of Elizabeth* (New York, 1961), p. 373, quotes a contemporary source which accuses the Middle Temple of being "pestered with Papists." Rowse implies that this tendency was initiated by the great lawyer who long resided there, Edmund Plowden.

need not have been a Puritan to have been fascinated by Travers because, as C. S. Lewis remarked about Elizabethan Calvinists: "In their own day they were the very latest thing. Unless we can imagine the freshness, the audacity, and (soon) the fashionableness of Calvinism, we shall get our whole picture wrong. It was the creed of progressives, even of revolutionaries. It appealed strongly to those tempers that would have been Marxist in the nineteen-thirties. The fierce young don, the learned lady, the courtier with intellectual leanings, were likely to be Calvinists . . . Youth is the taunt commonly brought against the puritan leaders by their opponents: youth and cocksureness." [8] Since the Inns were filled with fashion-conscious young men, the attraction was a natural one.

But if a recent argument by Christopher Hill is valid, there were deeper connections between Puritans like Travers and lawyers like Sir Edward Coke who were engaged in a vast effort to aggrandize the power and prestige of the common law. Hill says, "Coke was one of those who took notes at the lectures which Walter Travers . . . gave at the Temple . . . Sir Edward held the high Puritan view — or so he told Bacon — that it was sinful 'for a man to go against his own conscience, though erroneous, except his conscience be first informed and satisfied.' Coke was guardian to Roger Williams, a man not unlearned in the law. Williams regarded Coke as a 'blessed man,' who would have sympathized with his emigration to New England. So there was some affinity between Coke and those Puritans who, Sibthorpe complained, 'make the law above the King.' " [9]

Whether or not lawyers as a class were "infected with Puritanism," as one sympathizer with the Crown claimed,[10] the lawyers did join in an alliance with the Puritans against the encroachments of royal power. Notestein says of the lawyers, "To the Common Law their deepest loyalty was engaged; when James seemed to be undermining it they were ready to join the Opposition . . . Whatever the various reasons for their attitude, the lawyers were more than abettors of opposition to James, they made up a considerable part of the leadership of that opposition." [11]

As it happens, both of the main leaders of Parliament's op-

[8] *English Literature in the Sixteenth Century* (Oxford, 1954), p. 43.
[9] *Intellectual Origins of the English Revolution* (Oxford, 1965), pp. 249–250.
[10] Quoted by Wallace Notestein, *The Winning of the Initiative by the House of Commons* (London, 1924), p. 50.
[11] Ibid.

position to the Stuarts, Sir Edwin Sandys in the earlier Parliaments and John Pym later, had been members of the Middle Temple (see Appendix A). It is merely coincidence that they had been members of the same Inn; there is no evidence that any Inn had a monopoly on anti-Stuart sentiment. For example, no less than twenty-two of the regicides were listed on the rolls of Gray's Inn at one time or another.[12] Moreover, one could find inspiration for opposition from sources outside of Puritan doctrine or the common law. Sandys, in fact, derived his views about the limitations to a king's authority from Travers' opponent, the judicious Hooker, whose doctrine of an original contract was far from sanctioning theories of divine right.

How far the factional disputes of the nation were specifically affecting life at places like the Middle Temple is impossible to determine. The authoritative history of the Temple professes to see the influence of factionalism in the increasing unrest and disobedience of the younger members. The Middle Temple's minutes, it is claimed, "indicate a growing disposition to resent control and rebel against the discipline hitherto prevailing. No doubt this was only a reflexion of the general spirit of the age, and that tendency to resist constituted authority which, stimulated by the unwise pretensions of the Crown, was soon to find a fuller expression in the turmoil of the great rebellion."[13] Even as early as 1602, we get a sense of a new intractability among the young men. In a letter to Sir Robert Cecil, Sir John Popham announces that he has been able to get the Benchers of the Middle Temple to allot two hundred marks toward an entertainment for the Queen: "if the young gentlemen will be drawn in to perform what is of their part, I hope it will be effected. Some of the young gentlemen have their humors, but I hope that will be overruled."[14] One feels that the young gentlemen of Gray's Inn in 1594 would have vied for the honor of entertaining their Queen. Perhaps it was the same new spirit that provoked the young men at Lincoln's Inn to refuse to tread the measures in 1610 and that caused the turmoils at the Middle Temple in 1614 and, more importantly, in 1631. As far as I know, nothing comparable occurred at the Inns in the sixteenth century.

It would have been impossible for anyone to have remained totally detached from factiousness while residing at the Inns,

[12] Hill, *Intellectual Origins*, p. 256.

[13] John B. Williamson, *The History of the Temple* (London, 1924), pp. 286–287.

[14] Quoted in E. K. Chambers, *The Elizabethan Stage* (Oxford, 1923), I, 170, n. 1.

particularly when important Parliamentary committees had adopted the practice of deliberating in their very dining halls, most frequently at the Middle Temple's.[15] It happens that one of the former Prince d'Amour revelers, John Hoskins, became dangerously involved in the battle between King and Parliament. His reactions deserve some attention because they help to define an important aspect of the atmosphere at the Inns in the early seventeenth century.

Hoskins was an M.P. in James' earlier Parliaments and had become, with Sandys and Fuller, one of the leaders of the opposition.[16] Some of his remarks which have been preserved in note form in the *Commons Journal* show the very fundamental nature of his disagreement with King James. For example: "The regal power from God, but the activating thearof is from the people." [17] He asserted that the common law gave Parliament the right to limit the King's prerogative, that although the King "have custome *de jure,* yet the lymitation is *de pacto* by Parliament." [18] These statements make clear the risky course he was taking, but in 1614 Hoskins went further. Under circumstances which are obscure — some have claimed that he was put up to it by more powerful colleagues who assured him that he would be protected — Hoskins made a speech in the House in which he compared "the *Sicilianae Vesperae* to the Scots who consumed both king and kingdom in insolency and all kinds of riot." [19] Aubrey adds that he "made a Comparison of a Conduit, whereinto water came, and ran-out afarre-off. Now, said he, this pipe reaches as far as Edinborough." [20] For this speech Hoskins was jailed in the Tower for a year, as a *"close prisoner* there, i.e. his windowes were boarded up." [21]

We happen to have Hoskins' reactions to this event as well as those of his old schoolmate Henry Wotton. Wotton, it will be recalled, had had his career seriously hampered by one injudicious witticism, but in this instance the "noble studious Henry Wotton" (as Hoskins called him in the *Directions*)[22] was most unsympathetic to his old friend. In one letter, he says that Hoskins had acted as though he were a member of the "Senate

[15] See *Journals of the House of Commons* (London, 1803), I, 128–252 passim.
[16] Notestein, p. 32.
[17] Louise B. Osborn, *The Life, Letters and Writings of John Hoskyns* (New Haven, 1937), p. 35.
[18] Ibid., p. 35.
[19] Ibid., p. 38.
[20] *Aubrey's Brief Lives,* ed. Oliver Lawson Dick (London, 1949), p. 169.
[21] Ibid.
[22] Page 41.

of *Venice,* where the Treaters are perpetual Princes, then where those that speak so irreverently, are so soon to return (which they should remember) to the natural capacity of subjects." [23] Wotton also wrote that Hoskins was imprisoned for his "licentious baptized freedom: For I have noted in our House, that a false or faint Patriot did cover himself with the shadow of equal moderation; and on the other side, irreverent discourse was called honest liberty." [24] Once bitten, Wotton was twice careful, frankly admitting that "I like not the complexion of the place [that is, the Tower]." [25]

In a mood of rueful humor, Hoskins wrote a little poem from the Tower to his son in which he acknowledged his inability to control his tongue:

> Sweet Benedict whilst thou art younge,
> And know'st not yet the use of Toung,
> Keepe it in thral whilst thou art free:
> Imprison it or it will thee.[26]

To a limited extent Wotton was correct in his assessment of Hoskins: he would have spoken anywhere with the freedom of a Venetian Senator or a *terrae filius.* A comic incident involving his old colleague, the Prince d'Amour, Richard Martin, confirms what we have already learned, that an uncheckable tongue within this circle was not a constitutional malady but virtually a reflex conditioned by the peer group. At the time of the convocation of the Parliament of 1614, the one in which Hoskins got into trouble, the letter-writer Chamberlain noted that "Dick" Martin had chosen not to serve because (as the rumor went) "growing rich [he] is loth to venter his rising fortune upon his slipperie tongue." [27] But Chamberlain was most amused to report that in little more than a month Martin was betrayed by his own worst enemy. He had been allowed on the floor of Parliament as a councillor to plead a cause "but after a while having spoken but little in the cause he came for, he fell to ripping up what had passed since theyre sitting, taxing them for theyre slow proceding, for theyre disorderly cariage, and schooling them what they shold do, with divers odde

---

[23] Osborn, p. 40.
[24] Ibid., p. 234, n. 33.
[25] Ibid., pp. 40–41.
[26] Ibid., p. 203. Characteristically, Hoskins composed the same poem as a Latin epigram, also printed on p. 203.
[27] *The Letters of John Chamberlain,* ed. Norman McClure (Philadephia, 1939), I, 525.

glaunces, wherewith he so discontented them that after he was gon there was much arguing what course they shold take with him, and in the end yt was agreed he shold be called to the barre and aunswer his misdemeanure . . . Thus you see though he abstained from beeing of the parlement for feare of being transported and doing himself harme, yet yt was *in fatis* that he shold shame himself in that house." [28] Martin managed to save himself through a public apology.

Returning to the more serious troubles of Hoskins, it is interesting to note the terms in which he assessed his plight. He did not see himself as a pawn in a power struggle between King and Parliament, but as someone whose right to free speech had been abridged. In a noble letter from the Tower to his wife Benedicta, written after nine months of imprisonment, he reveals that it is alleged against him "that no obligacion will bynd my witt." He denies that he has ever been ungrateful or "unkynd in earnest or bitter jest." But he is being impugned by someone who "feares a jest and desires to imprison witt. It is like a man that cannot endure cheese and psuades others to sound at the sight of it as he doth . . . and suer he hath reade little history: for no man ever suffered for mere witt: but yf he lived not to requitt it hymselfe, yet the witt of all posterity took penaunce on his name that oppressed hym. Be cheereful noble Ben I cannot be psuaded that any man that hath witt of his own is afrayd of anothers witt as no good soldier that hath a sword feares another mans sword. and for my part I had rather dy with witt then live without it." [29] After his release, Aubrey tells us, "his Crest was graunted him (I believe) for his bold Spirit, and (I suppose) contrived by himselfe, viz. a Lyon's head couped or, breathing fire." [30]

The metaphor of the soldier's sword captures precisely the attitude toward wit of Hoskins and his circle. "Wit" was their highest honorific term, referring not merely to a faculty of the mind or to a way with words but to a whole style of life. It involved danger, but it was worth it to be esteemed one of the best swordsmen of his time. When Hoskins came to the Middle Temple, according to Aubrey, "His excellent Witt gave him letters of Commendacion to all ingeniose persons." And "his great Witt quickly made him be taken notice of." [31] All

---

[28] Ibid., p. 531.

[29] Osborn, p. 71.

[30] *Aubrey's Brief Lives*, p. 169. Hoskins managed to make his peace with the King without compromising his integrity and eventually received some preferment in the form of promotion to Sergeant.

[31] Ibid.

that he attained was "by his witt and industrie": he wrote an autobiography on that subject, unfortunately lost.[32]

Hoskins' experience was a minor early incident, but it does illustrate the direction in which events were moving. His metaphor about the conduits to Scotland sounds like a joke from a play by John Marston. It is astonishing how quickly after James' accession, nearly instantaneously, in fact, the playwrights at the private theaters responded with venomous satire to the new dispensation. Among them, Marston's satiric wit was, like his own Malcontent's, notably "halter-worthy at all hours." Eventually it, too, had to be silenced. How much Marston's political attitudes were inspired by the place in which he lived and by the people who surrounded him we cannot tell. But in the free-spoken, irreverent, independent atmosphere of the Inns, his criticism of the alien king, blinded by unscrupulous flatterers and unable to comprehend English customs and laws, would have gained an enthusiastic response.

[32] Ibid., p. 170.

VI "The Noblest Nourceries of Humanity and Liberty"

When George Turbervile lived in one of the Inns in the 1570's, he explained with unusual candor that he wrote love poetry because it was expected of him. The Inns were a place

> Where fond affection bore the cheefest sway,
> And where the blinded archer with his bow
> Did glaunce at sundry gallants every day
> And being there although my minde were free:
> Yet must I seeme love wounded eke to be.[1]

[1] *Tragicall Tales Translated by Turbervile* (London, 1587), fol. 199r.

The pressures on a writer in a restricted social circle are great; many produce what their peer group demands. In the 1570's one had to pretend to be lovesick. It was far otherwise in the 1590's when poor Turbervile, who lived longer than his popularity, was elegized in a heartless, but accurate parody of his outmoded style:

> Wth tricklinge teares ye Muses nine, bewaile o^r present woe
> Wth Drerye Drops of doleful plaintes o^r sobbinge sorrowes shewe,
> Put on y^r morninge weedes alas, pour forth your plaintes amayne,
> Ringe owte, Ringe out Ring out ye knell of Turbervile whom crewell death hath slaine, whom cruell death hath slaine.[2]

Not only had styles changed, but the prevailing attitude at the Inns, among the wits at least, was one of ridicule toward those who made love by "force of teares, and seeming languishment."[3] Yet the writing emanating from these surroundings was no less connected to its milieu than Turbervile's was. It had become a much more sophisticated world, but by its nature it was still a world in which a writer was constantly aware of his relationship to a specific audience.

The Latin epigrams of John Owen, who was connected, as we have seen, with the Wotton-Davies-Hoskins group, provide a clear-cut example. As Edward Bensly justly remarked, "It was the point and brevity which captured his auditors; the tastes of that audience are seen in Manningham's *Diary*. The Epigrammata would especially be welcomed by the members of the universities and inns of court, daily conversant with Latin, enamoured of verbal quips, impresses, and anagrams. They would find Owen singularly free from the two faults which rendered much modern Latin verse intolerable, namely insipidity and tediousness."[4]

Most of the men of letters in the Inns' circles tried their

---

[2] Quoted in John E. Hankins, *The Life and Works of George Turbervile,* University of Kansas Humanistic Studies 25 (Lawrence, 1940), p. 28. Although the manuscript containing this poem dates from 1605, the poem must have been written ca. 1595, when Turbervile seems to have died.

[3] *Poems of John Marston,* ed. Arnold Davenport (Liverpool, 1961), p. 153, l. 91.

[4] *Cambridge History of English Literature,* ed. A. W. Ward and A. R. Waller (Cambridge, Eng., 1907–1916), IV, 262–263.

hand at English epigrams: Campion, Donne, Harington, Davies, Guilpin, Bastard, Hoskins (with his epitaphs), and Rudyerd. The supreme practitioner in English in this genre, Ben Jonson, accurately and disdainfully described the epigrams of this period as "bold, licentious, full of gall,/Wormewood, and sulphure, sharpe, and tooth'd withall." [5] It is true that for most of these writers the epigram was an instrument for satiric wit. Often it was aimed at real people under the disguise of Roman names. Sir John Harington admitted that he engaged in this practice,[6] and we are able to identify enough victims (for example, "Matho" in Rudyerd's epigram about Davies, mentioned earlier) to deduce that it was widespread. The line between a satire and a "libel" was sometimes extremely thin; with some of the writers it was no more than the substitution of a name drawn from Horace or Juvenal.

Jonson also said that it was customary for the epigrams he disliked to use "lewd, prophane, and beastly phrase." [7] Here again we can find agreement from a practitioner: Guilpin says that "wanton words . . . are the language of an Epigrame." [8] This was not invariably the case; the clergyman Bastard prided himself on the purity of his language. But possibly because of its derivation from Martial, the epigram in the later sixteenth century was fully as licentious as the jokes in the revels.

One can sense in this epigram-writing something of a communal enterprise, of a group writing for private entertainment and shared animosities. Everyone in what was becoming known as "the town" would know who was being talked about, and no one reading the poems would be shocked by the licentiousness any more than he would be by the material in the revels. They knew that an epigrammatist, armed with his pen like a rapier in his fist, was, as Guilpin said in his last epigram, like "a carelesse Prince." [9]

At times we can detect what appears to be friendly rivalry in a verbal game. Davies brags that he has surpassed Heywood,[10] Bastard says that he has it in him to sing "Davy

[5] *Ben Jonson,* ed. C. H. Herford and Percy and Evelyn Simpson (Oxford, 1947), VIII, 27, ll. 4–5.

[6] *Letters and Epigrams of Sir John Harington,* ed. Norman E. McClure (Philadelphia, 1930), p. 319. Harington says that he will not reveal identies until his death, but "who gat some of them may soone be guest."

[7] *Ben Jonson,* VIII, 27, l. 11.

[8] Everard Guilpin, *Skialetheia or A Shadowe of Truth, in certain Epigrams and Satyres* (London, 1598), sig. B3r.

[9] Ibid., sig. B7r.

[10] *Poems of Sir John Davies,* ed. Clare Howard (New York, 1941), p. 47.

down," [11] Guilpin gives the prize to Davies as "Our *English Martiall*," [12] but Harington tells Davies that everyone is really pilfering from Martial [13] — as indeed they were. When the epigrams are not about friends, enemies, or recognizable public figures, they are imitations or adaptations of Martial's, often of the same ones which friends had attempted.

There is little distinguished poetry in these epigrams until we come to Jonson's very different type; in fact, they have a uniform, mass-produced quality. This springs from the fact that all were inspired by approximately the same attitude toward language, defined clearly by Harington in his contrast between the "sugred" sonnet and the epigram: "though I grant Suger may please the taste,/Yet let my verse have salt to make it last." [14] As Guilpin said in defending the use of such language, his Muse is but keeping "*Decorum* to the times,/To womens loose gownes suting her loose rimes." [15]

By such writing these epigrammatists played a part in what J. B. Leishman has described as the reaction "especially of University and Inns of Court men . . . against most of the literary ideals and fashions which had hitherto prevailed, . . . declaring, in so many words, that it is time to get down from one's stilts, to remove one's rose-coloured spectacles, . . . a disenchanted resolve to be at all costs realistic, to see things and show things as they really are, and to describe them (as Jonson put it) in 'language such as men do use.' " [16] This realistic and satiric tendency was a compound of the many elements I have been examining: youthful, self-conscious cynicism nurtured in the catalytic atmosphere of the law schools; a sense of belonging to an elite of wits in a world of gulls; a tradition of free and candid speech; upper-class condescension to the taste of professional writers; a tradition of plain style in language which tended to be associated with the Inns and the courtly writers; and perhaps the dominance of one powerful and admirable figure in Donne.

This reaction was expressed in various other genres, notably the formal verse satire (often merely an extended epigram), the libertine elegy, and occasionally, parodies of the popular romantic forms. Even in a love lyric like Hoskins' familiar an-

---

[11] *Chrestoleros* (London, 1598), p. 36.
[12] *Skialetheia*, sig. A6r.
[13] *Letters and Epigrams*, p. 306.
[14] Ibid., p. 163.
[15] *Skialetheia*, sig. B6v.
[16] *The Three Parnassus Plays* (London, 1949), pp. 41–42.

thology piece "Absence," [17] a special note appears, which it is not very enlightening to label "metaphysical." Rather it is a witty poem about the power and limitations of wit as an antidote to Fortune:

> Absence heare my protestation
> Against thy strength
> Distance and lengthe,
> Doe what thou canst for alteration:
> For harts of truest metall
> Absence doth joyne, and time doth settle.

This first stanza begins the demonstration of a witty paradox through an analytic process. The speaker seems to murder absence by dissecting it into its abstract components; in the ensuing stanzas, it is a triumph for reason as he pursues the proof that "Absence is present." But in a final rueful twist, at the same time tender and witty, he suggests that he has been protesting too much, that the process he has been praising is ultimately unsatisfactory despite the neat proofs:

> By absence this good means I gaine
> That I can catch her
> Where none can watch her
> In some close corner of my braine:
> There I embrace and there kiss her,
> And so enjoye her, and so misse her.

The poem exhibits a high degree of technical competence, especially in the controlled movement of the short lines against the long ones. Hoskins may have been an "amateur" — so also was Donne — but this did not prevent his being a sophisticated and adept artisan.

Next to Donne, Sir John Davies is today the best-known poet who lived at the Inns in the 1590's. I want to look at his work briefly in order to demonstrate how deeply he was tied to this milieu and to suggest how a consideration of this connection helps to clarify the tone of some of his poems. I have already quoted epigrams which demonstrate his close observation of Inns' manners. He was also an acute critic of literary fashions

[17] Printed in *Poems of John Donne*, ed. H. J. C. Grierson (Oxford, 1912), I, 428–429. An argument prefaces the poem in some MS versions and in Grierson's text: "That time and absence proves/Rather helps than hurts to loves." This seems to me to ignore the modifying force of "misse" in the last line.

among the Inns' poetasters and criticasters. His "Gulling Sonnets," written at the height of the sonnet vogue, mocked the extravagant gestures, the Petrarchan formulae, and the strained metaphors of the worst offenders in this fashion. One of them speaks in the voice of a sonneteering "puisne" from the Middle Temple.[18] Adopting the parlance of the Inns, he has Cupid admit himself "into the midle Temple of my harte," using his mistress' wit as his pledge. Cupid misbehaves ("he gan to revell it"), for which he and "his young pledge" are brought before "that old Bencher grave," Reason, who, under pressure from the prosecutor, "dilligence, yt slye and secreate knave," gave "this sadd sentence":

> That love and witt, for ever shold departe
> out of the midle Temple of my harte.

The three "Ignoto" sonnets appended to his epigrams are the complement to these parodies. In them, he expresses his anti-Petrarchan attitudes in unusually uninhibited terms, although no worse than many items in the revels. These, more than any other poems in a volume which also contained Marlowe's translation of Ovid's elegies, must have been the occasion for its inclusion in the famous bonfire at Stationers' Hall in June of 1599. It was Davies' amorous and satiric works which inspired the admiring estimate in the third of the "Parnassus" plays at St. John's College, Cambridge:

> Acute *John Davis,* I affect thy rhymes,
> That jerck in hidden charmes these looser times:
> Thy playner verse, thy unaffected vaine,
> Is graced with a fayre and sooping trayne.
> Martiall & hee may sitt upon one bench,
> Either wrote well & either lov'd his wench.[19]

A reputation as lover and satirist would seem to combine all that a young man in this milieu would hope for.

But Davies also wrote serious, long poems, and it is here that we encounter an apparent problem. As G. A. Wilkes remarks in an excellent essay on his poetry, "Davies' antagonism to the conventions he ridicules could not have been very deep, because they belong to a form of verse he practised himself." [20]

[18] *Poems,* ed. Howard, pp. 226–227.
[19] *Parnassus Plays,* ed. Leishman, p. 240, ll. 233–258.
[20] "The Poetry of Sir John Davies," *Huntington Library Quarterly,* 25 (1961–1962), 283–298.

Wilkes is here referring to the "Astraea" poems, twenty-six acrostics on the words "Elisabetha Regina." In fact, such acrostics were a popular pastime among the Templars, as Manningham's *Diary* attests, but there are solider grounds for explaining this apparent inconsistency. Published during his rustication in 1599, it is almost certain that they were written as part of Davies' determined effort to regain favor after his attack on Martin. This would explain why he reserved for the last three poems his praise of Elizabeth's justice, magnanimity, and moderation. Nor is the academic, philosophical poem *Nosce Teipsum* an anomalous performance. As Wilkes aptly says, Davies "argues for the immortality of the soul like an attorney with a brief." [21] The pared down, plain style and the heavily intellectual, reasoned arguments could only have been conceived with a scholastically trained audience in mind.

But what of *Orchestra*, which C. S. Lewis authoritatively pigeonholes as "Golden" verse? Unlike his other poetry in tone and manner, it is a highly idealized version of the "Elizabethan world picture" written in a relatively smooth, musical style. The poem, as Hoskins acidly says — his judgment came after Davies' attack on Martin — is an apt example of rhetorical amplification by "division." According to Hoskins, "This only trick made up J. D.'s *Poem of Dancing*: all danceth, the heavens, the elements, men's minds, commonwealths, and so by parts all danceth." [22] This is a fairly accurate description of the poem, but perhaps not a damning one. The title page explains that the aim is "Judicially prooving the true observation of time and measure, in the Authenticall and laudable use of Dauncing." [23] The basic action of the poem is, as Tillyard says, a disputation,[24] and with its origin in the Middle Temple, the poem may be read as a law school tour de force "judicially" proving that everything dances. It is the sort of exercise which might have entertained an audience at revels, particularly the Prince d'Amour's revels, for the major argument is that "Dauncing" (the prime activity at revels) is "Loves proper exercise." [25]

The idea that *Orchestra* may have been delivered at a public entertainment has recently been advanced by Robert Krueger on the basis of his discovery of a manuscript which reveals a

[21] Ibid., p. 296.
[22] *Directions for Speech and Style by John Hoskins*, ed. Hoyt H. Hudson (Princeton, 1935), p. 23.
[23] *Poems*, ed. Howard, p. 61.
[24] E. M. W. Tillyard, ed., *Orchestra or A Poem of Dancing* (London, 1947), p. 11.
[25] *Poems*, ed. Howard, p. 71, stanza 18.

new and complete version of the poem.[26] Previously, we had
two printed texts, those of 1596 and 1619. The latter added
some stanzas to the earlier text while suppressing Davies' dedication to Richard Martin and some praise of him and others
in the concluding stanzas. In the manuscript which Krueger
discovered in a commonplace book compiled by Leweston Fitz-
james of the Middle Temple, he detected two versions of the
poem: stanzas 1–108 plus 127–131 and an augmented version,
stanzas 1–126. The additions are devoted to praise of the Queen
and her Court, and it is upon the basis of these that Krueger
erects his hypothesis: "Stanzas 119–126 particularly suggest that
they might have been written for use in a court entertainment
at which the Queen was present. All the action narrated is such
that it could easily have been acted." [27] This would not have
been John Davies' only court entertainment, and while it is
longer than most, it would not take much longer than an hour
to present. Even if the action of the poem were not mimed, it
possesses an essentially dramatic structure through its nearly
total dependence on speeches by Antinous, Penelope, and Love,
with only a brief introductory comment by a narrator.

If *Orchestra* was, in fact, delivered as a courtly entertainment, it is all the more likely that it was originally conceived
for the Middle Temple's revels. This notion is given greater
credence by the fact that it was Richard Martin, at a later date
the perpetual Prince d'Amour, who was, according to Davies'
dedication, "first mover and sole cause" of the poem.[28] Perhaps
Martin requisitioned it for the revels: that Davies dashed it off
in fifteen days is consistent with this notion, as we saw from
the hasty way in which the 1597–98 revels were put together.
Further, Davies' dedication praises Martin's "mellifluous tongue,
whereon doth sit/*Suada* [persuasiveness] in majestie." [29] The entire action of the poem may be described as one of "persua-
sion": the word is used frequently to describe the speeches of
Antinous and of Love.[30] Thus it is possible that Richard Martin took one of the parts in the performance. Certainly it would
have been appropriate for whoever was Prince d'Amour to
have recited the lines of Love just as the Prince of Purpoole
played the hero's role in the "Masque of Proteus" at Gray's
Inn. But whether or not my extension of Krueger's hypothesis

[26] "Sir John Davies: *Orchestra* Complete, *Epigrams*, Unpublished Poems,"
Review of English Studies, 13 (1962), pp. 2–29, 113–124.

[27] Ibid., p. 23.

[28] *Poems*, ed. Howard, p. 63.

[29] Ibid.

[30] See stanzas 5, 32 (marginal gloss in 1619 ed.), 61, 118.

is accepted, the structural principle of *Orchestra,* to which Hoskins took exception, can be justified. Its verse may appear "Golden," but the dominant effect of the poem is one of calculated and extended wittiness of the sort which occurs frequently in quasi-academic "defenses" and in such genres as the paradox and the problem. This is not to deny serious overtones to the entire conception of the poem, but to suggest that the poem is a social celebration of the Elizabethan world picture rather than an exposition of it. Most of Davies' poetry was pre-eminently social, designed for the entertainment of his immediate circle and for the Court; clearly, it assisted his worldly advancement. But it was a sport of his youth. It is the clearest sign of the nature of his relationship to his milieu that once he had left the surroundings which had nurtured his wit and provided a ready audience, he wrote no more poetry of significance.

The effect of this milieu is apparent in the writing of many members of the Inns, but it was Ben Jonson who best described what the Inns collectively represented to an artist. Certainly no one was better qualified for the task. He was a close friend of many important members, and he had the objectivity of an outsider and of a professional writer who had to know his audience. His appraisal appears in the folio of 1616 as the dedication to *Every Man out of his Humour,* first performed in 1599 when his connection with the Inns was closest:

> To the Noblest Nourceries of Humanity, and Liberty, in the Kingdome: the Innes of Court
> I understand you, Gentlemen, not your houses: and a worthy succession of you, to all time, as being borne the Judges of these studies. When I wrote this Poeme, I had friendship with divers in your societies; who, as they were great Names in learning, so they were no lesse Examples of living. Of them, and then (that I say no more) it was not despis'd. Now that the Printer, by a doubled charge, thinkes it worthy a longer life, then commonly the ayre of such things doth promise; I am carefull to put it a servant to their pleasures, who are the inheriters of the first favour borne it. Yet, I command, it lye not in the way of your more noble, and use-ful studies to the publike. For so I shall suffer for it: But, when the gowne and cap is off, and the Lord of liberty raignes; then, to take it in your hands, perhaps may make some Bencher, tincted with humanity, reade: and not repent him.[31]

[31] *Ben Jonson,* III, 421.

Jonson stresses that it is not the institutions themselves but their inhabitants whom he is calling by the metaphor of "nour- ceries": collectively they provide nourishment for "Humanity and Liberty." His old friends, the circle of wits in the 1590's, inspired this description. They were, in fact, "great names in learning," authentic humanists. Hoskins was a solid classical scholar with a mastery of Greek and Latin beyond what even Winchester and New College usually produced. Aubrey claims to have seen the Greek lexicon that Hoskins compiled up to the letter *mu*.[32] He wrote witty and accomplished Latin poetry. As he himself admits, his study of rhetoric was so broad that "your Masters of the Universities have thought the author [that is, Hoskins] as great a reader and a greater observer thereof than themselves."[33] This vaunt was justified by the help he gave Ben Jonson and Sir Walter Raleigh in polishing their work as well as by the originality and learning of his book of rhetoric.[34] Davies and Martin cared enough about "humanity" to pay a visit to Lipsius' successor at Leiden, Paul Merula.[35] Such learned members are qualified "Judges of these studies." Jonson's term alludes, of course, to their legal roles, but any serious Elizabethan writer must have thought of the Inns as the home of his prime judges, a Court of Critics.

When the Benchers wore their gowns and caps, they were occupied with "studies" for the "publike." But they were also "nourceries" of "liberty." Clearly the prime meaning here is not political. Jonson is referring to the spirit which appears during the revels when the "Lord of liberty raignes": then "liberty plucks justice by the nose."[36] A "Bencher tincted with humanity" may assume this spirit at any time. "Humanity" flourished at the Inns when "Liberty" reigned; the poems and plays which were produced by or appreciated by members of the Inns were nourished in the kingdom of the Lord of Lib- erty.

But political connotations also lurk in Jonson's phrase. It was not only in a legalistic sense that the members of the Inns felt themselves to be living in a "liberty," a legal sanctuary. The triumph of the common law had thrust the lawyers into a unique and powerful position. As Wallace Notestein says, "By virtue of their manner of education and discipline, they had

---

[32] *Aubrey's Brief Lives,* ed. Oliver Lawson Dick (London, 1949), p. 169.
[33] *Directions,* ed. Hudson, p. 31.
[34] *Aubrey's Brief Lives,* p. 169.
[35] Robert Krueger, "Sir John Davies," p. 25.
[36] Shakespeare, *Measure for Measure,* I.iii.29.

become almost a class in society, a class with which the Government had to reckon as with the nobility and gentry." [37] Some young members, feeling that they were the cream of the kingdom, ran loose around the town until they ruined themselves. But even the wisest ones acquired a sense that they were a privileged class. When their liberties, defined for them by the common law, were endangered, their independent and critical spirit enabled some of them to risk everything.

A cluster of other terms are associated with these larger ones. "Liberty" suggests revelry, rebellion, uninhibited satire, relaxed playfulness, libertine wantonness, licensed fooling, and political freedom. "Humanity" suggests an interest in the linguistic and critical concerns of the humanists. Thus Jonson's formulation even brings to mind limitations perceptible in many Inns' writers: an excessive reliance on classical forms, often as defined by Renaissance humanists, and a concomitant disregard for what was vital in the evolving forms of popular art. And the notion that art appears in the reign of the "Lord of liberty" is connected to a concentration on comic forms and a general avoidance of the tragic. Both the consumers and the producers of literary art at the Inns favored a peculiar blend of learning and license, of the scholastic and the playful. In the rich, special senses that Jonson used the terms, it was a milieu that combined Humanity with Liberty.

[37] *The Winning of the Initiative by the House of Commons* (London, 1924), pp. 49–50.

Two
Playwright at the Inns of Court:
John Marston

VII John Marston's Early Writing

A character in one of Marston's plays observes that

> the sonne of a Divine
> Seldome proves Preacher, or a Lawiers sonne
> Rarely a pleader, (for they strive to Run
> A various fortune from their Auncestors).[1]

Such was the case with four of the most prominent writers at the Inns of Court. Thomas Overbury's and Francis Beaumont's fathers were judges, and John Ford's uncle was Sir John Popham, the Lord Chief Justice. Marston's father was a prosperous lawyer. He became a member of the Middle Temple in

[1] *The Plays of John Marston*, ed. H. Harvey Wood (3 vols., Edinburgh, 1934–1939), II, 242. For a chronology of events in Marston's life see Appendix B.

1570, and during the legal term he lived there for the rest of his life in chambers which he had built for himself. Admitted to the bar in 1577, he eventually acquired sufficient seniority and prestige to serve as Fall Reader at the Middle Temple in 1592. This position gives evidence not only of the elder Marston's legal scholarship but of his extreme affluence, for assumption of the office involved an extraordinary financial outlay. Often the expenses for three weeks of banquets and ceremonies cost the reader as much as £1,000; many otherwise qualified candidates preferred to forego this honor and pay a fine instead. It is fair to assume that Reader Marston's only son and heir was relatively wealthy after his father's death in 1599. Inherited wealth is a useful cushion for a scourge of villainy.

Not much about Marston's father has survived, but we know that as a resident of Coventry he was close to Stratford-on-Avon and represented the town corporation in some legal work.[2] Perhaps it was through this employment that he became acquainted with Shakespeare's cousin, Thomas Greene, who also became a prominent member of the Middle Temple and ultimately served as its Treasurer. In any case, Greene was sufficiently close to the Marstons to act as one of the "pledges," or financial guarantors, for the younger Marston when he was admitted to the Middle Temple.[3]

One story about Marston's father is often repeated. In his will he bequeathed "to s^d son John my furniture &c. in my chambers in the Middle Temple my law books &c. to my s^d son whom I hoped would have profited by them in the study of the law but man proposeth and God disposeth &c." [4] The son decided to run a various fortune from his ancestors, and his works contain many vicious slurs at lawyers. But he always takes pains to distinguish them from the "grave, and reverent legists . . . That ayde *Astrea*." [5] I mention this to qualify the impres-

[2] For information on the elder Marston's connection with the town of Strat-ford-on-Avon see Mark Eccles, *Shakespeare in Warwickshire* (Madison, Wis., 1961), pp. 138–139.

[3] On the basis of this connection, Leslie Hotson, *Shakespeare's Sonnets Dated and Other Essays* (New York, 1949), pp. 37–56, advances several startling conjectures about Shakespeare's *Troilus and Cressida;* though they are not improbable, they are wholly unsubstantiated.

[4] An abstract of the will appears in Alexander Grosart, ed., *The Poems of John Marston* (Manchester, 1879), pp. x–xi.

[5] *Poems of John Marston,* ed. Arnold Davenport (Liverpool, 1961), SV, VII, 93–94. Subsequent citations in the text refer to this edition. I indicate the title, whether *Pigmalion's Image* (PI), *Certain Satires* (CS), or *The Scourge of Villanie* (SV), followed by satire number (in Roman numerals), and line numbers.

sion of Marston which sometimes emerges from a rapid summary of the more notorious facts in his career. Superficially, he sounds like Lenton's gallant: first, disappointing his father's hopes by abandoning the law; next, writing poems burned by order of the Archbishop of Canterbury and plays which caused his imprisonment; finally, metamorphosing improbably from a prodigal into a clergyman of the Church of England.

But Marston sounds anything but rebellious in the modest prefaces to his plays, and one is struck by the respectability of his friends.[6] All his chambermates at the Middle Temple were serious enough to become members of the bar. The last of these was Henry Hall, with whom Marston shared rooms from 1600 to 1605. Hall became Reader, Bencher, and eventually Treasurer of the Middle Temple during this period. Meanwhile his roommate was acquiring a reputation as one of "the best and chiefest of our moderne writers," to quote the title page of *Loves Martyr* of 1601. His inclusion in many of the contemporary lists of important writers confirms this estimate.[7] It must have been a matter of some prestige to have had such a personage living in the Middle Temple with the Treasurer. By the end of his life, after he had long ceased to write, Marston was still something of a hero at the Middle Temple, his reputation matched by only one writer. An edict by the Prince d'Amour in the revels of 1635–36 declared "that noe person or persons whatsoever shall medd[le] in Poetry for that they have gathered with industry phrases out of Shakespeare Marston or the like or that they thinke they have a pretty vaine of lov[e wri]ting, but only such as our privy Counsell shall find habile or fitt for soe high a Calling." [8]

[6] It may be noted that one of Marston's close friends, possibly his closest, was Henry Walley, a stationer who was involved in the unauthorized quarto of Shakespeare's *Troilus* and who eventually became the Master of the Stationers' Company. Both Marston and his wife mention him in their wills; Mrs. Marston bequeathed her husband's picture to him. Since Marston lived outside London after he stopped writing, his friendship with Walley must date from the period when he was still an active playwright. A lasting friendship between men of such different social classes tends to soften the haughty, aristocratic impression which Marston gives in some of his writing. See my "Henry Walley of the Stationers' Company and John Marston," *Papers of the Bibliographical Society of America*, 56 (1962), 366–368. When I published that note, I was unaware that R. E. Brettle in "Bibliographical Notes on Some Marston Quartos and Early Collected Editions," *The Library*, 8 (1927), 340, had originally noticed this relationship.

[7] Among signs of his contemporary importance (as opposed to his undoubted notoriety) are his inclusion in the list of the most pregnant wits of the time by William Camden, *Remaines* (1605); quotation of fifteen passages from *The Scourge* by Robert Allot, *England's Parnassus* (1600); and selections from his poetry by John Bodenham, *Belvedere* (1600).

[8] *Shakespeare's Sonnets Dated*, p. 243.

We know very little about the younger Marston before his books appear.[9] After his birth in 1576, we next find him at Brasenose College, Oxford, from 1591 to 1594. At the completion of his B.A., he may have begun residence at the Middle Temple in 1594, although he was not definitely resident until 1595.[10] Nothing has survived about his early years at the Temple, but occasionally his works show an easy acquaintance with the intricacies of the law, which suggests that between 1594 and 1598 he gave Littleton more than a passing glance.[11] It was during the very period when he must have begun to write seriously that he was his father's chambermate, from 1597 until the latter's death in 1599.

The Hoskins-Martin-Davies circle was of a slightly earlier generation both at Oxford and at the Temple. There is no direct evidence of Marston's acquaintance with them, although physical proximity and their mutual friendship with Jonson make it a virtual certainty. It is scarcely credible that as an Inner Barrister with literary interests Marston would have had no part in the festivities of 1597–98; as I shall demonstrate, one of his plays, *The Fawne,* reveals close acquaintance with the revels of the Prince d'Amour. And the opening lines of the first satire in his first volume, *The Metamorphosis of Pigmalions Image and Certain Satyres* (entered in the Stationers' Register three months after Davies' attack), strongly suggest Marston's involvement in the feud. The satire, written on the theme "Quedam videntur, et non sunt" (CS, I, 67), begins with a portrait (ll. 1–18) which has a familiar ring. After the speaker says that he cannot change "like a Camelion" (l. 2), he describes "browne *Ruscus*" (l. 5), who acts as though he is invisible. In his "wits halfe capreall" (l. 7), he drops a letter for others to read which he has penned with commendations to himself. Also, he hangs onto important men in order to establish the impression that they esteem him. The speaker orders Ruscus to un-

[9] Almost all of the modern work on Marston's biography has been done by R. E. Brettle, beginning with his Oxford dissertation, *Abstracts of Dissertations* (Oxford, 1928), I, 20–31, and continuing in a succession of articles to this day.

[10] He was admitted as early as 1592 while still at Oxford because his father had taken advantage of his right as Reader to grant him a "special" admission. Such an admission carried certain privileges, among which seems to have been an immunity from the fines for absence during vacations. Thus, during his long residence, Marston was only present at the Middle Temple at his own pleasure.

[11] In SV, XI, 33–34, in which the speaker is ridiculing Curio for admiring Davies' *Orchestra* immoderately, he says, "O wits quick travers, but *sance ceo's* slow,/Good faith tis hard for nimble *Curio.*" Davenport's ingenious explanation of this passage (*Poems,* p. 358) implies that Marston knew a good deal of law; it certainly required a literate lawyer to comprehend the double meaning of "travers" as well as the legal Latin.

mask so that men can see that he is "vaine-glorious, impudent" (l. 18). This picture of a self-praising social climber sounds very much like the recently maligned Stradilax. Harold Littledale suggested in 1899 that it is a portrait of John Davies, noting that in *Orchestra* he speaks of the "half-capriole of my wit" and, in the "Gulling Sonnets," of his "Chameleon muse." [12] Littledale failed to notice that the likelihood of this identification is strengthened by Marston's references to Ruscus in the volume of satires published a few months later, *The Scourge of Villanie*. From a collocation of two references in Satire IV, Ruscus can be identified as an Inns-a-Court man. He is a reveler who is in debt for his reveling attire, which, like Stradilax, he has rented; he is also in arrears to his laundress, an omnipresent figure in satire of Inns' men. [13] In addition, Ruscus, like Stradilax, tells stupid old jokes; like Matho in Rudyerd's epigram, he affixes himself to great men. In Satire XI, we hear that Ruscus has written a "nastie lothsome brothell rime" (l. 146). This could refer to several of Davies' poems in the volume of epigrams consigned to the same fire as Marston's satires. [14] It all seems to point toward Davies, particularly when we recall that his notorious exploit was fresh in everyone's mind.

I have been attempting to identify Ruscus as Davies in order to link Marston to the elite intellectual group at the Middle Temple. But whether or not this identification is correct, it is clear that he is speaking about specific individuals, as he indicates in one of the passages about Ruscus:

> There is a crew which I too plaine could name
> If so I might without th' Aquinians blame.
>
> (SV, IV, 57–58)

[12] *Athenaeum*, No. 3727, April 1, 1899, p. 400. Davies' use of "capriole" as a noun is the first recorded in the *NED*, a fact which suggests that Marston was glancing at his peculiar usage. Littledale failed to note Davies' use of "chameleon" in *Orchestra*, stanza 130, where he refers to "Astrophel . . . Whose supple Muse chameleon-like doth change." Davenport rejects Littledale's identification because he claims that another figure, "Curio," is "certainly" Davies (p. 218). But a careful investigation of Curio's activities will show that none of them are characteristic of Davies except his love of dancing (e.g., SV, XI, 13–36). Curio is merely a dancing addict who uses Davies' poem as his justification, and in l. 32 he is clearly distinguished from the author of the poem.

[13] Cf. Edward Sharpham (of the Middle Temple), *Cupid's Whirligig* (London, 1607): "why doe your Innes-of-Court man lie with his Laundresse in a long Vacation, but because he hath no money to goe abroad" (sig. F1v).

[14] Davenport, *Poems*, pp. 362–363, points out the many similarities between Ruscus and another figure named Tuscus (SV, VI) and suggests the possibility of a misprint. Tuscus flatters great men, retails others' wit, pawns his clothes, and publishes epigrams which are really by others. I should mention that Davenport identifies Ruscus as Thomas Nashe. The various indications that Ruscus is of the Inns of Court make this extremely unlikely, and on pp. 218–219, Davenport virtually admits this.

In other words, "were I not adhering to the prudent example of Juvenal (born in Aquinium) and using false names in order to keep out of trouble, I could tell you quite specifically whom I am satirizing." He may well have intended "to note generall vices" while using "fained private names" (p. 176), as he claims in a formulaic disclaimer of libelous intention, but in his world personal satire was nearly inevitable.

We get some sense of the closed circle of intimates in which such satire was brewed when Marston and his friend (and relation) Everard Guilpin employ the same "fained private name" to discuss one clearly defined individual. In "Satyra Tertia" of *Skialetheia* (entered in the Stationers' Register just one week after *The Scourge of Villanie*), Guilpin reproaches an old college friend (apparently from Emmanuel College, Cambridge), whom he calls "Fabian," for his distant and unfriendly attitude now that he has become a reveler at the Inns of Court. At Cambridge he had studied philosophy, and apparently he has retained his interest in this subject, for Guilpin describes him as "New cast in mold of deepe philosophy." [15] But Fabian feels superior to his old friend because he has just participated in the Middle Temple's revels:

> But then a simple reveller, thou art more,
> Thou hast had som doings with the prince *d'Amore*
> And playd a noble mans part in a play.[16]

The satirist attacks Fabian for priding himself on such a slight accomplishment and adds

> and beside,
> thou mightst have had som doings with that prince
> which wold have made thee less proude ever since.[17]

Guilpin is referring to some piece of gossip about Richard Martin's "doings" which we may assume many of his readers would

---

[15] *Skialetheia or A Shadowe of Truth* (London, 1598), sig. D1r. In "Donne and Everard Guilpin," *Review of English Studies,* 14 (1963), 164–167, I demonstrated that Guilpin could not have been referring here to John Donne, as had been alleged. I also noted that Marston and Guilpin were related by the marriage of Marston's uncle to Guilpin's mother and of Guilpin to Marston's cousin. R. E. Brettle, "Everard Guilpin and John Marston," *Review of English Studies,* 16 (1965), 396–399, has established the dates of these marriages as 1592 and 1606/7 respectively.

[16] *Skialetheia,* sig. D1v. These must have been the revels of 1597–98 because the *Prince d'Amour* (p. 6) mentions that there had been no revels for eight years.

[17] Ibid.

comprehend. Guilpin could have heard it from his contact at the Middle Temple, Marston, who also refers to a "Fabian" in *The Scourge of Villanie*. We recognize him as the same figure because in his one appearance Fabian indulges his propensity for philosophizing, discussing the impossibility of changing bad habits. Marston's speaker condescendingly rejects his views ("I smile at thee," SV, IV, 1. 99) and offers a lengthy refutation. With the data that Guilpin and Marston supply (Emmanuel student of philosophy in the Middle Temple's revels), it would have been easy for anyone in the right circles to have identified Fabian.

These examples suggest that Marston was as enmeshed in the world of the Inns as Martin and Hoskins were. Thus it should come as no surprise that a large majority of his satires describe young men of the sort who lived at the Inns; they are Marston's favorite target. By contrast, Hall, who also lived in an academic community, concentrated largely on public and social matters: for example, the vices endemic to the various professions, the harm to English life from the decline of "house-keeping" and from the increasing fluidity of the social classes, the unfair practices of businessmen and landlords. His interests are usually sociological even when he does illustrate a vice with a particular fictitious character. Hall's pace is leisurely. He tends to pick a theme and develop it with a single example; then he moves to the next poem. When he does chastise an individual, it is usually an older man, often one living in the country.

The other important formal verse satirist of the 1590's, Donne, seems to have written at least his first three satires while at Lincoln's Inn, and the first two reflect this environment. Donne exhibits the "fondling motley humorist" of Satire I and the corrupt lawyer of Satire II at length, but he uses them largely as vehicles for the construction of the witty, sophisticated, disabused character of the speaker. The focus of the satire is on the speaker's copious wit directed at a single character.

Marston's poems possess a different unifying principle. They present a chaotic world in which a series of young fools troop rapidly by. Each receives a lashing for his personal vice, to be followed by the next who may or may not be connected thematically with his predecessors. In the first satire in his first volume, for example, Marston constructs a procession of hypocritical young men. It begins, as we have seen, with the "glavering" Ruscus, after whom comes Briscus, who courts his mistress with his "Gambo violl" but is otherwise inarticulate. Castilio follows, adept at all the courtly graces — horsemanship, reveling, sonnet-ing, among others — but although he is well-endowed, the sat-irist claims that all his accomplishments are superficial. The next unnamed hypocrite (ll. 51–62) is not clearly described. He appears holy, but "intends some damned villanies" (l. 54). The satirist then shows "troupes of gallants" (l. 64), among them Spero, resorting to Cornuto's shop to take advantage of the proprietor's wife, "chaste *Brownetta*" (l. 66). The next figure is described at length (ll. 69–88), but nothing is clear except that he receives public homage for the office he holds and that he acts pompously. Next is a vivid portrait of a familiar figure in Elizabethan literature, a *miles gloriosus* who gallivants with the gallants. The satirist concludes the satire by claiming that when he contemplates such hypocrites, he can put up with simple fools like the ever-dancing Curio, the tennis player Tullus, and the fencing addict Robrus. In this satire only two of the figures, those who are described vaguely, might not have been encoun-tered in the normal course of a day at the Middle Temple. Most are young gentry or their hangers-on who are involved in char-acteristically youthful forms of villainy or foolishness.

A similar analysis of the remainder of Marston's sixteen sa-tires reveals that a large majority of the men, nearly three fourths, are young gentry. In two (CS, IV; SV, X), part of a third (SV, IX), and scattered passages in other satires, Marston attacks Joseph Hall, but this confrontation is of the same order of interest as the satires on young gentry. It pits an Oxford man at an Inn of Court against a Cambridge academic, a free-speaking Londoner against (as Marston would claim) a Puri-tan.[18] The fifth satire in *Certain Satires* is another apparent ex-ception. It pretends to be about the gods, but as has been suggested,[19] it is probably an attack on the sexual habits of the Elizabethan nobility, hence once again a variety of libelous satire.

Only the first two satires in *The Scourge of Villanie* do not deal primarily with young men or with matters that would be of immediate interest to them. Their prominent position at the front of his better-known volume has given a false impres-sion of Marston's methods and preoccupations. By his own testimony, Satire I can be dismissed as a literary exercise in

[18] Cf. SV, X, 39–40.
[19] See Davenport, ed., *Poems*, p. 250. He agrees with a suggestion to this effect by A. José Axelrad, *Un Malcontent Elizabéthain: John Marston* (Paris, 1955), p. 43.

obscurity; its characters are largely derived from Juvenal.[20] Satire II has a few good passages, but it is a discordant and uncharacteristic performance. Although it uses the theme of Juvenal's first satire, it resembles neither its model nor Marston's other poems. In its vague, generalized satire on social mobility, religious practices, and the decay of learning in the universities, it is reminiscent of Hall's style until a few Marstonian characters appear at the end.

With these exceptions, the satires are largely filled with figures more or less like those in the last poem in *The Scourge* (XI) where, in succession, we see an addict to dancing, a playgoer, a fencer, an epigrammatist who steals ideas from others, a vaulter, a would-be critic, a whoremonger, a clothes-ape, and a self-praiser. At the conclusion the satirist finds himself depressed by his own vision:

> In fayth I am sad, I am possest with ruth,
> To see the vainenes of fayre *Albions* youth;
> To see their richest time even wholy spent
> In that which is but Gentries ornament. (ll. 186–189)

In this passage he is speaking only about the "Humours" characters of this last satire, but it is appropriate that he concludes his satires with a serious exhortation to the youthful gentry who have been his main subject:

> Gallants,
> Me thinks your soules should grudge, & inly scorne
> To be made slave, to humors that are borne
> In slime of filthy sensualitie. (ll. 204–207)

If the majority of the "villains" whom Marston is discussing are young gallants, this simple fact explains the amount of space he allots to the form of "villanie" which young men are most frequently guilty of and preoccupied with, illicit sexual activity. The revels give sufficient evidence of the primary importance of this topic to his audience. Compared with Hall, a Fellow of the Puritan Emmanuel College who was on the verge of ordination, Marston does speak more frequently and explicitly about sex. But it is difficult to find much difference be-

---

[20] See *Poems,* p. 100. Marston says that he wrote the first satire in SV for those who have a liking for obscurity and that it is "in some places too obscure, in all places misliking me."

tween Marston and strictly comparable figures from the same
milieu, men like Davies, Guilpin, or Donne. Most of Marston's
sexual references attack two eternal practices at men's colleges,
lechery and homosexuality. The following passages are representative:

> Who would not shake a Satyres knottie rod?
> When to defile the sacred seate of God
> Is but accounted gentlemens disport?
> To snort in filth, each hower to resort
> To brothell pits: alas a veniall crime,
> Nay, royall, to be last in *thirtith slime*. (SV, II, 38–43)

> *A man, a man:* peace Cynick, yon is one,
> A compleat soule, of all perfection.
> What? mean'st thou him that walks al open brested?
> Drawne through the eare with Ribands, plumy crested?
> He that doth snort in fat-fed luxury,
> And gapes for some grinding Monopoly?
> He that in effeminate invention,
> In beastly source of all pollution,
> In ryot, lust, and fleshly seeming sweetnes,
> Sleepes sound secure, under the shade of greatnes?
> Mean'st thou that sencelesse, sensuall Epicure?
>   (SV, VII, 28–38)

The first example is viciously sarcastic about the "disport" which
the gentlemen treated so casually in the revels. Some of the
language is vivid, but it is difficult to read anything but disgust
into the phrase "thirti[e]th slime," certainly not the "horrified
fascination" which has become the cliché about Marston's sexual attitudes. The second example exhibits Marston's propensity toward name-calling and unimaginative epithets, but its
defects are aesthetic rather than moral. Only by the narrowest
standards of the last century could either of these characteristic
treatments of sex be considered morally offensive.

However, the third satire in *The Scourge of Villanie* does
venture (uniquely, I would claim) into more exotic areas, particularly in two passages. In lines 34 to 52 he tells the story of
Luscus whose "Cynick Dad/Hath forc'd him cleane forsake
his Pickhatch drab" (ll. 35–36). Luscus has had to resort to a
substitute:

>   he hath his *Ganimede*,
>   His perfum'd shee-goate, smooth kembd & high fed.
>   At Hogsdon now his monstrous lust he feasts,
>   For there he keeps a baudy-house of beasts. (ll. 39–42)

The speaker advises Luscus' father to allow him his "Curtezan" before his son turns into a "monster," but the father's next step is to immure him in a "brick-built tower." Once again Luscus proves his resourcefulness:

>   Fayth, what cares he for faire *Cynedian* boyes?
>   Velvet cap'd Goates, duch Mares? tut common toies.
>   Detaine them all, on this condition
>   He may but use the Cynick friction. (ll. 49–52)

The second example is short enough to quote completely. The speaker has been criticizing Hall for treating "thrice-turn'd bone-pick'd subject[s]" when all about are forces which

>   Infect our soules with all polluting evill.
>   Shal *Lucea* scorne her husbands luke-warme bed?
>   (Because her pleasure being hurried
>   In joulting Coach, with glassie instrument,
>   Doth farre exceede the *Paphian* blandishment)
>   Whilst I (like to some mute *Pythagoran*)
>   Halter my hate, and cease to curse and ban
>   Such brutish filth? (ll. 120–127)

In both cases, Marston would say that his moral intention was clear. It is true that he treats the plight of Luscus as a joke, especially on the "Dad" whose enforcement of the Cynics' moral precepts left poor Luscus no recourse but "Cynick friction." Marston expresses his revulsion by saying that "luxurious incontinence" in "male stews" is almost justifiable by comparison. In the case of Lucea, Marston registers his disgust vehemently. But many critics would tend to agree with John Peter that Marston's purposes were far from moral: "The one common denominator between the passages on Lucea and Luscus is their capacity to shock, and he undoubtedly meant them to be shocking." [21] The issue of Marston's moral sincerity has frequently been raised. It is based, I would claim, on a very small percentage of his work. But to place it in a useful context, I

[21] *Complaint and Satire in Early English Literature* (Oxford, 1956), p. 172.

must make a digression about the work by Marston which moral critics have attacked most severely, *The Metamorphosis of Pigmalions Image.*

2

The Metamorphosis of Pigmalions Image has recently been examined by a fairly long list of scholars, including such authorities as C. S. Lewis, Douglas Bush, John Peter, and Arnold Davenport.[22] The poem is often used to illustrate certain tendencies in the writing of the 1590's or, since this was Marston's earliest publication, to show the fundamental cast of his mind. But from the first it has provoked disagreement: Marston hotly defended it against charges of immorality, but the author of the poem *Alcilia* (1617) mentioned it as suitable for a prostitute's library.

Recently the argument has centered on whether *Pigmalions Image* is an Ovidian amatory poem — it expands Ovid's fifty-five lines to two hundred thirty-four — in the manner of *Hero and Leander* (designed, some would claim, with lubricious intent), or a sophisticated burlesque of the Ovidian vogue by one of the new satirists.[23] It would seem unlikely that scholars as deeply versed in the poetry of the period as those mentioned above could be completely "wrong" in their divergent readings, and I propose to show that both sides in this controversy are partially right: that the poem is a serious attempt in the Ovidian mode (though not intentionally pornographic), but that it also has satiric elements.

Some kind of satiric intention is evident in the elaborate paraphernalia of dedication, argument, and invocation which precede the poem. The dedication to Opinion is clearly a burlesque, the first of several by Marston, of the fulsome, abject dedicatory style, as well as a sardonic comment on the world's

[22] *Pigmalion* is in that category of minor poem endlessly mentioned but (one suspects) not often re-examined. Among modern studies which attempt fresh appraisals or which are important for other reasons, I would cite in chronological order: Morse Allen, *The Satire of John Marston* (Columbus, Ohio, 1920), pp. 88–92; Douglas Bush, *Mythology and the Renaissance Tradition* (Minneapolis, 1932), pp. 177–180; C. S. Lewis, *English Literature in the Sixteenth Century* (Oxford, 1954), pp. 472–474; A. José Axelrad, *Malcontent Elizabéthain*, pp. 20–36; John Peter, *Complaint and Satire*, passim; and Anthony Caputi, *John Marston, Satirist* (Ithaca, 1961), pp. 14–22. There is also an article by Gustav Cross, "Marston's 'Metamorphosis of Pigmalions Image': a Mock-epyllion," *Etudes Anglaises*, 13 (1960), 332–336; and some useful material in Davenport's *Poems of John Marston.*

[23] Of the critics cited above, Allen, Lewis, Axelrad, and Peter read it as an amatory poem while Bush, Caputi, and Cross find varying degrees of burlesque of Ovidian poetry.

values: *"Thou soule of Pleasure, Honors only substance,/Great Arbitrator, Umpire of the Earth."* [24] It concludes:

> *But if thou wilt not with thy Deitie*
> *Shade, and inmaske the errors of my pen,*
> *Protect an Orphane Poets infancie,*
> *I will disclose, that all the world shall ken*
>   *How partiall thou art in Honors giving:*
>   *Crowning the shade, the substance praise depriving.*
> (p. 49, ll. 13–18)

Behind the humility we observe traces of a satirist who can distinguish shade from substance, as the world in general and the hero of his poem, Pigmalion, can not.

"The Argument of the Poem" which follows is a straightforward prose summary of the story, but at two points it shows the special twist to Marston's version. Pigmalion, it says, "was so deeplie enamored on his owne workmanship, that he would oftentimes lay the Image in bedde with him, and *fondlie* use such petitions and dalliance, as if it had been a breathing creature. But in the end, finding his *fond dotage*" (p. 50, italics mine), he obtained Venus' intercession and hence a compliant mistress. Marston directs us to view Pigmalion's love for a statue as a form of insanity, a "fond dotage."

The last introductory piece, "To his Mistress," is a typically Petrarchan plea to the poet's Angel, Saint, and Deitie for her grace:

>   *as thou read'st, (Faire) take compassion,*
> *Force me not envie my* Pigmalion.
> *Then when thy kindnes grants me such sweet blisse,*
> *I'le gladly write thy metamorphosis.* (p. 51, ll. 13–16)

He asks her to accept the lesson of the poem and to be metamorphosed from a statue-like saint who demands distant worship into a compliant mistress.

Tonally and thematically, these introductory pieces prepare us for Marston's special treatment of the Pigmalion story. Thus, in the first stanza of the poem, we see the shade-substance confusion which appears in the dedication to Opinion:

[24] *Poems*, p. 49, ll. 1–2. All page and line numbers interpolated in the text refer to this edition. In the case of *Pigmalion*, Davenport's edition provides stanza numbers only. For more precise reference I have also included the line numbers from volume III of A. H. Bullen's edition of *The Works of John Marston* (London, 1887).

> Love at length forc'd him [Pigmalion] to know his fate,
> And love the shade, whose substance he did hate.
>
> (stanza 1; ll. 5–6)

These lines also exhibit what we have seen in the "Argument of the Poem," the narrator's objective and ironic view of his "fond" hero. Marston intermixes two narrative methods. Though staying outside Pigmalion's consciousness, he usually confines his narrative to what Pigmalion sees and feels: a "limited omniscient" point of view. But he also employs first-person asides (probably copied from *Hero and Leander* and seen also in Ovid) which tend to mock the emotion or action just described; often these asides are long similes with a satiric overtone.

The satiric nature of the asides and similes has often been noticed, but the ironic effects achieved within the "limited omniscient" narrative are equally important:

> He thought he saw the blood run through the vaine
> And leape, and swell with all alluring meanes:
> Then feares he is deceiv'd, and then againe,
> He thinks he see'th the brightnes of the beames
>   Which shoote from out the fairenes of her eye:
>   At which he stands as in an extasie.
>
> Her Amber-coloured, her shining haire,
> Makes him protest, the Sunne hath spread her head
> With golden beames, to make her farre more faire.
> But when her cheeks his amorous thoughts have fed,
>   Then he exclaimes, such redde and so pure white,
>   Did never blesse the eye of mortall sight.
>
> (stanzas 5–6; ll. 25–36)

Pigmalion's fond dotage is such that he "thought he saw, . . . feares he is deceiv'd, . . . thinks he see'th." He works himself into an "extasie" and ascribes to the power of the sun what he himself has formed. Pigmalion's adoration is unmistakably in the language of the sonneteers of the 1590's ("such redde and so pure white"). There is, of course, no clear-cut distinction between the way a hero expresses his admiration in Ovidian and Petrarchan love poetry, but there is often a difference in the way he acts and feels. The poem continues:

Then view's her lips, no lips did seeme so faire
In his conceit, through which he thinks doth flie
So sweet a breath, that doth perfume the ayre.

(stanza 7; ll. 37–39)

Douglas Bush has pointed out that these lines echo some from
Hero and Leander:

Many would praise the sweet smell when she past,
When 'twas the odour which her breath foorth cast.[25]

By the use of "seeme," "conceit," and "thinks," Marston has
shifted the tone to stress the conceited, mental quality of Pigmalion's perceptions. Similarly, we have heard many a mistress's
breasts compared to ivory as are the statue's:

Her breasts, like polisht Ivory appeare,
Whose modest mount, doe blesse admiring eye.

(stanza 8; ll. 43–44)

But the point of the deadpan humor is that her breasts appear
that way because they are, in fact, ivory.

After several introductory stanzas which establish Pigmalion's
situation, the narrative proceeds by describing his reactions to
the various parts of his statue's body. Jumping, one stanza at
a time, from hair to lips to breasts in the manner of a Petrarchan
inventory, Pigmalion finally "discried Loves pavillion" (l. 50).
It is at this point that Marston inserts the first of the extended
similes which establish beyond doubt the author's attitude
toward his hero:

Who ever saw the subtile Citty-dame
In sacred church, when her pure thoughts shold pray,
Peire through her fingers, so to hide her shame,
When that her eye, her mind would faine bewray.

[25] *Works of Christopher Marlowe,* ed. C. F. Tucker Brooke (Oxford, 1912),
First Sestiad, ll. 21–22. Bush, *Mythology,* p. 179, taking the position that *Pigmalion* is an "ironic piece of studied excess" in the Ovidian style, claims that
Marston's echoes of Marlowe are part of his parody. Certainly Marlowe's poem
was on Marston's mind during the composition of *Pigmalion.* He appropriates
lines from it and distorts them in meaningful ways. On at least one occasion
(discussed below), Marston's argument is a condensed version of Marlowe's,
much clarified by reference to the earlier poem. But the main use Marston
makes of *Hero and Leander* is as a standard of comparison: the actions of Marlowe's protagonists are a measure of Pigmalion's absurd conduct.

> So would he view, and winke, and view againe,
> A chaster thought could not his eyes retaine.
>
> (stanza 10; ll. 55–60)

The farfetched comparison deflates Pigmalion's high imaginary passion; it also hints at a nasty voyeuristic side to his conduct. A little later his gaze falls lower:

> But when the faire proportion of her thigh
> Began appeare. O *Ovid* would he cry,
> Did ere *Corinna* show such Ivorie
> When she appear'd in *Venus* livorie?
>   And thus enamour'd, dotes on his owne Art
>   Which he did work, to work his pleasing smart.
>
> (stanza 12; ll. 67–72)

This stanza is compounded of ironies: the hero of Ovid's story is apostrophizing Ovid, but this also reminds us of the vast disparity between an ivory statue and the quite palpable Corinna of the familiar passage in the *Amores* (I.v) to which Pigmalion alludes. Additionally, the words Pigmalion utters are the often repeated Petrarchan boast of a mistress whose beauty exceeds that of legendary heroines, but here the narrator instantly points out that this particular lover is an artist admiring and emotionally affected by his own artifact.

The next of the long similes brings together the moral bases of Marston's attitude toward his hero. By now Pigmalion has completed his observation and is proceeding to action. He begins to kiss, to "dally with her Ivory breasts," to engage in several kinds of "wanton love-trick[s],"

> Whereby he thought he might procure the love
> Of his dull Image, which no plaints coulde move.
>
> (stanza 13; ll. 77–78)

In a characteristic Elizabethan association, Marston compares these actions to Catholic image-worship:

> Looke how the peevish Papists crouch, and kneele
> To some dum Idoll with their offering,
> As if a senceles carved stone could feele
> The ardor of his bootles chattering,
>   So fond he was, and earnest in his sute
>   To his remorsles Image, dum and mute.
>
> (stanza 14; ll. 79–84)

This stanza really contains a double comparison. Pigmalion's distracted conduct in adoring his own statue is like the "idolatry" of the Papists. But insofar as Pigmalion's love is a fierce, unrequited passion for an unresponsive mistress, Marston is comparing Petrarchan to "Papist" attitudes. This second comparison is admittedly rather submerged; it is elaborated in very similar language in a passage about a fond lover in *The Scourge of Villanie*:

> Publius hates vainely to idolatries,
> And laughs that Papists honor Images,
> And yet (ô madnes) these mine eyes did see
> Him melt in moving plaints, obsequiously
> Imploring favour, twining his kind armes,
> Using inchauntments, exorcismes, charmes.
> The oyle of Sonnets, wanton blandishment,
> The force of teares, & seeming languishment,
> Unto the picture of a painted lasse. (SV, VIII, ll. 84–92)

The passage continues in this sardonic vein for seventeen additional lines: what is obscure in *Pigmalion* through excessive condensation is here made explicit. Pigmalion's Papist-like idolatry qualifies him as a pre-eminent example of the foolish Petrarchan lovers who figure so extensively in the satires of the 1590's.

Thus far the poet has been mocking the hero and, by extension, a set of attitudes engendered by and typical of the Petrarchan sonneteers: not so much their frigid, formulaic style as their moral position. Marston is saying that people with this attitude toward love (and life) desire merely to indulge their emotions, not to involve themselves in love or other serious human relationships. They enclose themselves in a dream divorced from the objects of this world and remain tied to their own constructions. This is a subject to which Marston returns in his plays as well as his satires.

The poet becomes explicit on this point after Pigmalion realizes that he has deceived himself and that, like Ixion, he has "clipt a cloud in steede of heavens Queene" (l.108). The narrator proceeds to generalize about Pigmalion's plight:

> I oft have smil'd to see the foolery
> Of some sweet Youths, who seriously protest
> That Love respects not actuall Luxury,
> But onely joy's to dally, sport, and jest:

> Love is a child, contented with a toy,
> A busk-point, or some favour still's the boy.
>
> > (stanza 19; ll. 109–114)

The connection with Publius' arid, "Platonic" worship in *The Scourge of Villanie* is obvious: the "youths" do not expect nor do they want real human contact and sexual love. But for Marston love is more than a childish game or an organized ritual.[26]

Up to this point in the poem, Pigmalion resembles the young gallants whom Marston scourges in the satires for their puling love dotage.[27] But a change now takes place which commentators have missed. Frustrated by the stoniness of his mistress, Pigmalion refuses to be rebuffed; he insists on fulfillment. As a result, at precisely the halfway point in the poem, the twentieth of thirty-nine stanzas, a metamorphosis occurs in the narrator's attitude toward him:

> Marke my *Pigmalion,* whose affections ardor
> May be a mirror to posteritie.
> Yet viewing, touching, kissing, (common favour,)
> Could never satiat his loves ardencie:
> > And therefore Ladies, thinke that they nere love you,
> > Who doe not unto more then kissing move you.
>
> > (stanza 20; ll. 115–120)

Pigmalion is no longer an object of satire; he is a mirror, an amatory model. It is significant that the last two lines (above) echo Ovid's *Ars Amatoria* (as Davenport pointed out in his edition, p. 214):

---

[26] Perhaps Marston's conception of Pigmalion is derived from Gower's *Confessio Amantis,* which uses the story to combat "Pusillamite" in love by those "truantz" that "lacken herte" and out of "fere" "wexen doumb and dar noght telle" their love. Gower's Pigmalion is a positive example because he refused to be rebuffed by his statue's silence:

> He made such continuance
> Fro dai to nyht, and preith so longe,
> That his preiere is underfonge,
> Which Venus of hire grace herde . . .
> And if he wolde have holde him stille
> And nothing spoke, he sholde have failed.

(*Works of John Gower,* ed. G. C. Macauley [Oxford, 1901], Vol. II, Book iv, ll. 342–427 passim.)

[27] In some satiric lines "in prayse" of *Pigmalion,* Marston again makes the connection between the "sweet youths" and "our gallants" who are "Faint, and white liver'd" (p. 64, l. 24).

Oscula qui sumpsit, si non et cetera sumet,
Haec quoque, quae data sunt, perdere dignus erit.

This is a characteristic attitude of Ovid; it is equally characteristic of many Elizabethan Ovidian poems to stress the primacy
of passion. For example, an analogous passage, which serves
virtually as a gloss on Marston's views, occurs in another
Ovidian poem, *Hero and Leander*:

Like *Aesops* cocke, this jewell he enjoyed,
And as a brother with his sister toyed,
Supposing nothing else was to be done,
Now he her favour and good will had wone.
But know you not that creatures wanting sence
By nature have a mutuall appetence,
And wanting organs to advaunce a step,
Mov'd by Loves force, unto ech other lep?
Much more in subjects having intellect,
Some hidden influence breeds like effect.[28]

With respect to sexual fulfillment, Ovidian poetry is quite
unlike — one might almost say, it is opposed to — the tendency
of 1590's Petrarchanism. Petrarchan ladies refuse and rebuff;
Ovidian ladies like Venus and Hero often pursue. In other
words, Marston is fulfilling the traditions of the Ovidian genre,
almost defining them in this poem. It is therefore ironic that
the poem has often been read as a satire on the genre.

In the final section of the poem Marston makes explicit an
element latent in the story. Pigmalion's statue is an ideal
vehicle to image an obdurate Petrarchan mistress — willing to
be worshipped but, like the "sweet youths," uninterested in
going further.[29] Pigmalion begins to wonder whether women
were made only to "heate mens harts" (l. 125) and not to
"coole" them as well. He turns for help to Venus, whom he
now describes as "Queene of sportive dallying" (l. 133), one
whose "kingdome rests in wanton revelling" (l. 135). He desires
that his mistress "may equalize affection,/And have a mutuall
love, and loves desire" (stanza 24; ll. 141–142). Not until this
moment of prayer to Venus does Pigmalion "strip" himself

[28] *Works of Christopher Marlowe*, Second Sestiad, ll. 51–60.
[29] Petrarch himself noticed this in Sonnet LXXVIII:

Pigmalion, quanto lodar ti dei
De l'imagine tua, se mille volte
N'avesti quel ch'i' sol una vorrei!

"naked quite" (l. 149); until now he has not been a serious lover. The metamorphosis in Pigmalion causes one in his statue, and it is really Pigmalion's change that is described as a return from death:

> Doe but conceive a Mothers passing gladnes,
> (After that death her onely sonne hath seazed
> And overwhelm'd her soule with endlesse sadnes)
> When that she sees him gin for to be raised
> From out his deadly swoune to life againe.
>
> (stanza 30; ll. 175–179)

The statue having never lived could not return from the dead, but Pigmalion's change of heart amounts to a new life.

I pointed out in discussing lines 31–33 that Pigmalion thought his powers godlike; he confused his powers with the sun's. This mistake is recalled at the moment when his prayers are being successfully answered. It is Venus who has the sunlike power, for "Each part [of the statue] like Waxe before the sunne did melt" (l. 171). The same point is made in the lines that follow, where every word seems to require a double interpretation:

> And now, oh now, he finds how he is graced
> By his owne worke. Tut, women will relent
> When as they finde such moving blandishment.
>
> (stanza 29; ll. 172–174)

The simplest interpretation of these lines involves obvious contradictions: one is usually "graced" by someone else's work, and it can hardly be claimed that the statue relents through Pigmalion's blandishments. Only by "grace" can he enjoy his "owne worke," and thus the "worke" by which he succeeds is his prayer rather than his artistry. In fact, these lines echo a portion of his prayer: "make her relent,/And kindly yeeld to thy sweet blandishment" (ll. 137–138). It is through the "powerfulnesse" (l. 136) of Venus' "blandishment" that the statue relents.

The apparent becomes the real through a change in Pigmalion's attitudes. He has learned that however attractive the world of art, it can never be as satisfying as the gratification of the senses:

> when he proves & finds her wondrous kind,
> Yeelding soft touch for touch, sweet kisse, for kisse,
> He's well assur'd no faire imagery
> Could yeeld such pleasing, loves felicity.
>   (stanza 31; ll. 183–186)

And the poet asserts that the consummation to which Pigmalion proceeds is the normal and proper sequel which anyone in his position would have pursued.

Now Marston employs another device which suggests satiric intent. He plays a cat-and-mouse game with those who are reading his poem for lascivious enjoyment, that is, the same "sweet youths" who substitute art for life:

> And now me thinks some wanton itching eare
> With lustfull thoughts, and ill attention,
> List's to my Muse, expecting for to heare
> The amorous discription of that action
> Which *Venus* seekes, and ever doth require,
> When fitnes graunts a place to please desire.
>   (stanza 33; ll. 193–198)

He bases this refusal on a clearly defined distinction:

> Peace idle Poesie,
> Be not obsceane though wanton in thy rhimes.
>   (stanza 38; ll. 225–226)

The relevant NED meanings are, I believe, the following: *wanton* — "sportive, impelled by caprice or fancy, free, unrestrained"; *obscene* — "offensive to modesty or decency; expressing or suggesting unchaste or lustful ideas; impure; indecent; lewd." (Marston's use of "obsceane" in this place is the earliest listed usage with this meaning. Earlier it had meant "offensive to the senses.") This distinction is the point of the poem; the "kingdome" of love "rests in *wanton revelling*" (l. 135).

Are we to take what Marston says about this poem at his own valuation? Does he not present lines that "gaping eares [may] . . . swallow up" (l. 224)? My reading suggests that the only passages open to the charge of "obscenity" are those which depict Pigmalion's unhealthy state of mind. When he has been metamorphosed and is engaged in "wanton revelling," Marston leaves the action to our imagination: "Let him [that is, each of us] conceit but what himselfe would doe" (l. 199).

The concluding lines can re-enforce the defense against decadence or perversion:

> And chaster thoughts, pardon if I doe trip,
> Or if some loose lines from my pen doe slip,

> Let this suffice, that that same happy night
> So gracious were the Gods of marriage
> Mids't all there pleasing and long wish'd delight
> *Paphus* was got: of whom in after age
>   *Cyprus* was *Paphos* call'd, and evermore
>   Those Ilandars do *Venus* name adore.
> (stanzas 38–39; ll. 227–234)

A couplet by the "Authour in prayse of his precedent Poem" may serve as a comment on these lines:

> And in the end, (the end of love I wot)
> *Pigmalion* hath a jolly boy begot. (p. 65, ll. 27–28)

Venus, the goddess of healthy, sensual, propagative love, becomes the heroine or, perhaps, the conqueror of the poem. *The Metamorphosis of Pigmalions Image* describes an interlocking set of metamorphoses: the change in Pigmalion produces the transformation in his statue, and it is intended to produce one in the poet's mistress and in those who read poetry for the wrong reasons. Hence it is a "mirror to posteritie" for a healthy and fertile society. According to this reading, the various interpretations are not really contradictory. *Pigmalion* is an orthodox Ovidian amatory poem, its attitudes virtually epitomizing the genre. Nevertheless, when Marston later said that he was writing satirically and that the object of his attack was "loose lascivious rime," he was sincere, for the poem is also a criticism of Petrarchan poetry and the young gallants who admire it.[30]

---

[30] Marston made several comments about *Pigmalion* in his satires; they are defensive and obscure. Many interpretations of the poem have been influenced by these comments, but I have tried to interpret the poem without reference to them because I think they raise more questions than they solve. However, in "From Petrarch to Ovid: Metamorphoses in John Marston's *Metamorphosis of Pigmalions Image*," *ELH*, 32 (1965), 333–348, I have attempted to show that Marston's subsequent statements confirm the interpretation I have proposed above.

3

To return to the long deferred cases of Luscus the goat lover and Lucea with her obscene instrument in Satire III of *The Scourge,* it is evident that their villainies are of the same order as Pigmalion's before his metamorphosis. Lucea has a "glassie" rather than an ivory "instrument"; this she prefers to the sort of *"Paphian* blandishment" (SV, III, 124) which eventually gained Pigmalion his bliss on Paphos. Luscus' "Cynick friction" (SV, III, 52) is a mechanical activity far removed from "wanton revelling" (PI, stanza 23; 1. 138). These passages in *The Scourge* may well have been calculated to shock, as Mr. Peter asserts. Even the dry recital of case histories by Krafft-Ebing is shocking. But this is no reason to impugn Marston's "sincerity," as several writers have done. Had he been interested in writing a work of sensational pornography, he could easily have inserted more material of this sort and treated it in greater detail. Instead he criticized these activities from a clear-cut moral position. It is not a strictly Christian morality, but it does resemble the Prince d'Amour's distinction between "desires illuminated by the Celestial flame of Beauty" and "easie and low-prized Venery." [31] By substituting images for the joys of wanton reveling, Luscus, Lucea, and Luxurio, the rake, have lost "loves felicity" (PI, stanza 31; 1. 186).

I fail to detect any "insincerity" in these attitudes, but the satires do reflect an uncertainty about his role, which ultimately led Marston to abandon the writing of formal verse satire. Briefly, he became disturbed by the fact that he was read by those whom he disdained and, according to him, ignored by those whom he hoped to have as his readers. In his first volume, he was, quite naturally, unaware of the problem. *Pigmalion* was designed for a literate audience capable of responding to allusions and to complexities of tone. The appended satires require a comprehension of personal references, and the controversy with Hall in the third and fourth satires and the dark hints at scandal in the fifth presume a knowing audience. However, Marston was dismayed to discover that he was attracting unexpected and undesirable readers. In the sixth satire of *The Scourge,* in which he defends *Pigmalion,* he describes the responses of a series of characters to the first volume. Curio thought that *Pigmalion* was pornography. Muto lisped *"tis prety good/*And praiseth that he never understood" (ll. 79–80). Flaccus accused the author of plagiary on the basis of a misunderstanding of a Latin note, and Friscus, although unable to

[31] *Prince d'Amour,* p. 7.

read Latin, tried to claim that the poems were a jumble of lines picked out of the Roman satirists. Furious at such "vulgar prophanation" of his "very *Genius*" (ll. 108–109), Marston announced at the beginning of *The Scourge* that he was not directing this volume to a "vaine fantasticke troupe/Of puffie youthes" (p. 97, ll. 41–42). He realized that he could not drive such readers away, that they would in fact be the larger part of his audience, but he made it clear that he had nothing but contempt for the whole group whom he describes sarcastically as

> Castilios, Cyprians, court-boyes, spanish blocks,
> Ribanded eares, granado-netherstocks,
> Fidlers, Scriveners, pedlers, tynkering knaves,
> Base blew-coats, tapsters, brod-cloth minded slaves.
>
> (p. 97, ll. 31–34)

The sociological range is broad for satiric effect, but he knows that his main audience will be his fellow residents at the Inns, both young and old:

> Shall each odd puisne of the Lawyers Inne,
> Each barmy-froth, that last day did beginne
> To reade his little, or his *nere a whit*,
> Or shall some greater auncient, of lesse wit,
> (That never turnd but browne Tobacco leaves
> Whose sences some damn'd *Occupant* bereaves)
> Lye gnawing on thy vacant times expence?
> Tearing thy rimes, quite altering the sence?
>
> (p. 96, ll. 7–14)

To both categories, the "spruce pedant" (l. 77) and the "span-new come fry/Of Innes-a-court" (ll. 77–78), he sarcastically requests: "doe but raile at me,/No greater honor craves my poesie" (ll. 79–80).

But it is not accurate to say, as one critic has said, that Marston's satires display "a mixture of contempt for the vices he is attacking, contempt for the reader, and contempt for himself which gives a particular character to his work." [32] Marston does respect one class of prospective readers, although it would be more precise to describe his feeling as abject adulation. His poem "cheerfully . . . runnes" toward an intellectual elite whom he calls "diviner wits, celestiall soules,/Whose free-borne mindes no kennel thought controules." Such readers are the

---

[32] Hallett Smith, *Elizabethan Poetry* (Cambridge, Mass., 1952), p. 240.

"substance of the shadowes of our age, . . . True judging eyes, quick sighted censurers." The thought of them inspires him to conclude with an ecstatic ejaculation: "O rare!" (pp. 98–99, ll. 81–97 *passim*). The Castilios and Luxurios against whom he directed the main force of his satire read his work, but he hoped to gain the attention of the true wits, such Inns of Court men as Hoskins, Donne, Martin, and closely connected literary figures like "O rare Ben Jonson." Even more than in his first volume, Marston seems to have aimed *The Scourge* at a small, select audience. Twice he describes these satires as "deepe designes" (see below), and the philosophical framework, technical and academic terms, even the abortive attempt at obscurity in the first satire, show that he "sweat . . . out . . . [his] braine" to acquire a worthier audience. For that audience the manner of Horace or, in English, of Donne would have been ideal: casual, intimate, quietly sophisticated, sometimes even indulgent toward his victims. Instead Marston chose to emulate Juvenal at his angriest:

> Grim-fac'd *Reproofe,* sparkle with threatning eye
> Bend thy sower browes in my tart poesie.
> Avant yee curres, houle in some cloudie mist,
> Quake to behold a sharp-fang'd Satyrist.
> O how on tiptoes proudly mounts my Muse,
> Stalking a loftier gate than Satyres use.
> Me thinkes some sacred rage warmes all my vaines,
> Making my spright mount up to higher straines
> Then wel beseemes a rough-tongu'd Satyres part,
> *But Art curbs Nature, Nature guildeth Art.*
>
> (SV, IX, 1–10)

"Grim *Reprofe*" was the phrase Marston used to describe the tone in his earlier volume (CS, III, 1), and he uses it in two other passages in *The Scourge*. He seems proud of the fact — he is certainly accurate in his claim — that his "gate" is "loftier" than that of other satirists. No one had ever stood on tiptoes so long or scourged so noisily or claimed so much for his role. This arrogant and pretentious satiric persona was not a felicitous choice for someone hoping to attract the audience he desired. It was not enough that he had added philosophical passages to *The Scourge*; it was the part he had left unchanged that provoked distaste and, what was worse, amusement.

The special formula for Marston's later satire was an amalgam of "grim reproof" and philosophical generalization, mostly

directed against a specific group, the young gentry, and designed
to interest an audience of learned wits. Satire VIII of *The
Scourge* provides an especially clear example. Titled "Inamo-
rato Curio," it is a satire of manners on a subject which *The
Prince d'Amour* and *Pigmalion* also treat, the absurdities and
perversities of abject Petrarchan lovers and the dangerous implications of their conduct. It begins with portraits of a series
of lovers — first foolish gallants, then amorous gods, and finally
poets and poetasters — who are unmanned by their passion:

> If *Lauras* painted lip doe daine a kisse
> To her enamor'd slave, *ô heavens blisse*
> (Straight he exclaimes) *not to be match'd with this!*
> Blaspheming dolt, goe three-score sonnets write
> Upon a pictures kisse, ô raving spright!
>
> (SV, VIII, 138–142)

The extreme epithets, the commanding tone, the heavy sarcasm
conclude the section of grim reproofs, and the satirist next
proceeds to climb a ladder of progressively higher generalities
about the implications of these "villainies." First he expresses
concern at such "base dishonors of our sexe," but he realizes
that men are "guiltles Doves" compared with the gods who
"force foule rapes" and "Will turne themselves to any brutish
shapes" (ll. 149–150). From the evidence of men and gods, he
can only conclude:

> Lust hath confounded all,
> The bright glosse of our intellectuall
> Is fouly soyl'd. The wanton wallowing
> In fond delights, and amorous dallying,
> Hath dusk'd the fairest splendour of our soule.
>
> (SV, VIII, 165–169)

This bare generality is followed by an even more general conclusion, the importance of which is emphasized by italics:

> *Reason by prudence in her function*
> *Had wont to tutor all our action.*
> *Ayding with precepts of philosophy*
> *Our feebled natures imbecilitie:*
> *But now affection, will, concupiscence,*
> *Have got o're Reason chiefe preheminence.*
>
> (SV, VIII, 173–178)

Even this versifying of Epictetus[33] does not conclude the satirist's generalizations. He decides that he can "see, and can right plainly show/From whence such abject thoughts & actions grow" (ll. 183–184). The intellectual portion of the soul, according to his parable, began to "scorne his Land-lordes muddy slime" (l. 192) and reunited with his "celestiall" source, "leaving the sensuall/Base hangers on, lusking at home in slime" (ll. 198–199). Hence the body deflowers "chast time" (l. 208) and abuses his "organons of sence" (l. 210). He concludes with a prayer:

> Returne, returne, sacred *Synderesis,*
> Inspire our truncks, let not such mud as this
> Pollute us still. Awake our lethargie,
> Raise us from out our brain-sicke foolerie.
>
> (SV, VIII, 211–214)

It would not require one of the "diviner wits" to detect the contradictions and gaps in the logic of these philosophical preachments. If the instinct for right conduct (pretentiously called "synderesis," for which Jonson mocked him in *Every Man out of his Humour*[34]) has left the earth, Curio and the rest might fairly ask how they can conform to the speaker's moral strictures. It is not at all clear that it is within one's power to reform, and, as we shall see, Marston suggests in the fourth satire of *The Scourge* that we cannot. It is true that the speaker includes himself ("Inspire our truncks") among those who require the return of "Synderesis," but, as every reader of the satires must have asked, why then does he scourge others with such unmitigated disdain? Why is he not writing holy sonnets asking how he may repent? The speaker admits at one point that morally he is "not imaculate" (CS, II, 11), but this is merely another way of demonstrating that he is franker than the hypocritical Hall. In most of the satires, he speaks from on high as the last pure man. As he claims in the satire under discussion, he sees the truth with clarity and expresses it with plainness (SV, VIII, l. 183). Thus he has the right to reprove his victims with scornful sarcasm. Such inconsistencies may be inherent in the satiric mask, in fact are an integral feature of it according to Alvin Kernan,[35] but Marston does not exploit the

---

[33] Cf. Davenport, *Poems*, p. 346.

[34] *Ben Jonson*, ed. C. H. Herford and Percy and Evelyn Simpson (Oxford, 1927), III, 502.

[35] *The Cankered Muse* (New Haven, 1959).

persona skillfully. His infrequent assertions of involvement in vice sound like afterthoughts, and his rhetoric is that of an absolutist.

In the only full-length modern study of Marston in English, Anthony Caputi has recently claimed that Marston's moral absolutism was a "personal version of Neo-Stoicism" influenced by continental philosophers like Lipsius and Du Vair.[36] Almost simultaneously, the late Arnold Davenport's edition of Marston's poems was published. He tried to show, not for the first time but more specifically than anyone else had shown, the strong Calvinist tendency in the satires and some of the inconsistencies in Marston's philosophical positions. As Marston's most pretentious intellectual effort, the fourth satire in *The Scourge* must be the crux in settling this disagreement. It presents a succession of characters who promise to reform "tomorrow." In it, the would-be philosopher Fabian is confuted for advancing the view that bad habits are not easily uprooted. The speaker disagrees with him, claiming that vice is not the result

[36] Caputi, *John Marston*, p. 58. There are serious objections to Caputi's repeated claim that Marston was a Neo-Stoic. He acknowledges that he has been unable to discover any "concrete proof" (p. 59), but offers three major arguments in support of his contention. (1) He points out Marston's central use of the term "synderesis," derived from the Christian mystics. This he equates with the Neo-Stoics' use of the notion of "fire" and "spark" to define God. But nowhere does he demonstrate a connection made by any Neo-Stoic philosopher between these terms although Marston himself connects them. (2) He cites Marston's frequent references to "Opinion," but this term had very broad currency at that time: Shakespeare was particularly fond of using it to signify a vulgar or mistaken estimation of things. (3) Caputi's most important argument rests on Marston's use of a metaphor which, he claims, resembles the Neo-Stoic comparison of the relationship between God and man to that between a fountain and a plant. However, Marston's metaphor is not precisely the same (it strikes me as very different), for Marston describes man connected to God "As't were by pypes" (SV, VII, 191). It was, incidentally, not a uniquely Neo-Stoic notion but, as Davenport (*Poems*, p. 338) points out, one which Seneca offered. Moreover, Marston offers the image "tentatively and a bit grudgingly," as Caputi concedes (p. 67), since he introduces it by saying that he does not believe it to be literally true (1.188). Once Caputi establishes the pipe as a Neo-Stoic figure, he finds many other related figures, although he describes them as being treated "rather more tangentially" (making them tangents to an "axiome" which Marston says he thinks untrue). For example, "The [pipe] figure is distinctly operative when he uses the term 'purge'" (p. 67); he also relates Marston's many images of dirt to this master metaphor. But the cleaning away of dirt and purification by water can scarcely be called the unique task of Neo-Stoic satirists. Perhaps Caputi is correct in guessing that Marston thought of himself as a Neo-Stoic who had evolved a very special variety of the belief for himself, but it is so "special" that it might well be given other labels. I think he is quite right to stress the idealism behind Marston's writing, but I cannot see that it is the product of any consistently held body of beliefs. Marston's use of the pipe metaphor is typical of his method. He picked metaphors to suit his poetic purposes; some of them resemble those used by the Neo-Stoics, probably because he was well-read in the Stoicism of the ancients.

of habit but of inspiration. Hence he asserts that nothing but Divine Grace can effect a cure:

> In earnest thus, *it is a sacred cure*
> *To salve the soules dread wounds; Omnipotent*
> *That Nature is, that cures the impotent,*
> *Even in a moment; Sure Grace is infus'd*
> *By divine favour, not by actions us'd.*
> *Which is as permanent as heavens blisse*
> *To them that have it, then no habite is.*
> *To morrow,* nay to day, it may be got:
> So please that gracious Power clense thy spot.
>
> (SV, IV, 114–122)

We are doubly alerted — by the speaker's assertion that he is "in earnest" and by the italics — that this pronouncement is a deeply held belief. Nothing could be more Calvinist than the notion — as a theologian paraphrased the passage — that since grace "is solely the work of Christ (man being utterly corrupt and incapable of in any way earning God's grace) it cannot be acquired by any actions or habits of our own." [37] At this point the satire turns into an academic disputation. The language is at once obscure, technical, colloquial, and angry. After the passage on grace, the speaker offers an illustration to clarify his view that vice is not the result of habit. His disputant responds by establishing a quick distinction between two senses of the term "intellectual" in order to maintain the thesis that virtue is a habit:

> For *Sustine pro nunc* doth bend his brow,
> And old crabb'd *Scotus* on th'organon
> Pay'th me with snaphaunce, quick distinction,
> *Habites that intellectuall termed be,*
> *Are got, or els infus'd from Deitie.* (SV, IV, 130–134)

The satirist easily demonstrates that this distinction is self-contradictory:

> Dull Sorbonist, flie contradiction.
> Fye, thou oppugn'st the definition.
> If one should say, *Of things term'd rationall,*
> *Some reason have, others meere sensuall.*

[37] Quoted by Davenport, *Poems*, p. 310. I am relying heavily on Davenport's paraphrases of obscure passages in this satire.

> Would not some freshman reading *Porphirie,*
> Hisse, and deride such blockish foolerie?
> *Then vice nor vertue have from habite place,*
> *The one from want, the other sacred grace.*
> *Infus'd, displac'd, not in our will or force,*
> *But as it please* Iehova *have remorce.* (SV, IV, 135–144)

Then he proceeds to refute Zeno, the Cynics, and, at greater length, the Stoics, whom he shows to be confused by their simultaneous belief in destiny and free will.

I have quoted long passages from this satire in order to show how unmistakably Marston commits himself to a Calvinist view. But I also wanted to illustrate how academic the language in *The Scourge* can be. It is strained, self-conscious, and learned, but insofar as the Calvinist view is seriously offered, the endeavor of such satire is illogical. The satirist scourges his victims for their villainy, yet explains that it is not really within their power to reform. All they can do is to "implore obsequiously" (l. 163) for grace. Moreover, he describes their impotence in language that only the "diviner wits" could have understood, although he does not presume to be the moral censor of such "rare" creatures. What makes Marston's satiric persona more interesting than Hall's is that he is capable of concluding this satire by expressing his awareness of the absurdity of what he is doing:

> But I forget; why sweat I out my braine,
> In deepe designes, to gay boyes lewd, and vaine?
> These notes were better sung, mong better sort,
> But to my pamphlet, few save fooles resort.
> (SV, IV, 167–170)

He realizes that he has been singing the wrong words to the wrong audience.

We have seen that in the last satire of *The Scourge* the satirist addresses himself directly to the gallants and exhorts them to reform. Obviously this is inconsistent with his views on grace. Perhaps Marston permitted himself this contradiction in order to make his endeavors as a satirist appear less self-defeating at the end of the volume, but it is equally likely that he simply did not notice that he was assuming contradictory positions. The impression from the satires as a whole is that no one label — not Neo-Stoic, Calvinist, or Anglican — would serve to cover the range of positions that Marston intermittently adopted. At one point he expresses the wish that he might emulate Hercules' achievement in cleansing the Augean stables (SV, p. 149, ll. 19–20); at another, he uses Hercules as an example of a hero emasculated by inordinate lust (SV, VIII, 29–39): so, with his Stoicism and anti-Stoicism, his fatalism and voluntarism. Yet something like a unity of vision does emerge from the satires. It is of a fallen world inhabited by fools and villains so hopelessly unreformable that the cynic satirist is entitled to flay them remorselessly despite the futility of his task. The noise of the scourge deafens and keeps us from noticing the inconsistencies in his thought.

Doubtless it was some form of idealism which inspired Marston's violent tone, but it was an aesthetic mistake to have adopted such an extreme version of the satiric persona because it gave an impression of the poet as a malcontented, uncontrolled ranter, virtually a Thersites, which to this day is the dominant complaint against his work and his personality. The objection was never better expressed than by the undergraduates of St. John's College, Cambridge, in their brilliant description of Marston in the second part of *The Return from Parnassus*:

> IUDICIO. What *Monsier Kinsayder,* lifting up your legge and pissing against the world? Put up man, put up for shame.
>
> INGENIOSO. Me thinks he is a Ruffian in his stile,
> Withouten bands or garters ornament.
> He quaffes a cup of Frenchman's Helicon,
> Then royster doyster in his oylie tearmes,
> Cutts, thrusts, and foines at whomesoever he meets,
> And strewes about Ram-ally meditations.
> Tut, what cares he for modest close coucht termes,
> Cleanly to gird our looser libertines?
> Give him plaine naked words stript from their shirts
> That might beseeme plaine dealing *Aretine.*
>
> IUDICIO. I, there is one that backes a paper steed
> And manageth a pen-knife gallantly,
> Strikes his poinado at a buttons breadth,
> Brings the great battering ram of tearms to towne,
> And at first volly of his Cannon shot
> Batters the walles of the old fustie world.[38]

---

[38] *The Three Parnassus Plays*, ed. J. B. Leishman (London, 1949), pp. 241–242, ll. 267–284. Since "Ram-ally" was a disreputable spot which was located within the Temple's liberty, this may represent an attempt to link Marston with the Inns of Court.

I quote this passage in order to stress that it is not merely modern taste nurtured on Pope and Dryden that finds Marston's satires using inordinately heavy artillery. This is also Ben Jonson's objection in the *Poetaster* of 1601 — it may, in fact, have influenced the *Parnassus* authors — when he has the Marston-figure "boldly nominate a spade, a spade." [39]

As in all good literary satire, the judgments presented here are not totally fair since there are some variations in Marston's style. Marston was capable of comic touches, as in his description of the gestation and birth of a pastoral romance by a balladeer in Satire VI and in his well-known description of an inveterate playgoer who could speak of "Naught but pure *Juliat* and *Romeo*" (l. 39) in Satire XI of *The Scourge*. On a few occasions he exploits the possibilities in the couplet form for sardonic wit, as in his attack on the doctrine of transubstantiation:

> Deride their frenzie, that for policie
> Adore Wheate dough, as reall deitie.
> Almighty men, that can their Maker make,
> And force his sacred body to forsake
> The Cherubines, to be gnawne actually,
> Deviding *individuum*, really:
> Making a score of Gods with one poore word.
>
> (SV, II, 82–88)

All these passages occur during the infrequent moments when the speaker's manner is relatively relaxed and his aims are comic. Even in his normal angry tone he is capable of writing lines that jump from the page with concentrated fury:

> I thinke the blind doth see, the flame God rise
> From Sisters couch, each morning to the skies:
> Glowing with lust. (SV, II, 21–23)

We see the world lit by lust, not light — an incestuous lust so dazzling that the blind are endowed with moral vision by it; its continuation is as remorseless as the diurnal cycle ("each morning").

But for most of the 2600 lines of the satires one must agree with the *Parnassus* authors that Marston's major satiric weapon was the battering ram. As C. S. Lewis put it in his general assessment of the Elizabethan verse satirists: "it must

---

[39] *Ben Jonson*, IV, 306, l. 276.

be confessed that the formal satires of the nineties are, in the aggregate, a weariness. They have their happy moments; but there is far too little irony and invention, and far too much direct denunciation. The shapeless Roman model was a fatal encouragement to the Elizabethan love of facile moral ferocity. Nothing is easier, or less interesting, than to proclaim with raucous conviction that whores are unchaste, misers ungenerous, and hypocrites insincere: and the raucous passes with equal ease into the falsetto." [40] This appraisal is more accurate than Lewis' claim for Marston's own satires, that "we seldom go far without coming to some passage which is almost as spirited as Nashe's prose." [41] This is precisely what one would hope to find but rarely does amidst Marston's noisy fury. Name-calling and denunciation can make very exciting reading, but it would seem that invective (in this respect, perhaps, like pornography) works best in prose or in poetry less structured than the couplets used by the satirists of the nineties. We are constantly reminded that their material has been molded. But great invective like that of Nashe seems to spring from the unconscious. It sounds unchecked and unpremeditated; it is rarely just, but it compensates for this by being wildly and inventively copious.

In Marston's satire a sense of conscious effort pervades even the angriest scourging. He was aware of this potential danger, as he reveals in his poem "Ad Rithmum" (by which he means rhyme):

> Then hence base ballad stuffe, my poetrie
> Disclaimes you quite, for know my libertie
> Scornes riming lawes; Alas poore idle sound
> Since I first *Phoebus* knew, I never found
> Thy interest in sacred Poesie.
> Thou to Invention add'st but surquedry,
> A gaudie ornature, but hast no part,
> In that soule-pleasing high infused art.
> Then if thou wilt clip kindly in my lines,
> Welcome thou friendly ayde of my designes.
> If not? No title of my sence let change
> To wrest some forced rime, but freely range.
> (pp. 128–129, ll. 25–36)

But Marston often allowed the "gaudie ornature" to take precedence, and one rarely gets the sense which Nashe conveys of

[40] *English Literature in the Sixteenth Century,* p. 477.
[41] Ibid., p. 474.

surprising twists or even of new ways of saying old things. Although the satires ostensibly deal with various themes, they tend to monotonous repetition of the same attitudes, often by means of the same epithets.

This is, of course, a retrospective judgment; at the time, *The Scourge* had a strong and immediate impact on the reading public. It rapidly went through three editions, and its manner was aped by many poets. For one moment, Marston's ferocity, like Allen Ginsberg's in *Howl,* struck exactly the resonant note. But before the cacophony could grow deafening, in June of 1599 the Bishop of London and the Archbishop of Canterbury ordered that both of Marston's volumes, along with the one by Everard Guilpin and the epigrams by the still-rusticated John Davies, be burned. The churchmen's motives are not clear. Some have guessed that they were trying to halt an outbreak of satire potentially dangerous to the stability of the commonwealth. But the fact that, among other works, two anonymous volumes entitled *The 15 Joyes of Marriage* and *Marriage and Wyvinge* were also burned suggests that they found the works obscene. Whatever the motives, they also ordered that "noe Satyres or Epigrams be printed hereafter." [42]

But no one seems to have noticed that even before the bishops' ban Marston had publicly announced his abandonment of verse satire.[43] Within *The Scourge* we may detect three successive stages, one growing out of the other, in his attitude toward his readers. We have seen his contemptuous description of the various misreaders of *Pigmalion,* but despite his scorn for such fools, his language also reveals a certain thin-skinned sensitivity to the criticism which public exposure entails:

> What though the sacred issue of my soule
> I heare expose to Ideots controule?
> What though I bare to lewd Opinion
> Lay ope to vulgar prophanation
> My very *Genius.* (SV, VI, 105–109)

Because he felt his work was caviar to the general, he invited a learned audience of wits to read his second volume. I have

[42] *Transcript of the Register of the Company of Stationers of London, 1554–1640,* ed. Edward Arber (London and Birmingham, 1875–1894), III, 677.

[43] In making this point, I am not referring to his poem at the conclusion of the SV volume, "To everlasting *Oblivion,*" where he claims that he will henceforth be silent. There seems to be little conviction behind this promise since he adds that he will write again if "some hound doe wake me from my place" (p. 175, l. 17).

been suggesting that the greater obscurity, the parade of learning, and particularly the philosophical passages in the later volume were part of a concerted effort to interest this audience. But in a mood of insecurity not yet warranted by a public response, he concluded his fourth satire, the most pretentious effort in this direction, by saying pessimistically (in a passage quoted earlier) that the verses were designed for a better sort than the fools who resorted to them. Thus, after disappointment at the reception of his first volume and pessimistic premonitions concerning the second, the first edition of *The Scourge* was exposed to the *profanum vulgus,* and the response was as he had feared: great popularity among the "lewd boys," public satire by a Cambridge don, and the violent opposition, moral or political, which eventually led to the conflagration in Stationers' Hall.

It is against this background that we must read the new poem which Marston inserted into the second edition of *The Scourge* in 1599. It is titled "Satyra Nova," but it would be more precise to call it a verse epistle with satiric passages. It is written "To his very friend, maister E. G.," that is, Everard Guilpin, and it concludes with the conventional "Vale" of an epistle. A Latin motto at the head of the poem, *"Stultorum plena sunt omnia,"* describes the theme, the point being that he has been a fool to write seriously for the sort of audience he has acquired:

> For pre-thee *Ned,* I pre-thee gentle lad,
> Is not he frantique, foolish, bedlam mad,
> That wastes his spright, that melts his very braine,
> In deepe designes, in wits dark gloomie straine?
> That scourgeth great slaves with a dreadlesse fist,
> Playing the rough part of a Satyrist,
> To be perus'd by all the dung-scum rable
> Of thin-braind Ideots, dull, uncapable?
> For mimicke apish schollers, pedants, gulls,
> Perfum'd Inamoratoes, brothell trulls? (SV, X, 9–18)

This repeats nearly verbatim the language he used at the conclusion of his philosophical disputation on grace: "why sweat I out my braine,/In deepe designes, to gay boyes lewd, and vaine?" (SV, IV, 167–168). He writes as a disappointed man obsessed by the disparity between the effort expended and the response received. His aim was profundity; his reward, notoriety among the very gallants he had been satirizing. Meanwhile, as he complains to "Ned" Guilpin — it is Marston speaking, not his satiric persona, although he lapses into it briefly — his writing has placed him in a position in which he must endure the condescension of fools like a certain stupid, immoral person called Dromus, clearly somebody known to both "Ned" and Marston.[44] He has also allowed himself to be publicly libeled by Guilpin's former college mate, Hall, who caused an insulting and childishly inept epigram to be pasted in every copy of *Pigmalion* in Cambridge. He finds it incomprehensible that such a person could gain a high reputation; it is merely another confirmation of how mad the world is. Suddenly he realizes that he is once more engaging in the mad occupation of writing a poem. He refuses to be "seduced" by "poesie" any longer; his love for it has turned to hate and he renounces the role of poet:

> Out on this humour. From a sickly bed,
> And from a moodie minde distempered,
> I vomit foorth my love, now turn'd to hate,
> Scorning the honour of a Poets state.
> Nor shall the kennell route of muddy braines,
> Ravish my Muses heyre, or heare my straines
> Once more. No nittie pedant shall correct
> Aenigmaes to his shallow Intelect.
> Inchauntment, *Ned* hath ravished my sence
> In a Poetick vaine circumference.
> Yet thus I hope, (God shield I now should lie)
> *Many more fooles, and most more wise than I.*
> VALE (SV, X, 73–85)

Thus it was not the bishops' ban but a gradual disenchantment with the role of satirist which silenced the scourger of villainy. But in this farewell to Guilpin and to his once-loved "Poets state," he inadvertently hit upon the proper tone for the audience he had courted unsuccessfully. Speaking intimately to one of the wits, his manner sounds tired and defeated as he reproaches himself for his vain efforts. From this stance he can indulge in the pleasures of invective without leaving himself open to the accusation of holier-than-thou arrogance. This is the angry but self-critical, even modest tone we hear in some of the prologues and prefaces to his plays. Clearly what Marston required was an audience with whom he could feel at ease. This he obtained, or pretended to have obtained, when the private theaters were reopened at the end of the same year, 1599. It is difficult to understand why he immediately felt comfort-

[44] Cf. Davenport, *Poems*, pp. 353–354.

able with an audience which would have been nearly identical with the readers of verse satires. Perhaps it was the economic exclusiveness of the private theaters which gave Marston the illusion that at last he had the ear of "diviner wits, celestiall soules."

4

But before Marston ever wrote a play for the private theaters, he seems to have produced a dramatic work called *Histriomastix*. Published anonymously in 1610 with no indication of where it was produced, it has been universally attributed to Marston on the basis of strong stylistic similarities to his verse satires. Since Jonson's *Every Man out of his Humour* makes a reference to it in 1599, it must be Marston's earliest dramatic work.[45] However, almost all commentators have felt that Marston merely revised an earlier play. They have offered three major arguments for this view: (1) that Marston's style (by which they mean the style of his verse satires) is only intermittently evident; (2) that various incongruities in the action show evidence of patchwork; and (3) that the play is in a long-outmoded genre, that of the morality play. With regard to the evidence from style, it seems unreasonable to demand that all of the characters in a play speak identically; there are only certain moments in the action when the language of a verse satirist is appropriate. It is true that there is one inconsistency in the plot. The author forgot from one act to the next how some wives were paired with their husbands, but the wives are minor figures in an exceedingly complex plot with a large cast of characters.

The weakness of the evidence for revision has recently been demonstrated by Alvin Kernan through an analysis of the structure of the play. He shows that it is all of a piece, and since there is no external evidence for revision, he attributes the whole play to Marston.[46] I agree with Kernan's view and would make the further point that a morality play of this sort was not at all old-fashioned for an academic audience at the end of the sixteenth century. The *Parnassus* plays of about 1600 reflect an acute awareness of the latest literary developments in London; yet they employ allegorical figures and a morality play framework. Even Nashe utilized a morality play structure when he wrote *Summer's Last Will and Testament* in 1592 for performance at Archbishop Whitgift's palace at Croydon.

[45] See Appendix B for my view of the chronological order of Marston's plays.
[46] "John Marston's Play, *Histriomastix*," *Modern Language Quarterly*, 19 (1958), 134–140.

There is no indication of where *Histriomastix* was performed, and I have attempted to show elsewhere that there are many reasons for believing that it was designed for revels at one of the Inns of Court.[47] To summarize my conclusions, *Histriomastix* was written before the first of the boys' companies, the Children of Paul's, was revived.[48] If it was not designed for a private theater — a public theater is out of the question, and from Jonson's allusion we know that it was produced somewhere — the only remaining possibility is an academic setting. Chambers long ago suggested that the *"proto-Histriomastix"* (that is, the play before Marston's putative revision) was "a University or possibly an Inns of Court, not a choir-boy, play." [49] Marston's membership at the Middle Temple suggests production during revels, and there is a substantial amount of internal evidence to confirm this hypothesis. The size of the cast alone — one hundred twenty according to G. B. Harrison's calculation[50] — would seem to require the kind of manpower that only an academic environment could supply. We have seen that at this time the Middle Temple had about one hundred fifty Inner Barristers, so that with the usual twenty percent rate of absence during the Christmas vacation the figure conforms remarkably to the requirements of *Histriomastix*.

An Inns of Court setting would explain the number of references to lawyers, the use of recherché legal terminology, and, in at least one instance, the reference to an Inns' intramural

---

[47] "John Marston's *Histrio-Mastix* as an Inns of Court Play: A Hypothesis," *Huntington Library Quarterly,* 29 (1966), 223–234. M. C. Bradbrook *"The Comedy of Timon:* A Reveling Play of the Inner Temple," *Renaissance Drama,* 9 (1966), 83–103, has recently made the same kind of effort — very convincingly, in my opinion — for another play. Since the Inns offered dramatic entertainments intermittently throughout the sixteenth and seventeenth centuries, it would be surprising if further examples were not discovered.

[48] To place the play in late 1599 requires us to believe that more than a year after the appearance of the verse satires, Marston was writing in the same style, but that a few months later (in *Jack Drum's Entertainment*) he was writing differently. In the article cited above, I point out two topical allusions which suggest the earlier date. Since writing the article I have noticed another strong argument against production by Paul's Boys. In *Jack Drum* (firmly dated in 1600: see E. K. Chambers, *The Elizabethan Stage* [Oxford, 1923], IV, 21) Marston has someone express the hope that the new company will someday be invited to perform at Court (*Plays,* ed. Wood, III, 234). Our text of *Histriomastix* indicates two endings, one of which was clearly designed for performance before the Queen. Paul's Boys had not yet achieved this distinction, but, as we have seen, it was quite normal for the Inns to offer entertainment for the Queen during revels. Chambers, IV, 17, notes this ending, but says that there was "no court performance at the end of the century available for it." There is no reason to believe that Court records were complete; and, in addition, the Queen might have watched the performance at the Middle Temple.

[49] IV, 17–18.

[50] *Elizabethan Plays and Players* (Ann Arbor, 1956), p. 207.

regulation. It would also account for the extremely academic language used by the curious figure Chrisoganus. At one point this philosopher-satirist-Stoic attempts to teach the liberal arts to a group of nobles during a period of plenty:

> that knowledge (that considers things
> Abjunct from sencive matter) is exacter
> Then that which joynes it selfe with elements;
> *Arithmetick* ever considers numbers
> Abstract from sencive matter; *Musick* still
> Considers it with sence, as mixt with sound:
> Therefore *Arithmeticque* is more exact,
> And more exact then is *Geometrie:*
> Since *unitas* is still *simplicior puncto,*
> And number simpler then is magnitude.
> For *Unitas* may still be *sine puncto,*
> But *Punctus* never without Unitie,
> Nor; *Magnitudo sine Numero,*
> Dum (enim) punctus ponitur, ponitur (ex necessitate)
> unitas.[51]

Were this a play by Ben Jonson, this passage might well have been designed as a piece of pretentious jargon in the manner of the pseudo-learning displayed in *The Alchemist*. But not only does this passage make sense; it happens to express a view — the superiority of intellectual abstractions over sense perceptions — which Marston took very seriously.[52] Once more he sweated out his brain in deep designs, but this time it appears that he had an audience in which many were trained in formal philosophical disputation.

Many scholars have seen in the character Chrisoganus a representation of Marston's friend, Ben Jonson, and hence the opening shot in the so-called War of the Theaters.[53] The identification is plausible, but it is important to realize that within the play Chrisoganus is a totally admirable figure. It is he who maintains standards and who shows the path to reformation through law at the end. An admiring portrait of Ben Jonson within the friendly surroundings of the Middle Temple seems entirely fitting. Yet it is also easy to understand why Ben might

---

[51] *Plays*, III, 249.

[52] See Davenport's comment, *Poems*, pp. 342–343.

[53] It is fairly certain that Chrisoganus did represent somebody because, as in the case of Fabian described above, Everard Guilpin, *Skialetheia*, sig. A8v, uses the same name in an epigram about an ugly man who "teacheth . . . his face" how to appear fearful to people. In *Satiromastix* Dekker stresses Jonson's ugliness and his desire to terrify.

have resented the broad strokes of the characterization, particularly since Marston put several speeches into Chrisoganus'
mouth which sound like quotations from *The Scourge,* a poem
Jonson thought ridiculous.

In view of the fact that there is no evidence that *Histriomastix* was produced by a private theater and that an interlocking
set of probabilities points to the Inns of Court, I have suggested
that Marston wrote the play for the Christmas revels of 1598–99.
This date not only meets all the chronological requirements
(described in note 48 above) but is consistent with the fact that
the Middle Temple tended to sponsor plays only during the
Christmas season.

If I am correct, Marston made his first venture into the
drama by constructing a quasi-pageant for the edification and
glorification of his Society and of his Queen. He dramatizes a
cyclical view of history in which a commonwealth passes through
periods dominated by Peace, Plenty, Pride, Envy, War, and
Poverty until finally Peace is restored. In each act the author
exemplifies the state of the kingdom under its particular presiding allegorical deity, first by means of general statements and
then by the introduction of a succession of characters — nobles,
lawyers, merchants, actors, and so forth — who depict a cross
section of the commonwealth. All are satirized, but the harm
that bad lawyers can do is emphasized. At the conclusion, the
author's spokesman, Chrisoganus, affirms the central position
of the law:

> Your lawes appoincted to be positive
> (By *Warre* confounded) must be brought againe.
> For law is that which Love and Peace maintaine.
>
> (III, 296)

When the citizens understand this and order themselves, Peace
is once more enthroned. In the second ending (clearly visible
within the first and apparently designed for court performance),
Astraea, the goddess of justice, returns to earth in the image
of Queen Elizabeth, and Religion and the Arts regain their
rightful places.

It is a mistake to discuss this made-to-order professional entertainment as though it were an inept first effort at drama by a
satirist forced to write plays. We must remember that a play for
Inns' revels would have been designed to afford opportunities
for declamation by as many young gentlemen as possible. *Histriomastix* met all the necessary specifications in form and atti-

tude, and the result is as mechanical and stolid as the gravest ancient might have desired; he would not have had to take off his gown and cap to have enjoyed its edifying message.

Within this traditional celebration of law and order Marston emphasized the contribution of the liberal arts and its learned masters to the health of the commonwealth. The centrality of this theme is underlined by the otherwise enigmatic title. It refers to the newly framed act which authorized the whipping of "Fencers, Bearwardes, common Players of Enterludes and Minstrelles . . . taken begging vagrant wandering and mys-ordering themselves in any part of this Realme." Rogues who were deemed especially dangerous or incorrigible were also liable to "be banysshed out of this Realme."[54] The play demonstrates the wisdom of this act by following the actions of a group of base mechanicals who have formed themselves into a company of players. They are about as literate and artful as Bottom's group, though considerably less endearing. They are talentless, sturdy, "Proud Statute Rogues" (III, 275) who wander about living immorally, becoming wealthy, and acting generally in a disorderly manner. Marston presents the learned moralist Chrisoganus (perhaps Jonson) as a contrasting type of artist. In time of plenty the nobles and professional men reject his tutelage and instead promote the illiterate pretenders to art. Chrisoganus remains true to his values and starves. But when peace is once again restored, Chrisoganus gains an honored place while the actors and the poetaster who wrote for them are shipped out of the realm. We are made to realize that peace and plenty go hand in hand with the cultivation of the arts.

This traditional article of humanistic faith is offered in *Histriomastix* with as few qualifications as the other orthodox attitudes in the play. Such a work from a man of Marston's background and tastes should not surprise us. We have seen how readily Davies could produce his "Astraea" poems, how easily the men of Gray's Inn could move from the worldly joking of the revels to the "Masque of Proteus," and how integral to the revels of the Prince d'Amour was the idolatry shown Queen Elizabeth. It must have been a comfort to the sometime Reader of the Middle Temple to note that even if his son and chambermate was not actively pursuing his legal studies, he too revered Astraea.

Histriomastix adds the extra touch needed to fill out the portrait of Marston as a representative Inns of Court literary man. It will require a close look at his more important work to

[54] Chambers, IV, 324.

see how deeply he was based in this environment and to what degree such a relationship can be used to explain his work. But we have already seen that he had many of the characteristic Inns' manners and attitudes. He was violent and contentious, aggressively free-spoken, arrogant and contemptuous, prone to personal satire. His poetry shows the expected preference for satire, parody, and harshness, together with a disdain for popular styles. But in spite of the bishops' fears, there was no more reason to worry about Marston's orthodoxy than there was about that of John Davies. Nothing thus far in Marston's work questions the inherited framework of things, and he is viciously satiric about deviations from this order.

Within this conformity to type, what appears quite early in his work as a special and personal note is a fierce urge to be heard. Chrisoganus' accession to the status of moral and intellectual mentor of a commonwealth at the end of *Histrio-mastix* sounds like an ego fantasy of the scourge of villainy. Through the sweat of his brain, Marston strained to communicate deep designs, and the strain is often apparent. "Art" did not "curb Nature" sufficiently. He showed more "negligence" than "diligence," more "Liberty" than "Humanity." The "quick sighted censurers" among the "diviner wits" quickly censured him for his violations of decorum. This is not to say that he ever approached the linguistic anarchy of someone like Stanyhurst; in fact, the satires are not really representative of Marston's general linguistic practice. As an examination of his first professional play will show, even in this one area of apparent heresy, his divergence from the precepts of the "true judging eyes" was not great.

VIII *Jack Drum's Entertainment*: Speech and Style at Highgate

If my argument about *Histriomastix* is correct, Marston began his professional playwriting career with *Jack Drum's Entertainment,* produced in 1600 by the newly revived dramatic
company, the Children of Paul's.[1] For an affluent young man
from an old family to have become a professional playwright at
this time was an unprecedented move. Clearly, his decision was
not based on even a temporary financial embarrassment, for

[1] Published anonymously, attributed to Marston on the basis of an ascription
in Edward Pudsey's commonplace book (Bodleian MS. Eng. Poet. d.3), fol. 40v,
as well as on the basis of its obvious similarities to Marston's work. E. K. Chambers, *The Elizabethan Stage* (Oxford, 1923), IV, 21, was able to establish the
date with unusual precision.

his father had just died and provided for him amply. His choice is a clear sign that the vocation of playwright was becoming respectable, and Marston's entry into the field created a precedent for other members of the gentry, notably Beaumont, Fletcher, and Ford.

Apparently Marston wanted so fervently to write plays that he even enlisted in the most plebeian company. Henslowe's Admiral's Men, for a brief period. But the revival of the private theaters must have eased Marston's role considerably. Soon after he received forty shillings from Henslowe for his share in an unspecified collaboration, the boy chorister company named the Children of Paul's was reactivated. After a hiatus of about ten years, a London theatergoer could once more see plays acted by boys in small indoor theaters. The audience at these performances was undoubtedly wealthier and, on the average, better educated than that at the large "public" theaters. The private "houses" were located very near the Inns of Court; by all accounts the percentage of Inns' members in the audience was high, and the audience was very similar, probably even in age, to the spectrum at the Inns described in Chapter I. It is impossible to assess precisely the nature of this audience, but one general term will cover the majority of its members: "gallants." It was a term which applied to everyone from Hoskins to "Luscus," and its connotations for Marston were mixed. Possibly because the price of admission limited the social range, Marston chose to find in such an audience a "choise selected influence." [2] The audience apparently reciprocated his admiration. Almost instantly he seems to have become a successful playwright, and the Children of Paul's was for a time a thriving financial enterprise.

Thus, it is fascinating to imagine *Jack Drum's Entertainment* in its moment in history. The "new poet" (as Henslowe described him) has suddenly become the new playwright for the new company of children. So far, they have been producing "mustie fopperies of antiquitie" (III, 234), but from Marston it would be reasonable to expect something à la mode. What did he concoct to attract the attention of a sophisticated, worldly audience which had the choice of going to see *As You Like It* instead? Speaking for the playwright and themselves, the players make a promise in the "Introduction"

[2] *Plays of John Marston,* ed. H. Harvey Wood (3 vols., Edinburgh, 1934–1939), III, 179. Hereafter, unless otherwise noted, page references in the text will refer to the volume of Wood in which the play under discussion is located.

> not to torment your listning eares
> With mouldy fopperies of stale Poetry,
> Unpossible drie mustie Fictions. (III, 179)

Marston fulfilled at least part of this manifesto for a new drama of antipoetical realism by setting the action of his play in the present time and in the London suburb of Highgate, the small village on a hill north of the city. By a dozen references scattered through the play to the town, the hill, and the neighboring village of Holloway, Marston kept the audience aware that most of the events were occurring around a great house on Highgate Green owned by one Sir Edward Fortune. About Fortune we soon learn (1) that he is a courtier (III, 181–182), although not a very ambitious one (III, 184–185); (2) that he enjoys the revelry of country festivals in the spring (III, 182); (3) that he conducts his household with old-fashioned, lavish hospitality (III, 183–184); (4) that he has two daughters named Katherine and Camelia; (5) that his wife is dead and that she was "Poore, but of good dissent" (III, 187); and, slightly later in the play, (6) that he likes stage plays and might sponsor one at his house (III, 234).

It happens that a well-known contemporary courtier matches Sir Edward in almost every one of these distinguishing marks. I refer to Sir William Cornwallis (?–1611), sometimes referred to as "the elder" to distinguish him from his nephew, the well-known essayist, with whom he is confused in the DNB.[3] About Sir William's celebrated mansion on Highgate green, which was later named Arundel House, the *Survey of London* says: "John Norden wrote in 1593, 'At this place ——— Cornwalleys, Esquire, hath a very faire house from which he may beholde with great delight the staitlie city of London, Westminster, Greenwich, the famous river of Thamyse, and the country towards the south very farre.' The house must indeed have been an attractive dwelling place, on the brow of the hill, with the village green in front to the north and the slopes of Highgate Hill behind with open country all the way to the city, affording a splendid panorama, Old St. Paul's being only some four miles away." [4]

---

[3] I derive most of these facts from R. E. Bennett, "The Life and Works of Sir William Cornwallis" (unpublished Harvard dissertation, 1931).

[4] *London County Council Survey of London, Village of Highgate* (London, 1936), XVII, 48. In context, Norden's description in *Speculum Brittaniae. The First parte* (London, 1593), p. 22, makes it clear that this was the most important house in Highgate.

With a house as prominent as this mentioned so frequently in the play, no further identification would have been necessary, but in nearly every detail Marston's portrait of Sir Edward Fortune follows what we know about Sir William Cornwallis: (1) Sir William was a courtier under Elizabeth and James, though his role was always relatively subordinate, never high enough to be (in Sir Edward's words) "One day ador'd, and next pasht all in peeces" (III, 185). (2) May Day seems to have been an especially notable holiday at the Highgate house, for Sir William entertained Elizabeth and James there on that festive occasion. (3) He entertained lavishly and was visited by sovereigns on four occasions. His father once berated him for his extravagance — Sir Edward is similarly attacked in the play — describing him as "prodigal and therefore needy," [5] though there is ample evidence that he was quite wealthy. (4) Sir William had four daughters, but even here Marston was not simplifying matters out of dramatic necessity, since the two older ones were already married and no longer living at Highgate. The remaining two were named Cornelia and Anne, but the former seems to have been called "Catherine." [6] Perhaps because he has unkind things to say about the other daughter, Marston changed her name to Camelia. (5) The only discrepancies from fact concern Sir William's wife. She was indeed "of good dissent": her father was John, Lord Latimer, her mother was a daughter of Henry, Earl of Worcester, and her sister was the wife of Lord Burleigh's elder son, Thomas. Thus, I can only assume that "poore" is a rather heavy joke.[7] (6) Sir William did sponsor one dramatic entertainment by Ben Jonson in honor of the King's visit in 1604. This was subsequent to *Jack Drum*, but Sir William's interest in the drama is also evident from his patronage of the poet and playwright Thomas Watson.[8]

[5] Quoted by Bennett, p. 49.

[6] Ibid., p. 32. However, Catherine was the younger sister.

[7] Also, she was still alive, but since she was seriously ill for many years before her death, her absence from the play may have been a nearly accurate version of the situation at Cornwallis' house.

[8] Chambers, III, 506. It may be noted that Marston could have learned details about Sir William from his friend and relative Everard Guilpin, whose family lived in Highgate for a long time. There is even a tenuous link between Guilpin and Sir William, which suggests that they were not of altogether disparate rank. Both Guilpin's father (d. 1591/2) and Sir William served as governors of the Highgate Grammar School, the former in 1580, the latter in 1591 (*Survey of London*, XVII, 141). Moreover, I have recently discovered some kind of connection between Marston and some member of the Cornwallis family. On the title page of a first edition of Spenser's *Fairie Queene* (1590), recently acquired by the Vassar College Library in a bequest from the late Mabel L.

In short, Marston began his career as a professional dramatist with a clear portrayal of a well-known public figure. The private theaters soon became notorious for their personal and political satire, and Marston was one of the leading offenders. On paper, the satiric nature of this particular portrait is not always clear. At the beginning, Sir Edward appears to be a sympathetic figure, virtually the author's spokesman. Later he does become an object of satire through his absentminded and over-rapid resort to the consolations of food and drink whenever anything unfortunate happens to his daughter. If we recall that he would have been portrayed by a young boy, the likelihood of a ridiculous portrait is high. There can be no question of Marston's attitude toward Sir Edward's daughter Camelia, who is shown to be very stupid and fickle.[9] It seems inconceivable that Sir William could not have stopped this production, but perhaps Marston caught the various authorities by surprise. They were certainly alert to this kind of danger in later private theater productions, but censorship did not deter the boys' companies from continuing the practice and, as we shall see, from taking far greater risks.

This daring portrayal of a public figure is consistent with Harbage's conception of the private theaters. He claims that they tried to achieve financial success by purveying scandal and obscenity calculated to titillate the gross sensibilities of a small coterie. However, the same sort of thing is known to have occurred at public theaters. For example, Chambers cites a

---

Rossbach, the autograph "John Marston" appears in large, somewhat faded script; it resembles Marston's known autographs in every respect. Under ultraviolet light more writing is evident on the upper right-hand corner of the same page. On three successive lines one can detect the following: "Darlow [or Marlow]/ex dono [followed by something indecipherable]/mi[?] Cornwallis." The "D" in "Darlow," as my brackets suggest, might be an "M"; and some connection between Christopher Marlowe and Sir William Cornwallis, the elder, through their mutual acquaintance with the poet Thomas Watson is possible. However, the "Darlow/Marlow" signature does not greatly resemble Marlowe's one extant autograph. Moreover, unless more of the faded writing can be deciphered, there is no way to be certain which member of the Cornwallis family is involved here. More work must be done on problems raised by the Vassar *Fairie Queene*, but the appearance of the names of Cornwallis and Marston on the same page is a relevant, if tantalizing, addition to the argument of this chapter. I should add that I detected the writing on the title page two years after I had arrived at my conclusions about *Jack Drum* and Cornwallis.

9 The little I can discover about this daughter corroborates Marston's picture. As the play predicts, she did not marry for a long time, and although she married well, her reputation was clouded by one scandalous report. She was reputed to have had a child by the famous actor in Shakespeare's company, Nathan Field. At least, she was faithful to her father's interest in the theater.

nearly contemporaneous incident: "On 10 May 1601 the Privy Council sent an order to the Middlesex justices to examine and, if need be, suppress a play at the Curtain, in which were presented 'the persons of some gentlemen of good desert and quality that are yet alive, under obscure manner, but yet in such sort as all the hearers may take notice both of the matter and of the persons that are meant thereby.'" [10] Nonetheless such entertainment was far more frequent at the private theaters.

The rest of the play, by far the more important part of it, was also designed for a "select" audience, but its interest is of a very different sort. Most of the play is devoted to four interrelated plots, three of which might be called "romantic." In one, Sir Edward's younger daughter Katherine is courted by a fool named Puffe and a villainous usurer named Mamon, while she herself is passionately devoted to her ardent lover Pasquill. Sir Edward's fickle older daughter Camelia shifts her affections from Brabant Jr. to the fool John Ellis and then to the temperate Planet. Her inclinations are completely under the control of her maid Winifred, who directs her from one lover to the next after accepting bribes from each. Winifred, in turn, is wooed by the servant Jack Drum and by a comically lustful Frenchman, John fo de King. An additional, nonromantic strand exposes Brabant Sr. as a ridiculous gull for collecting a group of fools expressly to laugh at them.

Summarized thus, the plot sounds like a 1590's romantic comedy, the very sort of "mustie Fiction" Marston had promised to avoid. But a closer look discloses that it is quite the opposite. In part, Marston used these plots as a vehicle for satirizing the linguistic mannerisms of "gallants" (a term used repeatedly in the play). His standard was essentially the same as — perhaps it was influenced by — John Hoskins' *Directions*. Thus, after John Ellis is rejected by the fickle Camelia, he says, "Truly as a Mill-horse, is not a horse Mill, and as a Cart Jade, is not a Jade Cart, even so will I go hang my selfe" (III, 225). Marston appropriated the "Mill-horse" simile from Hoskins' memorable "fustian" oration in the 1597–98 revels, designed, it will be recalled, "in derision of vain rhetoric." [11] Hoskins also used this

---

[10] Chambers, I, 324.

[11] *Directions for Speech and Style by John Hoskins,* ed. Hoyt H. Hudson (Princeton, 1935) , p. 13. As Hudson points out, Hoskins borrowed this example from Bishop Wilson's *Arte of Rhetorique,* but Marston's quotation repeats Hoskins' phrasing. Wilson says, "There is a difference betwixt an Horsmilne and a Milne horse" (quoted by Hudson, p. 69). Hoskins' fustian oration says, "For even as a Mill-horse is not a Horse-mill . . ." (p. 112).

example in his *Directions* to illustrate the figure "Antimetabole or Commutatio . . . a sentence inversed or turned back." He concedes that this may be "a sharp and witty figure and shows out of the same words a pithy distinction of meaning, . . . [but] use this or any other point, unseasonably, it is as ridiculous as it was in the fustian oration." [12] The character Puffe speaks an elaborate variety of fustian called "compliment":

> PUFFE. Most accomplisht wit, exquisitly accoutred, (*Puffe*) Judgement, I could wish my abilitie worthie your service, and my service worthie your abilitie.
>
> PLANET. By the Lord fustian, now I understand it: complement is as much as fustian. (III, 209)

Hoskins had defined "compliment" as "performance of affected ceremonies in words, looks, or gesture." [13] Marston presents Puffe as an automaton totally addicted to such performances. When he is rejected by Katherine, Marston's final twist is to have him retreat from the world to study at the Inns of Court: "I leave love, and fall to the (*puffe*) Lawe, I will interre my selfe in *Ploydens* Coffin, and take an eternall *Conge* of the world. And so sweete gallants farewell" (III, 210). He may be leaving the world of the play, but, it is implied, he is a figure one might well see in commons or at the theater. Manningham, for example, notes in his *Diary* the existence of "One Parkins of the Inner House a very complementall gentleman; a barrester but noe lawyer." [14]

But it is not only the obvious gulls who utter fashionable absurdities. The servants, Jack Drum and Winifred, parrot their masters:

> DRUM. Truly Mistresse *Winifride,* as I would be willing to be thankfull, and thankfull to finde you willing to prostrate your faire partes to my pleasure, so I hope you will remember your promise and promise what you now remember, if you have forgot, I would be glad to put you in minde of it
>
> WINI. Truly friend *John,* as I would be loth to breake my promise, so I would be unwilling to keepe my word to the dishonesting of my virginitie. (III, 220)

[12] Ibid., p. 15.
[13] Ibid., p. 44.
[14] *Diary of John Manningham,* ed. John Bruce, Camden Society Publication 99 (London, 1868), p. 53

Even the wittier gallants express their love in romantic hyperboles which reveal them to be in a condition of "fond dotage," to use Marston's term from *Pigmalion* (p. 50). The similarity among all the lovers, high and low, is illustrated at the beginning of the second act. Marston constructs a balcony scene in which three successive lovers try to play Romeo to Katherine's Juliet. First Puffe approaches in an ardent, poetical vein: "Burnes not that light within the sacred shrine?/I meane the chamber of bright *Katherine*" (III, 195). Katherine disconcerts him by mocking his repetitive compliments, and he leaves, defeated by her sallies of wit. Next comes Mamon, "the Usurer, with a great nose" (III, 241), speaking lines that travesty some from *Romeo*: "Why then ô Love, ô Gout, ô goutie Love, how thou torments olde *Mamon*" (III, 197).[15] He woos Katherine in language which foreshadows Volpone's attempted seduction of Celia:

> the wrinckling print of time
> Err'd, when it seald my forehead up with age:
> I have as warme an arme to entertaine
> And hugge thy presence in a nuptiall bed,
> As those that have a cheek more lively red. (III, 197)[16]

But Katherine deflates his heroic vaunts and his bribes by taunting him with his age: "hence with your gold,/Leave the green fields, tis deawy, youle take cold" (III, 197).

Finally, the third and true Romeo appears. His name, Pasquill, has rather equivocal associations since it means "lampoon" or "libel." But although he is, according to Mamon, a "lowe ebd gallant" (III, 198), he is intelligent, young, and a perfect match for Katherine. They are deeply in love and given to unending expressions of their passion:

> PASQUIL. I'le chaunt thy name, and so inchaunt each
>   eare,
> That *Katherinas* happie name shall heare.
> My *Katherine*, my life, my *Katherine*.
>   KATHE. My *Ned*, my *Pasquil*, sweet I come, I come,
> Even with like swiftnes, tho not with like heart:
> As the fierce Fawcon stoupes to rysing fowle
> I hurrey to thee. (III, 198)

[15] Cf. *Romeo and Juliet*, I.i.182.
[16] His later speech on p. 216 is a more precise precursor.

Certain ludicrous touches indicate that Marston is satirizing their lovemaking as hyperbolic and cloying. In *Romeo*, Shakespeare's heroine wishes that she had a "falconer's voice/To lure this tassel-gentle back again." [17] Katherine swoops fiercely down on her prey like the falcon itself. They begin to kiss, but Pasquill grows "wanton" and bites her lip (III, 199). Suddenly, in mid-sentence, their aria shifts from the romantically mellifluous to the unmistakable accents of the scourge of villainy, as Pasquill says:

> In faith you Jest, I did but softly sip
> The Roseall Juice of your reviving breath:
> Let clumsie judgements, chilblaind gowtie wits
> Bung up their chiefe content within the whoopes
> Of a stuft dry Fatt: and repose their hopes
> Of happinesse, and hearts tranquilitie,
> Upon increase of durt. (III, 199)

They soon return to their romantic vein, and at their parting we are once more reminded of *Romeo* when Katherine says,

> Farewell, yet stay, but tis no matter too,
> My Father knowes I thinke, what must ensue.
> Adieu, yet harke, nay faith, adieu, adiew. (III, 200)

Pasquill's answer reminds us that this Juliet resembles a "fierce Fawcon": "Peace to thy passions, till next enterview" (III, 200).

The balcony scene ridicules "mouldy fopperies of stale Poetry" (III, 179) in various ways. It literally dislodges Juliet from her perch, and shows that the language of the romantic lovers is very similar to that of the gulls and fond doters. At times they repeat their very words:

> KA. Heaven of Content, *Paphos* of my delight.
> PAS. Mirrour of Constancie, life-bloud of love.
> KA. Centre to whom all my affections move.
> PAS. Renown of Virgins, whose fame shal ne're fleet.
>
> (III, 215)

Puffe has anticipated Katherine's geometrical metaphor in an elaborate "compliment" to Brabant Sr.: "your perfection is the center to which all the paralels of my affection are drawne"

---

[17] *Romeo and Juliet*, II.iii.159–160.

(III, 210). The doting lover Brabant Jr. employed one of Pasquill's epithets just a moment earlier when he called his unworthy mistress, Camelia, the "Life of love" (III, 211). Such epithets of adoration are used promiscuously by the fools, the love doters, and by Pasquill. To Marston, immoderate expressions of love are a form of "compliment."

There is a further implication that such linguistic habits are dangerous. As we have seen, Brabant Jr. dotes on Camelia, using the same sort of language as the other gallants:

> thoult sweare, that I am blest
> Beyond infinitie of happinesse,
> When thou beholdest admired *Camelia* . . .
> Oh when she clips, and clings about my necke,
> And suckes my soule forth with a melting kisse. (III, 203)

We are probably supposed to notice the echo of Faustus' speech to Helen in the last line, and this speech occurs at the start of yet another balcony scene. But in this case the deserving Romeo is ignominiously rejected in favor of the gull John Ellis. Despite several clear signs of Camelia's stupid and fickle nature, even after being enjoined not to love her, Brabant Jr. remains absurdly enamored:

> How not presume to love or fancie you?
> Hart, I will love you, by this light I will
> Whether you will or no, I'le love you still.
> Spight of your teeth I will your love pursue,
> I will by heaven, and so sweet soule adieu. (III, 213)

An idolator in his dotage can easily turn fanatic. On the basis of the flimsiest evidence he decides that his best friend Planet has surreptitiously won Camelia, and he orders his servant to kill him. After the murder has apparently been committed, he learns directly from Camelia of Planet's utter loyalty. Brabant Jr. realizes his folly, but this only leads him into deeper despair, and he is barely prevented from committing suicide. It is true that Marston rigidly controls the plot so that we never believe that the comic surface will be disrupted by tragedy, but it is a mistake to think that Brabant Jr.'s plight is merely used to satirize romantic comedies about lovers perpetually on the brink of disaster. Brabant Jr.'s romantic idealization has blinded him to the unworthiness of the object he dotes upon, and nothing but near-disaster can bring him to his senses. This is an early version of the problem Marston dramatizes at length in *The Dutch Courtesan*. Like *Pigmalion,* the satire is not primarily literary; it is concerned with dangerous attitudes which false literary and linguistic practices can engender.

When Brabant Jr. commissions his page to kill Planet, he is acting as basely as the arch-villain Mamon did when he hired the Frenchman to kill Pasquill. This suggests some kind of moral similarity between the two, at least during the period when Brabant Jr.'s jealousy amounts to a state of temporary insanity. In the same way, a similarity between the hero Pasquill and the villain Mamon is implied by the fact that they go insane at nearly the same moment. The common factor behind their madness is that they have invested all their hopes in the mutable gifts of the Goddess Fortune. Such theological moralizing is necessary in a play where the name Fortune is often played upon, where one character is named Mamon and another Planet (referring to his connection with the realm of unchanging things). The fickle Camelia ("chameleon") is specifically equated with the Lady Fortune when Winifride informs her that the "greatest Lady in the Land affects" John Ellis:

> CA. . . . what Lady, good sweet *Winifride?* say quick good wench.
> WINIF. The Lady *Fortune.*
> CAMEL. Why my name's *Fortune* too.
> WINIF. Then you must needs favour him,
> For *Fortune* favours fooles. (III, 188)

Mamon's name suggests the god to whom he has entrusted his life. When he loses all his possessions, he loses his mental stability. Similarly, Pasquill commits his entire life to the love of one woman:

> Oh how a kisse inflames a Lovers thought,
> With such a fewell let me burne and die,
> And like to *Hercules* so mount the skie. (III, 199)

This intemperate wish, uttered in a fit of passion, is ironically fulfilled when Pasquill goes mad and identifies himself with the mad Hercules of Seneca's *Hercules Furens:*

> PAS. *furens. O dira fata, saeva, miseranda, horida*
> *Quis hic locus? Quae Regio? quae Mundi plaga?*
> *Ubi sum?* Katherina, Katherina, *Eheu* Katherina.
>
> (III, 217)

Now that he is mad, his name fits him. He does nothing but spout "pasquills" (the inverse of "compliments") which sound exactly like *The Scourge* in its more bombastic moments:

> Poore, poore *Astrea,* who blurs thy orient shine?
> Come yons the Capitoll of *Jupiter,*
> Letts whip the Senate, els they will not leave
> To have their Justice blasted with abuse
> Of flattering *Sycophants.* (III, 226)

Mad, Pasquill's language is as literary as it was when he was doting for love. Mamon's idols, his "Obligations" and "Bonds" (III, 218), his ship and his house are totally destroyed, and so he is doomed to rave in Bedlam. But once Katherine Fortune's fortunes improve, Pasquill exchanges one intemperate mode of expression for another, reverting to his love language, which remains unchanged in the purity of its idolatry. Planet calls Camelia, Brabant Jr's "*Hygate* Mammet" (III, 189). Katherine is no less Pasquill's "Mammet." She is worthy of "infinit respect" (III, 229), according to Planet, but not of adulation.

In this world of eloquent and literary lovers, the Frenchman John fo de King (his name alludes to an obscene ballad) provides a refreshing contrast. In the words of *Pigmalions Image,* "viewing, touching, kissing, (common favour,)/Could never satiat his loves ardencie" (PI, stanza 20, ll. 117–118). He can scarcely speak English, but he approaches every woman with unabashed lust. Finally, he meets success in an incident which links the love plots to the strand involving Brabant Sr. This portion of the play has provoked much scholarly discussion, mostly because of its supposed connection with the "War of the Theaters." Brabant Sr. collects a group of gulls who amuse him by exhibiting their humors. As he says, "tis the recreation of my Intellect, I thinke I speake as significant, ha, ha, these are my zanyes, I fill their paunches, they feed my pleasures, I use them as my fooles faith, ha, ha" (III, 193). Several times he is shown provoking them into exhibitions of their follies. One of his jokes involves introducing the Frenchman to his wife: "I to gull the Foole, have brought him to my wife, as to a loose lascivious Curtezan, she being a meer straunger to the Jest"

(III, 239). Almost instantaneously, John fo de King appears, satisfied and exultant at his successful encounter, but Brabant Sr. assumes that he is bluffing:

> BRA. SIG. He would perswade you now that he toucht her, with an immodest hand. Ha, ha, ha.
>
> JOHN. Tuch her, by Gor mee tuch her, and tuch her, and me tuch her, mee nere tuch such a venche, de finea foote, de cleanest legge, de sleekest skin: and mee tell a sure token, shee hath de finest littl varte you knowe veare: hee by Gor mee nere tuch such a vench. (III, 239–240)

Everyone realizes that Brabant Sr. has "brew'd a headie Jest" (III, 240), and he is crowned with the "Coronet/Of Cuckolds," to the merriment of all.[18] But Marston does not exploit this fabliau-like incident in order to excite "some wanton itching eare/With lustfull thoughts" (PI, stanza 33, ll. 193–194). Instead, after a quick laugh, he shifts the focus to a consideration of the moral implications of Brabant Sr.'s conduct.

Some historians of the War of the Theaters have identified Brabant Sr. as Ben Jonson; this is an utterly groundless guess.[19]

[18] Since the play is so clearly set in Highgate, it is possible that the conclusion alludes to a well-known local custom, the so-called "ceremony of the horn." Almost every tavern in Highgate displayed a set of animal horns. When new travelers alighted from their coaches after the trip up the hill, they were inducted into the "freedom of Highgate" with a joking ceremonial that involved kissing the horns or drinking from a horn cup. In the seventeenth century, the inevitable connection with cuckoldry was made, as in this doggerel poem of 1625:

> Thence to Highgate, where I viewed
> City I so dearly lo'ed
> And i' the horn of matriculation
> Drank to the Freshmen of our nation,
> To his memory saluted,
> Whose branched head was last cornuted.

(Quoted by John H. Lloyd, *History, Topography, and Antiquities of Highgate* [Highgate, 1888], p. 376; for the "ceremony of the horn," see pp. 373–383.) It is merely my conjecture that this ceremony was being re-enacted in the last scene, but the lighthearted conclusion does suggest something formal and ritualistic. Planet plants the horns on Brabant Sr., who defiantly accepts them: "Weare the horne? I, spite of all your teethe/Ile weare this Crowne, and triumph in this horne" (p. 240). Then Sir Edward turns it all into a merry game by announcing plans for some sort of formal induction. In a Highgate setting, an allusion to the best-known local custom sounds very likely.

[19] Even the normally conservative Chambers says flatly, "There is little doubt that the critical Brabant Senior is Jonson, and that the play is that in which he told Drummond that Marston staged him. The cuckolding of Brabant Senior is based upon a story narrated by Jonson to Drummond as one in which he had played the active, not the passive, part. If he had imparted the same

But in his influential book, *Comicall Satyre and Shakespeare's "Troilus and Cressida,"* O. J. Campbell has made an interesting suggestion about the episodes involving Brabant Sr.[20] He claims that *Jack Drum* was one of a group of satiric comedies developed to circumvent the bishops' edict of 1599 against satire. In his view, Jonson and Marston tried to develop within their respective plays a proper representative for their own point of view, a satiric commentator who could both judge the action and yet remain involved in it. In *Jack Drum,* according to Campbell, Planet is "the agent of the author's satire." [21] As we have seen, this analysis is not completely accurate because Sir Edward, Pasquill, Brabant Jr., and others are liable to break into satire that is almost indistinguishable from Planet's. Campbell's companion point is provocative. He suggests that Planet's method of satire is contrasted with Brabant Sr.'s in order to show that there is a right and wrong way to satirize. It is significant that it is Planet who first objects to Brabant Sr.'s method:

> I do hate these bumbaste wits,
> That are puft up with arrogant conceit
> Of their owne worth, as if *Omnipotence*
> Had hoysed them to such unequald height,
> That they survaide our spirits with an eye
> Only create to censure from above,
> When good soules they do nothing but reprove. (III, 229)

This is an accurate criticism of Brabant's odious, inhumane condescension: the gulls are, after all, harmless "good soules," and he himself hardly qualifies as a true wit. Planet's speech also seems to echo the speaker in *The Scourge* who described himself as "I, which was create to whip/Incarnate fiends" (SV, VI, 15–16). We may also recall that in this play an amorist begins to sound unmistakably like *The Scourge* only after he has lost his wits.

---

story to Marston, he not unnaturally resented the use made of it" (IV, 21). But it is difficult to see what Jonson could have resented beyond the appropriation of a good story. Brabant Sr. is shown to be a foolish gallant proud of his gentry ("by my Gentry," p. 193), inadequate with words ("Complement, is as much as [what call you it] tis derived from the Greeke word, a pox ont," p. 209), and wealthy (he "makes costly suppers to trie wits," p. 190). He is not a writer, nor does he possess any of the distinguishing marks which make the portrait in *Satiromastix* so unmistakable. (Cf. my discussion of a similar problem in connection with the character Lampatho Doria in *What You Will,* Chapter X.)

[20] (San Marino, Cal., 1938).
[21] Ibid., p. 165.

Planet's criticism of Brabant Sr. rings true, but it is not easy to detect anything new in his own role. He is merely an extension of the old satiric persona, and he is not even as distinct from Brabant Sr. as Campbell would have us believe. For example, when Brabant Jr. invites Planet to observe his older brother's collection of gulls, the following exchange occurs:

> PLA. Oh we shall be overwhelmd with an inundation of laughter. Come, where are they?
> BRA. Here at this Taverne.
> PLA. In, in, in, in, I long to burst my sides and tyer my spleene with laughter. (III, 191)

This is precisely what Brabant Sr. would say. During most of the play Planet stands outside the events and criticizes a variety of vices, being, in his own words, "as sociable as *Timon* of *Athens*" (III, 190). Nevertheless, through Planet's address to Brabant Sr. at the conclusion of the play, Marston does express a new attitude toward satire:

> Why Foole, the power of Creation
> Is still Omnipotent, and there's no man that breathes
> So valiant, learned, wittie, or so wise,
> But it can equall him out of the same mould
> Wherein the first was form'd. Then leave proud scorne.
> (III, 240)

Rather than exhibiting a tentative solution to the problem of how a satiric commentator ought to be incorporated in a play, these lines constitute a public attack on uninvolved, condescending, satiric commentators who order "guzzell dogs" to quake when they appear. The speech, in fact, sounds like the recantation of an attitude Marston now found odious.

Marston weaves these separate strands of love and satire into a plot that is highly conventional. As we would expect from the satires, the comedy displays young gallants blinded by fashions and pursuing false gods, but the harshest attack, surprisingly, is directed at someone who censures gallants "from above." It is easy to see why *Jack Drum* has been ignored. Its satire may have broad implications, but its terms and its allusions are parochial and transient. It is also easy to see how it might have been a success. Marston concocted a product designed for an audience he knew intimately. He combined daring personal satire with precisely the kind of satire of manners which suited "the humorous ages backs/With cloathes in fashion" (III, 234).

IX The *Antonio* Plays: "What Men Must Be"

After the relatively unpretentious scope of *Jack Drum,* Marston's next effort appears to be an attempt at major work: *Antonio and Mellida* and *Antonio's Revenge* are a unique comic-tragic diptych filled with lofty matter. They may also have been a canny commercial venture. If, as I believe, both plays appeared after *Hamlet* (see Appendix C), the *Revenge* especially must have derived some of its appeal from its close resemblance to Shakespeare's play. Marston's plays would then represent an effort by the little "apes" at Paul's to capitalize on a success by their rivals, to "carry away . . . Hercules and his load too." [1]

[1] *Hamlet,* II.ii.378–379.

Although these plays have many significant interconnections and possess a larger unity, it is best to begin by studying the comedy, *Antonio and Mellida,* with no thought of its tragic sequel. Clearly it was designed to stand by itself, to induce, as the Prologue states, "dimpled smiles" from its "Select, and most respected Auditours" (I, 11). The *Revenge,* in contrast, hoped to "obtaine but teares" (I, 133). As the title to the comedy suggests, Marston was once again playing changes on the *Romeo and Juliet* story. The events take place in Venice rather than Verona, with warring dukes rather than feuding families necessitating secret meetings, agonized separations, and chance reunions. The "comick crosses of true love" (I, 62) rather than the malevolence of the stars frustrate the lovers temporarily, but all ends in miraculous happiness.

Once the Italianate facade is stripped away, however, it appears that fully half the play is devoted to an assortment of gallants very similar to those in the satires.[2] Most of them are "amorists" who possess "humors that are borne/In slime of filthy sensualitie."[3] Often they convict themselves through their absurd behavior, but Marston also included two characters, a free-spoken court lady and a Stoic, to make satiric comments on them. Sometimes these are formal set pieces reminiscent of the revels, as when the witty lady Rossaline speculates on the potential sexual prowess of a series of gallants on the basis of their physical appearance (I, 16–17), or again, when she catalogues imperfections in men which make her wary of marriage (I, 56–57). Her maid Flavia offers entertainment of the same order when she sings a "descant" upon the obscene names of the servants Catzo and Dildo (I, 22).

The bulk of the satire is delivered by a "happy" Stoic with the significant name Feliche, who is described in the Induction as "so impregnably fortrest with his own content, that no envious thought could ever invade his spirit" (I, 8). Twice he delivers orations on his personal contentment, his freedom from envy, and the superior spiritual power with which his philosophy has endowed him:

> [I am] amply suted, with all full content:
> Lord, how I clap my hands, and smooth my brow,

[2] There is also at least one sign of the kind of personal satire that we would expect of the boys and of Marston. The fool Balurdo says, "By Jesu, I think I am as elegant a Courtier, as ———. How lik'st my sute?" (I, 38). Clearly the name of a prominent courtier was inserted in the performance.

[3] SV, XI, 206–207.

> Rubbing my quiet bosome, tossing up
> A gratefull spirit to omnipotence! (I, 36)

From his "height of contemplation" (I, 35) he can criticize and satirize the parasitic flatterer, the "moderne *Bragadoch*" (I, 7), and the other varieties of foolish courtier whom he encounters. In doing so, he uses language and expresses attitudes very similar to the speaker's in *The Scourge*. But Marston's portrait of Feliche is complicated by the fact that he clearly lacks the quality on which he most prides himself, contentment. It may be true, as Anthony Caputi claims, that "there is no contradiction . . . between his speaking at one moment of his serenity and his attacking at the next the depravity of Piero, Forobosco, and Castilio." [4] But it is undeniably the case that, like Marston's later malcontent Malevole, Feliche "cannot sleepe" as he walks "unbrac't" around the court looking for examples of vice (I, 34), that he has unsuccessfully wooed the ladies of the court (I, 36), and that he is so enraged by Castilio's lies about amorous success that he administers a bastinado to him (I, 37). Clearly Stoicism did not fortress him impregnably from events in the world. Withdrawal and inner contentment are impossible in a world where evil and folly reign.

Feliche's values are beyond reproach, and often he expresses them impressively. But the disparity between his sentiments and his actions provides one of the main links between the atmospheric background material and the main plot. In a Romeo and Juliet situation we would expect to find a bold, intrepid young man, willing to combat every obstacle in order to win his lady. Instead, the hero is yet another "amorist," who spends the first two acts in women's clothing and much of the play lying on the ground, weeping helplessly. Antonio's most frequently expressed desire is not for his "adored Mellida," but for death. As if to disenchant our expectations immediately, Marston opens the play with his sad hero trooping across the stage disguised as an Amazon. Clearly we are to feel forewarned that this man with the Arcadian name of Florizell has a "sensuall weaknes" in the "reasonable parte of . . . his soule," as, in *The Arcadia*, Mucedorus claims when he reprimands Pyrocles for adopting a similar disguise. [5] Antonio frames his behavior according to his clothing, as he constantly regrets that he must live and strive:

[4] *John Marston, Satirist* (Ithaca, 1961), p. 137.

[5] Sir Philip Sidney, *The Countesse of Pembrokes Arcadia*, ed. A. Feuillerat (Cambridge, Eng., 1912), p. 77.

> Could not the fretting sea
> Have rowl'd me up in wrinkles of his browe?
> Is death growen coy? or grim confusion nice?
> That it will not accompany a wretch,
> But I must needs be cast on *Venice* shoare,
> And try new fortunes with this strange disguise?
> To purchase my adored *Mellida*. (I, 13)

The situation demands rapid and heroic action, but Antonio invariably collapses under stress, throwing himself on the ground and raving impotently against his bad fortune (for example, I, 40 and 47). Antonio enjoys and seizes upon every such occasion to indulge in histrionics. His speeches are filled with the bombastic rhetoric for which Marston is notorious. But I think it can be demonstrated that Antonio's manner of speech was constructed to reveal his absurdities: the Poetaster in this play is not Marston but Antonio. From Jonson onward, the language in the *Antonio* plays has provoked much hostile criticism. Yet if my reading of the play is correct, most of the adverse linguistic criticism is invalid. Each character defines himself by a special, often an absurd, type of language. It ranges from nearly total nonsense in the case of the fool Balurdo to highly self-conscious, "pretty" poetry in Antonio:

> Come downe, she comes like: O, no Simile
> Is pretious, choyce, or elegant enough
> To illustrate her descent: leape heart, she comes,
> She comes: smile heaven, and softest Southern winde
> Kisse her cheeke gently with perfumed breath.
> She comes: Creations puritie, admir'd,
> Ador'd, amazing raritie, she comes. (I, 17–18)

He selects his similes with finicky care:

> But come sweete creature, thou shalt be my home;
> My father, country, riches, and my friend:
> My all, my soule; and thou and I will live:
> (Lets thinke like what) and thou and I will live
> Like unmatcht mirrors of calamitie. (I, 29)

When Antonio unexpectedly encounters his love in the marsh, English is apparently too gross a language to indicate the depth of their emotion, and so he and Mellida hide their tender sentiments in Italian.

To make such claims for the language of the play might seem to be dogmatizing about the author's intention, but the Induction suggests just such a doctrine of linguistic decorum:

> MATZAGENTE. By the bright honour of a *Millanoise,*
> and the resplendent fulgor of this steele,
> I will defende the feminine to death;
> and ding his spirit to the verge of hell,
> that dares divulge a Ladies prejudice . . .
>
> FELICHE. Rampum scrampum, mount tuftie *Tamburlaine.* What rattling thunderclappe breakes from his lips?
>
> ALBERTO. O, 'tis native to his part. For, acting a modern *Bragadoch* under the person of *Matzagente,* the Duke of *Millaines* sonne, it may seeme to suite with good fashion of coherence. (I, 7)

In the same way, Antonio's speech fits his character as it is described in the Induction: "an Hermaphrodite; two parts in one" (I, 7). Without the Induction we would share the perplexity of one of the actors who was uncertain "in what mould we must cast our Actors" (I, 5). But with its aid and additional hints from the costuming (women's clothes) and careful stage directions (for example, the frequent falling), we can see Antonio clearly as an object of satire.

The satiric tone, established in the portrait of the hero, frequently becomes so extreme as to verge on farce in the portrait of the villain Piero. He first appears as a prideful Machiavellian villain-prince, disdainfully dismissing Jehovah, Heaven, Fate, Eternity, and the examples of Rome and Babylon with the blasphemous *"Dimitto superos, summa votorum attigi"* (I, 14), which Seneca put into the mouth of Atreus in *Thyestes.* But, at least in the first play, his talk is more formidable than his acts. At the one moment in the action when villainous talents are required, he responds with something less than Iago-like resourcefulness. He has just discovered the letter which betrays his daughter's intention to run off with Antonio:

> PIERO. . . . *Forobosco, Alberto, Feliche, Castilio, Balurdo?* run, keepe the Palace, post to the ports, goe to my daughters chamber: whether now? scud to the Jewes, stay, runne to the gates, stop the gundolets, let none passe the marsh, doe all at once. *Antonio?* his head, his head. Keep you the Court, the rest stand still, or runne,

or goe, or shoute, or search, or scud, or call, or hang, or
doe doe doe, su su su, somthing: I know not who who
who, what I do do do, nor who who who, where I
am . . .

> *O trista traditriche, rea, ribalda fortuna,*
> *Negando mi vindetta mi causa fera morte.* (I, 39)

Piero's recourse to Italian in a moment of emotional stress,
his pleasure in rant, his inability to act in a crisis — all suggest
that he is a fitting antagonist for Antonio.

Andrugio, the father of Antonio, is another serious figure
treated in a partially satiric way. He first appears in the third
act, a duke recently defeated in war, speaking like a Stoic prince
who has renounced worldly pretensions:

> I have no excellence to please.
> Pree the[e] observe the custome of the world,
> That onely flatters greatnesse, States exalts . . .
> Good, flatter not. (I, 31)

But a moment later, after reading a notice for his life which
Piero has posted, Andrugio turns passionate, and the resemblance to his son becomes more obvious. In the most impressive speech in the play, he denies the Stoic claims for a natural
moral order and concludes thus:

> O thou all-bearing earth,
> Which men doe gape for, till thou cramst their mouths,
> And choakst their throts with dust: O chaune thy brest,
> And let me sinke into thee. Looke who knocks;
> *Andrugio* cals. But O, she's deafe and blinde.
> A wretch, but leane reliefe on earth can finde. (I, 32)

Philosophy tells him one thing, but he *feels* another. He shunts
aside the lessons of philosophy and gropes his way from one
frightening image to the next, finally ending in a despairing
death wish. All he finally desires (and the sound tells the story)
is that the earth "chaune" her breast, but instead she "cramst"
and "choakst."

This is not attitudinizing on the part of Andrugio. The ter-
rifying image of the earth as a deaf and blind monster who eats
her young induces a despair that is both convincing and pathetic, although we may remind ourselves that the speaker is
supposed to be an arch-Stoic. It is the very essence of Stoic

doctrine that the earth is unstable and gives only "leane re-liefe." But the mood swiftly passes when his servant reminds him that a Stoic should be indifferent to Fortune. Andrugio remembers what he should say in such situations:

> There's nothing left
> Unto *Andrugio*, but *Andrugio*:
> And that nor mischief, force, distresse, nor hel can take,
> Fortune my fortunes, not my minde shall shake. (I, 32)

Yet when his servant asks him to discard his conspicuous armor for safety's sake, he promptly forgets this maxim and begins to rant:

> Come soule, resume the valour of thy birth;
> My selfe, my selfe will dare all opposits:
> Ile muster forces, an unvanquisht power:
> Cornets of horse shall presse th' ungratefull earth;
> This hollow wombed masse shall inly grone,
> And murmur to sustaine the waight of armes. (I, 33)

From cosmic despair to Stoic constancy to Tamburlaine heroics in three speeches! The next speech completes the cycle: when he is admonished to do nothing rash, he asserts a faith in the moral order:

> *Andrugio* lives, and a faire cause of armes,
> Why that's an armie all invincible! . . .
> O, a faire cause stands firme, and will abide.
> Legions of Angels fight upon her side. (I, 33)

Andrugio's remaining speeches in the scene continue in like manner,[6] and Marston's anatomy of inconstancy here serves to introduce an entire act (the third) in which instability is the keynote. In it Antonio and (as we have seen) Piero fall to pieces under the necessity of forthright action, and Feliche loses his Stoic detachment.

The implication of Andrugio's and Feliche's fluctuations is clear. Stoicism may be satisfactory as a philosophy, but it does not take into account the whole of man's nature. This criticism

---

[6] Charles Lamb, "Specimens of the English Dramatic Poets" in *Works of Charles and Mary Lamb*, ed. E. V. Lucas (New York, 1904), IV, 62, n. 2, described Andrugio's speeches in this scene as a picture of "royal impatience, a turbulent greatness, an affected resignation."

was a familiar one in the Renaissance; and the terms in which
Stoicism was rejected were sufficiently uniform to require only
suggestion, not explicit statement, from Marston.[7]

The criticism of Stoicism continues in Act IV. Andrugio
again mouths Stoic precepts, and mere mention by Andrugio
of his enemies "Unkings me quite, makes me vile passions
slave" (I, 45). Subsequently, a tearful, unexpected reunion with
his son occurs. He suggests to Antonio that the two of them
forget what they once had been and retire to a mean abode,
where they will pass the time in what we may feel to be a
curious mixture of Stoic resignation and passionate yearning.
Finally, Andrugio decides that resignation will not win him
happiness and that only courageous action can alleviate his
suffering. He specifically rejects the counsel of patience from
his Stoic servant:

> What patience, friend, can ruin'd hopes attend?
> Come, let me die like old *Andrugio*:
> Worthy my birth. O blood-true-honour'd graves
> Are farre more blessed then base life of slaves. (I, 51)

The familiar jeer at Stoicism is touched on in the last lines: the
morality designed by a slave for slaves is fit only for slaves. By
rejecting Stoicism, he becomes free to act, and he proceeds to
Piero's court.

The final scene in the play recapitulates rather than resolves
what has gone before. No real "conversions" are effected; everyone behaves in character. With all the heroics of Andrugio's
last speech, one is led to expect a violent course of action from
him. Instead, he passively throws himself on the mercy of his
inveterate enemy. All his inconsistencies appear in the speech
with which he gives himself up:

> Then here, *Piero,* is *Andrugios* head,
> Royally casked in a helme of steele:
> Give me thy love, and take it. My dauntlesse soule
> Hath that unbounded vigor in his spirits,
> That it can beare more ranke indignitie,
> With lesse impatience, then thy cancred hate
> Can sting and venome his untainted worth,
> With the most viperous sound of malice. (I, 59)

[7] See Henry W. Sams, "Anti-Stoicism in Seventeenth- and Early Eighteenth-
Century England," *Studies in Philology*, 41 (1944), 65–78.

He ascribes to himself the very virtue he is farthest from possessing, patience. Andrugio's trick scarcely redounds to his credit; as he himself knows (I, 60), his heroism is born of impulsiveness, his fortitude of despair. He is a curious mixture of manly and feminine traits, an androgyne. Antonio (the "hermaphrodite" [I, 7] son of Andrugio) plays a trick similarly consistent with his character. Since he has constantly clamored for death, it is a macabre joke for him to arrive in a coffin. He lies in it safely until he hears that everything has been solved, that all has been forgiven. When he does emerge, Piero is caught off guard and responds by saying, "We are amaz'd, our royall spirits numm'd/In stiffe astonisht wonder" (I, 60). Antonio replies in kind: "Stand not amaz'd, great states:/I rise from death that never liv'd till now" (I, 61). Amazement is, indeed, the proper response to a play filled with such a succession of shocks and surprises.

For the most part, the soliloquies and long tirades of the central characters show them to be essentially like the fools of the following stage direction:

> Enter *Balurdo,* backward; *Dildo* following him with a looking-glasse in one hand, & a candle in the other hand: *Flavia* following him backward, with a looking glasse in one hand, and a candle in the other; *Rossaline* following her. *Balurdo* and *Rossaline* stand setting of faces. (I, 37)

The main characters mistake the cosmetic-covered images in their mirrors for their real selves and meanwhile walk backward in the world. Misconceptions about themselves lead them to frequent displays of emotional instability. The plot is designed to give them the maximum number of opportunities for despair; their mental state is conveyed through the recurrent theatrical images of men falling on the ground and flailing at it or walking crazily in a circle.

All ends confusedly and "happily" in *Antonio and Mellida* with the conventional conclusion of peace and the promise of marriage. Yet as a conclusion, it is "amazing" to all. The play presents a sordid world governed by an absurd, prideful, and unjust ruler. The protagonists respond by uttering cries of anguish and by making theatrical, impotent gestures of defiance. Marston rigorously controls the action and the characters so that we see a comic vision: sensitive, melancholic, would-be tragedians mouthing Seneca and, absurdly, gaining a fragile success through the benevolence of their bitterest enemy.

But it is a distortion of the strange mixture of elements that constitutes this play to say that it is a burlesque or a parody or that Antonio and Andrugio are totally satiric figures. When Antonio learns that he is on the verge of capture in Piero's court, he characteristically collapses into despair and eloquence:

> Each man take[s] hence life, but no man death:
> Hee's a good fellow, and keepes open house:
> A thousand thousand waies lead to his gate,
> To his wide-mouth'd porch: when niggard life
> Hath but one little, little wicket through.
> We wring our selves into this wretched world,
> To pule, and weepe, exclaime, to curse and raile,
> To fret, and ban the fates, to strike the earth
> As I doe now. *Antonio,* curse thy birth,
> And die. (I, 40)

Since he (and he alone among the characters in any of Marston's plays) responds with nearly automatic effusions of "speckling melancholie" (as he describes a similar moment in the next act, I, 43), it is clear that Marston's attitude toward him is a complicated one. This speech is an impressive, carefully wrought passage of poetry; Marston's rendition and expansion of Seneca give it a surprisingly vivid colloquial twist. The same careful art is apparent in some of Andrugio's speeches, particularly his magnificent lamentation on deaf and blind Mother Earth who "eates her children" (I, 31–32). In these speeches the poetry may strike us as supererogatory, but it is nonetheless moving. The sentiments are in excess of the speakers' plight, but they have a general truth about them. These passages serve the same function as the many quotations from Seneca which somehow ballast this comedy.[8] Thus, read carefully, even in isolation from its sequel, for which it is a subtle preparation, the happy conclusion to *Antonio and Mellida* does not falsify the basic vision of the world which the play has been offering. The heroes ought not to trust their "happiness" any more than anything else which this earth, "this monstrous animal," belks up. *Antonio and Mellida* is a Senecan comedy.

[8] See J. W. Cunliffe, *The Influence of Seneca on Elizabethan Tragedy* (London, 1893). Cunliffe lists nearly as many Senecan sources for *Antonio and Mellida* as he does for *Antonio's Revenge.*

2

Antonio's Revenge opens with a prologue which sets the scene in winter and announces that a "sullen tragick Sceane" will match the season "with pleasing congruence" (I, 69). In fact, the setting does not alter much, but now the characters are placed in a genre where their rhetoric and actions will be congruent. Between the plays, Piero has murdered Andrugio and Feliche, and he opens the action "unbrac't, his armes bare, smeer'd in blood, a poniard in one hand bloodie, and a torch in the other" (I, 71). He crows in maniacal exultation at his "toplesse mount/Of unpeer'd mischiefe"; he "can scarce coope triumphing vengeance up,/From bursting forth in bragart passion" (I, 71). As he babbles on, refusing to be interrupted and demanding praise for each lurid action, we gradually see that the absurd Cambyses-like ranter of the first play is no longer an inept *miles gloriosus*. He is more like the gleeful Hitler doing his jig of triumph after the fall of France. The comparison is not unjust, because Piero's ambitions are similar, and he goes part of the way toward achieving them:

> *Venice, Florence, Genoa,* strongly leagu'd.
> Excellent, excellent. Ile conquer *Rome,*
> Pop out the light of bright religion:
> And then, helter skelter, all cock sure. (I, 117)

Marston's ironic portrayal makes Piero at once farcical and lethal. He reaches his most comic and destructive height when he coaches his accomplice, the strangler Strozzo, to make a confession. As a sign of contrition, Strozzo is to appear with a cord around his neck, confess, and be forgiven. But after he has done what Piero wishes, the Duke promptly strangles him with the cord. We must laugh incredulously at the trick and yet agree that his "bloodie crudities" (I, 125) must at all cost be stopped.

Antonio, in this play, remains much the same, with his lamentations and gestures of anguish, but our attitude toward him also changes after his troubles become tragic:

> My father dead, my love attaint of lust:
> Thats a large lye, as vast as spatious hell:
> Poore guiltlesse Ladie. O, accursed lye.
> What, whome, whether, which shall I first lament?
> A deade father, a dishonour'd wife. (I, 82)

In fact, according to the Prologue, only those who can sympathize with Antonio's anguish will be welcome to this play. It is not written for the person

> Uncapable of waightie passion
> (As from his birth, being hugged in the armes,
> And nuzzled twixt the breastes of happinesse)
> Who winkes, and shuts his apprehension up
> From common sense of what men were, and are,
> Who would not knowe what men must be. (I, 69)

In other words, to have lived in uninterrupted happiness stunts the growth of "common sense," defined here by Marston in a highly unusual way. It involves two notions: the ability to respond with passion to suffering (one's own or another's) and an awareness of man's lot as fundamentally tragic. The only way to acquire this "sense" is through personal experience:

> if a breast
> Nail'd to the earth with griefe: if any heart
> Pierc't through with anguish, pant within this ring:
> If there be any blood, whose heate is choakt
> And stifled with true sense of misery:
> If ought of these straines fill this consort up,
> Th'arrive most welcome. (I, 69–70)

Since this description fits Antonio perfectly, the unique requirement for admission to Paul's is, apparently, resemblance to the anguished, sensitive young lover who serves as the protagonist.

Antonio is by no means an Everyman, but we are shown that his manner of responding to misery represents "common sense." Marston stresses this through an elaborate contrast with two types of creatures who lack "sense." One is a Stoic, the father of the murdered Feliche. Pandulpho Feliche is an even firmer believer than his son in the doctrines of Epictetus and Seneca. His response to the announcement of his son's death and dishonor is characteristic:

> Would'st have me cry, run raving up & down,
> For my sons losse? would'st have me turn rank mad,
> Or wring my face with mimic action;
> Stampe, curse, weepe, rage, & then my bosome strike?
> Away, tis apish action, player-like. (I, 83)

He is noble and incorruptible and for most of the play seems utterly unaffected by the tragic events that surround him. He is above passion.

The subhuman fool Balurdo is also "senseless." His first words in *Antonio and Mellida* tell us that his senses are muddled: "Oh, I smell a sound" (I, 14), and he persists in this unwitting synesthesia in the *Revenge* (for example, I, 105). In both plays he echoes, sometimes burlesques, serious characters. After Antonio delivers a long speech describing his dream of foreboding on the night of the murders, Balurdo proceeds to tell one of his own dreams (I, 78). Its effect is to mock slightly Antonio's Senecan rhetoric, but it also shows that Balurdo has virtually no comprehension of the seriousness of what has been said. As Antonio says of fools,

> Had Heaven bin kinde,
> Creating me an honest senselesse dolt,
> A good poore foole, I should want sense to feele
> The stings of anguish shoot through every vaine, . . .
> I should be deade of sense. (I, 110)

Neither a Stoic stock nor a senseless dolt, Antonio has "common sense"; he responds like a human. The play demonstrates what happens to such a creature, what "men must be," under the pressure of extreme circumstances. For two acts his anguish increases as he rejects the easy comforts of Seneca:

> Pish, thy mother was not lately widdowed,
> Thy deare affied love, lately defam'd,
> With blemish of foule lust, when thou wrot'st thus.
> Thou wrapt in furres, beaking thy lymbs 'fore fiers,
> Forbidst the frozen Zone to shudder. Ha ha: tis naught
> But fomie bubling of a fleamie braine,
> Naught els but smoake. (I, 91–92)

Frustrated by unprovable suspicions against Piero, separated from his beloved Mellida, whom Piero pretends to have found in Feliche's embraces, watching Piero make advances to his mother, Antonio finds it "strange" that he has not yet gone mad (I, 95). Finally at midnight, alone in St. Mark's Church, Andrugio's ghost appears and tells him of the murders. This revelation seems to push Antonio to insanity, at least for the remainder of this act. He pledges vengeance in Latin, apparently with such stage byplay as to make his mother say: "Alas my son's distraught. Sweete boy appease/Thy mutinous affections" (I, 100). Antonio continues to utter oaths, now in English, in a rhythmic, almost barbaric chant. He rants against Man, finding him worse than swine, wolves, scorpions, dogs, toads. When he has an opportunity to kill Piero, he restrains himself, not for Hamlet's reasons, but to "force him feede on life/Till he shall loath it" (I, 102). Finally, when he encounters Piero's son, Julio, all his restraint dissolves. He decides to begin his vengeance on the innocent child:

> Gratious, ô bounteous heaven!
> I doe adore thy Justice; *Venit in nostras manus*
> *Tandem vindicta, venit & tota quidem.* (I, 103)

As he speaks the very words of Atreus in *Thyestes,* Antonio becomes a bloody conscienceless killer. He has come to resemble Piero, who thinks that Heaven approves his actions. It is nearly farcical for Piero to say: "O, let me swoone for joy. By heaven, I thinke/I ha said my prayers, within this month at least" (I, 73). But for the sensitive Antonio to think that this murder is heaven-approved demonstrates his degeneration into madness.

It was a delicate piece of work for the Elizabethan playwright to preserve the sympathy of the audience for his revenging protagonist. But at this point Marston was not interested in preserving that sympathy. By a "hellish wit," as Malheureux calls similar reasoning in *The Dutch Curtezan,*[9] Antonio excuses his acts to his victim:

> Come, prettie tender childe,
> It is not thee I hate, not thee I kill.
> Thy fathers blood that flowes within thy veines,
> Is it I loath; is that, Revenge must sucke.
> I love thy soule: and were thy heart lapt up
> In any flesh, but in *Piero's* bloode,
> I would thus kisse it: but being his: thus, thus,
> And thus Ile punch it. Abandon feares.
> Whil'st thy wounds bleede, my browes shall gush out
>   teares. (I, 103–104)

With such words as "sucke," with the kiss followed by the punch of the knife, Antonio sounds like a psychopath, and one's sympathy is further alienated by the sharp pathos of

---

[9] *Plays of John Marston,* ed. H. Harvey Wood (3 vols., Edinburgh, 1934–1939), II, 93.

Julio's innocent replies: "So you will love me, doe even what you will" (I, 104). After the murder, Antonio does not stop with a continual "punch[ing]" of his rapier into Julio's corpse; he "mangle[s]" it (I, 104), makes incense of the blood, sprinkles the gore on the hearse of Andrugio, and ends the scene by screaming for more objects of vengeance. In the next scene the stage direction and Antonio's speech bring to mind the opening image of Piero and his exultant bragging: "Enter *Antonio*, his armes bloody: a torch and a poniard . . .

> Looke how I smoake in blood, reeking the steame
> Of foming vengeance. O my soule's inthroan'd
> In the tryumphant chariot of revenge.
> Me thinks I am all ayre, and feele no waight
> Of humane dirt clogge. This is *Julio's* blood.
> Rich musique, father; this is *Julio's* blood. (I, 107)

Unlike Hamlet's father, Andrugio's ghost spurs him to further violence, nearly repeating Piero's very words: "be pearelesse in revenge" (I, 108; cf. I, 71).

The sensitive, poetic young lover has become a remorseless, bloodthirsty murderer. We do not see much of Antonio's "character" in either play, but this transformation is psychologically credible. For seven acts Marston has displayed his neurasthenic unsteadiness. Finally, in the sanctity of a church, the voice of his father, emanating from the grave, has precipitated a collapse. Marston stresses the extremity of his transformation by inventing little Julio for the occasion.

Antonio becomes his opposite, but this is not the only distinction which collapses as the play goes on. The difference between the sensitive and insensitive, the perceptive and foolish also dissolves in the fourth act when (as will be discussed below) the fool Balurdo acts like a hero and Antonio adopts "a fooles habit, with a little toy of a walnut shell, and sope, to make bubbles" (I, 109). Antonio explains his choice of disguise in a very complicated mixture of tones. As with Erasmus' Folly, it is difficult to determine what direction the compound of irony, satire, and self-criticism is taking. At first he merely defends his disguise by satirizing the ways of the world:

> Why friend, a golden asse,
> A babl'd foole are sole canonicall,
> Whil'st pale cheekt wisdome, and leane ribd arte
> Are kept in distance at the halberts point:

All held *Apocrypha,* not worth survey.
Why, by the genius of that *Florentine,*
Deepe, deepe observing, sound brain'd Macheveil,
He is not wise that strives not to seeme foole. (I, 109)

The "new" Antonio, the dedicated revenger, takes (or pretends
to take) the same devilish mentor that has inspired Piero. But
Antonio turns this praise of folly into an ambiguous shaft at
men with pretensions to wisdom:

> the chub-fac't fop
> Shines sleeke with full cramm'd fat of happinesse,
> Whil'st studious contemplation sucks the juyce
> From wisards cheekes: who making curious search
> For Natures secrets, the first innating cause
> Laughes them to scorne, as man doth busie Apes
> When they will zanie men. (I, 110)

From the point of view of the "first innating cause," "wisards,"
too, are fools. And he concludes his paradoxes by saying that
if he were "an honest senselesse dolt" he

> could not thus run mad,
> As one confounded in a maze of mischiefe,
> Staggerd, starke feld with brusing stroke of chance.
> (I, 110)

Folly is at least no worse than the price he has paid for his
sensitivity — madness. Mellida, in her dying words, is quoted
as saying, "O world thou art too subtile/For honest natures to
converse withall" (I, 118). For we are all "honest senselesse
dolts" (at least all but the villains) *sub specie aeternitatis,* as
Antonio, lying on his back in his fool's habit, perceives after
Mellida's death:

> I Heaven, thou maist, thou maist omnipotence.
> What vermine bred of putrifacted slime,
> Shall dare to expostulate with thy decrees! (I, 118)

He, too, is numb, and only lives

> to numme some others cursed bloode,
> With the dead palsie of like miserie.
> Then death, like to a stifling *Incubus,*
> Lie on my bosome. (I, 119)

Once again we are reminded of Piero, who also "nummes" people and has an "incubus" (I, 73). To blend distinctions further, Piero's one piece of self-knowledge is that he is a kind of fool when he speaks of "the unglewd joints" of his "shaken wits" (I, 112). He is a dangerous fool, a figure who can be seen at once as absurd, yet productive of tragedy. We are all fools, whether sensitive, senseless, or villainous.

Marston's view of men as lonely and helpless fools is underlined by imagery which suggests Nature's relation to the world of the play. Images of light and dark, dramatic as well as verbal, abound in *Antonio's Revenge*. For the most part, these images are attached to very careful descriptions of the diurnal cycle. Perhaps more consistently and accurately than anywhere else in Elizabethan drama, the *Antonio* plays detail the passage of time and the changes from darkness to light and from light to darkness again. At the beginning of the *Revenge*, the emphasis on darkness appears to be simply the standard fare of Senecan tragedy. But Marston does not permit this awareness of time to lag. Piero concludes the first scene by noticing that time has passed:

> For see, the dapple gray coursers of the morne
> Beat up the light with their bright silver hooves,
> And chase it through the skye. (I, 74)

Even after a night of blood and corpses he can perceive the chaste freshness of Nature's beauty — a beauty totally unrelated to man's actions.

The next scene takes place while "yon faint glimmering light . . . peeped through the crannies of the east" (I, 74–75). This does not set the time with sufficient precision for Marston's purposes, for we next learn that it is five o'clock. By the end of the scene, "tis cleare day" (I, 76).

Antonio starts the third scene with a description of the morning:

> Darknesse is fled: looke, infant morn hath drawne
> Bright silver curtains, 'bout the couch of night:
> And now *Auroras* horse trots azure rings,
> Breathing faire light about the firmament. (I, 76)

There must be something objective and unchanging in the return of day to inspire similar lyric outpourings from both Antonio and Piero.

With similar care, Marston traces the time changes throughout the rest of the play. What soon becomes clear is the total
lack of relation between nature and man. The sun and moon
take their places in turn, completely unaware of the convulsions
occurring below. As with the "deafe and blind" earth of
Andrugio's soliloquy in Part I, Nature cares nothing for man's
lonely existence in "this lodge/Of durts corruption" (I, 132).

With the universe indifferent to all of man's actions, a passive
acceptance of the world's indignities becomes both the natural
reaction of fools and the trained response of Stoics. But action
is ultimately necessary: not to act would be to acquiesce in the
villainous folly. Merely to rail (as Antonio did in the first play)
is to cast serious doubts on one's sensibleness. When the most
subhuman of fools is impelled to make a protest, mere railing
would make a sensible person look foolish. With a ruler like
Piero, even a "chub-fac't fop" cannot remain silent forever.
After Alberto is unjustly treated in the fourth act, Balurdo
suddenly comes to life and blurts out, "Gods neakes he has
wrong, that he has: and S'fut, and I were as he, I would beare
no coles, lawe I, I begin to swell, puffe . . . nay, but as poore
as I am, I will sweare the fellowe hath wrong" (I, 116–117).
Piero tries to ignore him, but Balurdo continues to criticize
the Duke's judgment until he is sent to the dungeon for his
momentary rebellion. By this time his innocence and helplessness have made him, through a speech (I, 124) too long to quote
here, a moving and pathetic example of unjust suffering.

Then it is Pandulpho's turn to come to his "senses." It is
difficult for the heavily committed Stoic to shift his views. Even
after he has become convinced of Piero's guilt, even after he
has been banished and deprived of all his property, even, in
fact, while burying his son, he sermonizes "in the old cut,"
using Seneca's *De Providentia* as his Bible. He recites his
characteristic sentences for about thirty lines, but then suddenly
turns on himself:

> Man will break out, despight Philosophie.
> Why, all this while I ha but plaid a part,
> Like to some boy, that actes a Tragedie,
> Speakes burly words, and raves out passion:
> But, when he thinks upon his infant weaknesse,
> He droopes his eye. I spake more then a god;
> Yet am lesse then a man.
> I am the miserablest sowle that breathes. (I, 121)

(It is a nice touch to have the boy actor use himself as a visual metaphor of man's powerlessness.) Henceforth Pandulpho sounds indistinguishable from Antonio. He sees Stoicism as a false and theatrical stance; and by the end of the play, he too "raves out passion," screaming as he plunges a rapier into Piero, "Murder for murder, blood for blood doth yell" (I, 131).

Thus the pressure to physical vengeance becomes irresistible; Piero's accumulated outrages have transformed the activity from private revenge into a political assassination, with all elements of society allied against him. The "citizens [have] growne sick/ With swallowing" his acts; "graver States-men" agree "this must not be." There is only one answer: "A royall vengeance, or a royall grave" (I, 125). It is indeed a royal and unique vengeance: every figure of any importance in the play is implicated in the plot against Piero.

What follows is probably the most painful revenge — certainly it is the most horrible onstage murder — in Elizabethan drama. It begins with a dramatic irony which imperceptibly prepares the way for an altered attitude toward Piero: "PIERO. Call *Julio* hither; Where's the little sowle?/I sawe him not to-day" (I, 128). After Julio arrives in the form of sweet meats, "the conspirators binde *Piero,* pluck out his tongue, and tryumph over him" (I, 129). They taunt him and indulge in name-calling: "Scum of the mud of hell . . . Slime of all filth . . . Thou most detested toad" (I, 130). Pandulpho says, "let him die, and die, and stil be dying," after which "They offer to runne all at *Piero,* and on a sodain stop" (I, 130). Finally Antonio, followed by the rest of the conspirators, "run all at *Piero* with their Rapiers" (I, 131). During this onslaught, Piero must sit silently weeping, making pitiable gestures: "*Piero* seemes to condole his sonne" (I, 130). With no chance to cringe abjectly or to scream in cowardice, Piero in spite of himself becomes an object of sympathy, almost a Julio, while the mad revengers act like villainous fools.

The moral distinction between Piero and his victims is all but obliterated, and Justice, in the form of a group of Venetian senators, implicates itself in the ruthless murders by judging the murderers "sacred" (I, 131). Instead of the usual punishment for revengers, Antonio and his friends are offered the "cheefest fortunes of the Venice state" (I, 132) (apparently the dukedom, although this is not absolutely clear). Marston points out the abnormal nature of this conclusion by having Antonio say, "We are amaz'd at your benignitie" (I, 132).

It is a play filled with "amazing" gestures, but the senators' "benignitie" is not a mere *coup de théâtre*. Benignity is in order in a world where all are guilty, "must be" guilty. Only Mellida remains pure. She deserves to be immortalized for her "virgine faith," according to Antonio (I, 133), but her "unmixt puritie" (I, 117) could not survive the world's subtle shifts. Pandulpho says, "We know the world, and did we know no more,/Wee would not live to know" (I, 132). They have learned reasons for suicide, but there is a canon against self-slaughter. Thus they will "Purge hearts of hatred" and withdraw to "holy verge of some religious order" until the "dread power cals . . . [their] soules appearance" (I, 132).

Fredson Bowers finds in this conclusion "the imposition of Roman callousness on the conventional English ethical view of the limits to which a revenger could go and the methods he should pursue." [10] It is indeed an unconventional ending, but it is far from callous. Men are "vermine bred of putrifacted slime" (I, 118) whose passions annihilate themselves or others. But there is no one to punish them, no one to establish a new order in Venice after the convulsion, for Marston is describing a general condition. This is what "men were, and are, [and] . . . must be" (I, 69). Nothing but grace when the "dread power cals" will save them.

This vision is as darkly pessimistic as any in Elizabethan drama. Put grossly, a "sensible" man can easily become passion's slave, capable of any horror. Hamlet was aware of this danger, but able to resist it. In Hamlet's universe, "there's special providence in the fall of a sparrow." [11] In Antonio's, "Omnipotence" treats vermin with the contempt they merit, and the natural order proceeds, indifferent to the puny passions enacted below. Marston's vision is consonant with his satires, although much more shocking in dramatic form.

The *Revenge* merely deepens attitudes implicit in *Antonio and Mellida* and his previous work, but undoubtedly some kind of shift occurred in Marston's interests between the two parts of the play. The earlier play is largely out of the same mold as *Jack Drum*, another variant on *Romeo*, with some parody and a great deal of *Scourge*-like satire. The leading character Antonio, at once sympathetic but passive and effeminate, resembles the portraits of "sweet" gallants which appear in most of Marston's previous work. The idea of inserting this figure into a *Hamlet* play was consistent with Marston's practice at this time. It would thereby connect both *Antonio* plays with

[10] *Elizabethan Revenge Tragedy* (Princeton, 1940), p. 124.
[11] *Hamlet*, V.ii.231.

famous plays in the Chamberlain's Men's repertory. It would also permit Marston to express another, possibly a "truer," version of Shakespeare's plot. The *Hamlet* story suggested a new and fruitful question to Marston: what happens to an Antonio when he is forced to act in this depraved and villainous world? This was to become one of Marston's most serious and persistent themes.

The choice of revenge as the metaphor for action produced an extreme vision, one of almost unprecedented darkness. In the twentieth century we can no longer dismiss it as a demonstrably false version of reality; indeed, the *Revenge* resembles the many recent works which emphasize cruelty as a fundamental element in human nature. Most readers have been too much repelled by the texture of the *Antonio* plays to notice their larger aims. Jonson was merely the first to ridicule the language, but such criticism must meet the clear evidence of the Induction that Marston was attempting to characterize and individuate through absurd or unusual linguistic practices. Antonio was my example, but the stiff contortions of Piero, the patent nonsense of Balurdo, the high nobility of Pandulpho, all show the same effort.

A more valid objection might be that the plays lack a linguistic common denominator, that they resemble Hieronimo's little play in *The Spanish Tragedy* in which each character is assigned a different language.[12] However, this is to assume that the *Revenge* is, like *Hamlet*, a mimetic tragedy. If we try to imagine an actual production, a somewhat different impression emerges. The stage directions indicate that much of the play takes place on a dark stage lit only by torches; that there is a great reliance on instrumental music and songs by the choir boys for mood effects; and that there are no less than three dumb shows and a notable number of visual effects. Among these are the sudden opening of the curtain to disclose Feliche hanging dead and the tableau-like placement of Feliche's corpse on the prone body of Antonio in his fool's costume. As we have seen, one of the play's most important "intellectual" points, that Antonio has come to resemble Piero, is conveyed through the use of a nonverbal stage metaphor — the unexpected entry of each after committing a murder, smeared with fresh gore. In short, the element of spectacle is unusually prominent in the *Revenge*. Marston's techniques verge on those of the masque rather than on those of mimetic tragedy. At the end, the re-

[12] See Thomas Kyd, *The Spanish Tragedy*, ed. Philip Edwards, The Revels Plays (Cambridge, Mass., 1959), p. 107, ll. 172–178.

vengers do become participants in a kind of "masque of the passions." It is easy to imagine the murder as a frenzied but patterned dance, and we must remember that the actors added an extra element of stylization by being boys. Thus, as I imagine it, a Mannerist production could easily have handled the otherwise difficult discontinuities between the characters' styles of speech. Without a precise knowledge of the acting and staging techniques at the boys' theaters, we can never be certain, but an abstract, stylized performance could have turned the *Revenge* into a compelling theatrical experience. However, this was not the type of play Marston was interested in developing. We have to look to the *Revengers' Tragedy* for the perfection of what Marston, probably only half-consciously, produced. What interested him in this play, at least what appeared here for the first time, was its theme: the moral cost of immersion in the destructive element. This became the central concern of most of his later work.

X *What You Will* or
Don Kynsayder's Descent from Parnassus

Among Marston's professional plays, *What You Will* would
seem best suited for an evening of pleasant entertainment at
an Inns of Court revel. Its main plot of mistaken identities
resembles *The Comedy of Errors,* with which Shakespeare entertained Gray's Inn in 1594. *What You Will* also shares many
attributes besides its title with Shakespeare's contribution to
the Middle Temple's celebration on February 2, 1602, *Twelfth
Night, or What You Will.* However we do not know anything
about the performance of Marston's play, not even which acting

company did it, and even the generally agreed upon date of 1601 is conjectural.[1]

In fact, the literary histories speak about this play with much more certainty than the facts warrant. Most discussions assign it a role in the so-called War of the Theaters, and various elements do connect the play with the brief outburst of animosity between Jonson and Marston which culminated in Jonson's *Poetaster* and Dekker's *Satiromastix,* both of 1601. It seems fairly certain, as Roscoe Small long ago demonstrated,[2] that *What You Will* reacts at various points to Jonson's *Cynthia's Revels* and *Every Man out of his Humour.* These few moments are not vital determinants in the shape of the play, but it is also claimed that one of its main characters, Lampatho Doria, was meant to represent Ben Jonson. This identification has never been seriously questioned, but it seems to me highly dubious.

Probably the most effective way to portray a public figure on the stage is to stress his best-known characteristics. We do have a definite portrait of Jonson in *Satiromastix.* It shows him to be a professional man of letters, someone who earned his living by writing. It alludes to most of the stale pieces of scandal and gossip which had been attached to his name: that he had been a bricklayer and an actor, that he had saved himself from hanging by penning "neck verses," and that he was dark and ugly. *What You Will* mentions none of this about Lampatho or any other character. Aside from a few references to his dark cloak and his "taber face" — most of the characters are described as beardless, probably to accentuate the fact that they are chorister-actors — the only specific description of Lampatho Doria is given by Meletza, the wittiest and most levelheaded woman in the play, when she first sees him: "A pretty youth, a pretty well-shapt youth, a good leg, a very good eye, a sweet ingenious face, and I warrant a good witte, nay which is more, if hee bee poore I assure my soule hee is chaste and honest, good faith I fancy, I fancie him, I and I may chance — well, Ile thinke the rest" (II, 280). As the last words suggest, Meletza, an heiress with ten thousand crowns, instantly falls in love with Lampatho and is about to marry him at the conclusion of the play.

[1] It was entered in the Stationers' Register on Aug. 6, 1607, and printed the same year. All arguments for an earlier date derive from its alleged connections with the War of the Theaters and subjective impressions of Marston's stylistic development.

[2] *The Stage Quarrel between Ben Jonson and the So-Called Poetasters* (Breslau, 1899), pp. 101–114.

Not only does Lampatho not resemble Jonson; his background is also significantly different. He had been a scholar with a special interest in philosophy. Moreover, he pursued his studies in an academic environment: "Lamp-oyle, watch Candles, Rug-gownes & small juice,/Thin commons, foure a clock rising, I renounce you all" (II, 278). Disillusioned with the aridity and fruitlessness of his endeavors, he turned into a "railer" and, one gathers from a sample of his style, into a verse satirist. We learn that he also wrote plays, one of which was to be produced for the entertainment of the Duke. Its title, *Temperance,* adds more doubt about Lampatho's representing Jonson, for this is the kind of play a cloistered academic might write for intramural entertainment, as we saw in the case of *Histriomastix.* If Lampatho did represent Jonson, it is difficult to detect an unpleasant, satiric portrait like that of Crispinus (Marston) in *The Poetaster* or of Horace (Jonson) in *Satiromastix.* Instead of receiving an "untrussing" in the fifth act, Lampatho wins the most attractive woman in the play; and although some of his actions are foolish, he is given the play's most impressive speech.

If Lampatho "represents" anybody, several details point to Marston himself. At one point he is called by the name with which Marston signed *The Scourge of Villanie* (a name well enough known to have been applied to him in one of the *Parnassus* plays): "Away Idolater, why you *Don Kynsayder*/ Thou Canker eaten rusty curre" (II, 248). Also, Marston's satires reveal a detailed, technical interest in philosophy. After leaving Oxford, he did become a "railer," one whose poems sounded very much like some of Lampatho's speeches, and he did write a play, *Histriomastix,* which came closer to a morality play than anything Jonson ever wrote. I am not suggesting that Marston was representing himself on the stage, merely that Lampatho embodies some of his traits and almost none of Jonson's.

Whatever its role in the War of the Theaters, Marston's achievement in *What You Will* was to dramatize the world of his verse satires without recourse to an intrusive representation of his own point of view. The Venice of this play (far less Italianate than in the *Antonio* plays) swarms with young gallants performing familiar antics. There is a love-sick amorist, an assortment of clothes-crazy, mindless ninnies, a faithless wife, and a libertine prince. It is a world where "*Pitty* and *Piety* are long since dead"; where only "a mad man would terme *Fortune* blind," since she can "see to wound desert so right/Just in the speeding place" (II, 238). Governed by a Duke who burns petitions unread and demands ever-new sensual delights, "The *Venice* state is young, loose, and un-knit,/Can rellish naught, but lushious vanities" (II, 259). Because clothes are more important than what is beneath, the hero, Albano, has a nearly impossible task in trying to prove his identity inasmuch as an impersonator is wearing his clothes. Although the impersonator is a perfumer and vastly different from the sometimes heroic Albano ("thrice was he made,/In dangerous armes *Venice providetore*" [II, 241]), he can easily perform his assignment because, as someone laments, "Ap-parail's growne a God" to the "Idolatrous vulgar, that worship Images" (II, 260).[3]

It is a matter of some urgency for Albano to prove that the rumors of his drowning are untrue because his wife, having already waited three months, like King Hamlet's wife,[4] is on the verge of marriage to an impecunious French knight. Albano's brothers and one of the knight's rivals have disguised the perfumer in order to block the marriage or, at least, provide their sister-in-law with a more suitable match. Unfortunately, the news of the plot quickly leaks out so that when the real Albano appears on the scene, everyone treats him like an im-poster. To all this, the hero responds with angry diatribes which degenerate into stuttering incoherence, followed by the despairing phrase, "What You Will." The tone is one of boisterous gaiety in the tradition of "festive comedy," as Marston reminds us: "Ist not some feast-day? you are all ranke drunke!" (II, 269).

But Marston complicates the tone by providing the returned husband with serious speeches in the vein of *The Scourge of Villanie*. At times, Albano sounds like an absolute idealist in this world of clothes and appearances:

> If love be holy, if that mistery,
> Of co-united hearts be sacrament,
> If the unbounded goodnesse have infus'd
> A sacred ardor of a mutuall love

[3] In a subplot, by the simple process of dressing a page as a woman, the fool Simplicius is gulled out of his money by some witty pages.

[4] The connection is frequently made: "thinke whose wife she was" (II, 241); "Me thinkes I see him now how he would walke" (II, 241); "his wifes most infamous lewd hast [in remarrying]" (II, 244). Albano's page indicates the length of their separation, "Thrice hath the horned mone — ," but is interrupted by Albano's diatribe against Celia's inconstancy (II, 262) in language reminiscent of Hamlet's against Gertrude in the closet scene.

> Into our *Speties,* if those amorous joyes,
> Those sweetes of life, those comfortes even in death
> Spring from a cause above our reasones reach,
> If that cleere flame deduce his heate from heaven,
> Tis like his cause eternall, alwaies one,
> As is th'instiller of devinest love
> Unchanged by time, immortall mauger death.
>
> (II, 262–263)[5]

But he also sounds like the speaker in the Satires, employing the very voice we became familiar with there:

> the soule of man is rotten
> Even to the core; no sound affection.
> Our love is hollow-vaulted, stands on proppes
> Of circumstance, profit or ambitious hopes. (II, 263)

In the world of "what you will," he asks whether anything "exists" apart from one's opinion of it:

> Doth not *Opinion* stamp the currant passe,
> Of each mans valew, vertue, quality?
> Had I ingross'd the choice commodities
> Of heavens trafike, yet reputed vile
> I am a rascall . . .
> . . . if *Albanos* name
> Were liable to scence, that I could tast or touch
> Or see, or feele it, it might tice beleefe,
> But since tis voice, and ayre, come to the Muscat boy,
> *Francisco,* that's my name tis right, I, I,
> What do you lack? what ist you lack? right, that's my
>   cry. (II, 269)

In Venice, it is better to be vile than vile esteemed. A positivist epistemology is pervasive, expressed most explicitly by the Epicurean Quadratus: *"Naughtes knowne but by exterior sence"* (II, 252).

Albano's problem is to gain acceptance from a Venice which already has one more Albano than it wants. In the subplot we watch another character, Lampatho Doria, being cajoled into accepting the society of Venice. The stages of his career would have been as familiar to Marston's audience as the terms

---

[5] I have incorporated the editor's suggested emendations, as I do with several subsequent quotations.

used to describe it. As a scholar he had been obsessed with ascertaining the true nature of the soul:

> I was a scholler: seaven use-full springs
> Did I defloure in quotations
> Of crossd oppinions boute the soule of man;
> The more I learnt the more I learnt to doubt,
> Knowledge and wit, faithes foes, turne fayth about.
>
> (II, 257)

But as he expatiates on the theme of his fruitless quest, he is frequently interrupted by a fool summoning him to join a company of "sweet gallants." This places the speech, one of the most vivid in Marston's plays, in an ironic framework because renunciation of his old studies apparently leaves him no alternative but acceptance of the values of the so-called "honest" Epicure. Nonetheless, it is a speech which must have awakened sympathetic recollections in most of Marston's audience:

> Honest *Epicure.* Nay marke list, *Delight,*
> *Delight* my spaniell slept, whilst I bausd leaves,
> Tossd ore the dunces, por'd on the old print
> Of titled wordes, and stil my spaniell slept.
> Whilst I wasted lampoile, bated my flesh,
> Shrunk up my veines, and still my spaniel slept.
> And still I held converse with *Zabarell,*
> *Aquinas, Scotus,* and the musty *sawe*
> Of antick *Donate,* still my spaniell slept:
> Still went on went I, first *an sit anima,*
> Then and it were mortall, O hold! hold!
> At that they are at braine buffets fell by the eares,
> A maine pell mell togither — still my spaniell slept.
> Then whether twere Corporeall, Local, fixt,
> Extraduce, but whether't had free will
> Or no, ho! Philosophers
> Stood banding factions all so strongly propt,
> I staggerd, knew not which was firmer part.
> But thought, quoted, reade, observ'd and pried,
> Stufft noting bookes, and still my spaniell slept.
> At length he wakt and yawned, and by yon sky,
> For aught I know he knew as much as I. (II, 257–258)

The brilliance of this speech, with its precise references, its sense of physical battle, its breathless inclusiveness, and its refrain-like use of the contrast to the semiallegorical spaniel, has obscured the implications of the intellectual tradition in which it must be placed. As writers like Cornelius Agrippa had shown, Lampatho's project was a prime example of the "vanity" of learning; it was as foredoomed to failure as squaring the circle. Thomas Nashe (under Agrippa's influence) speaks in *The Anatomie of Absurditie* about people who ask "such unnecessary questions": "Wherefore, even as he that enterpriseth to saile over the endlesse Ocean, whiles he cannot passe any further is constrained to returne by the way he came, so these men [who study the soul] beginning to sound the infinite depth of these misteries in ignorance, are faine to cease in ignorance." But Nashe points a moral which Lampatho fails to notice: "let them therefore refraine from such folly, and not seeke that which is not to be found, least they find not that which is to be found." [6] However impressive Lampatho's studies may sound, they have been a form of folly; but so also is his decision to throw over the pursuit of all knowledge on the basis of the futility of these endeavors. Socrates arrived at the same conclusion as Lampatho's despairing "I know, I know naught, but I naught do know" (II, 258), but for him this was a form of knowledge, a discovery, not the cause of despair.

Lampatho goes on to describe what happened when he left the academic cloister:

> when I crept abroad,
> Finding my numnesse in this nimble age,
> I fell a railing. (II, 258)

By "railing" Marston wants us to understand that Lampatho became something like a formal verse satirist; as I mentioned earlier, he is even called by Marston's satiric pseudonym, "Don Kynsayder." Marston ascribes Lampatho's satiric activity to bitterness. Not only has his scholarship been fruitless, it has left him too "numb" to make his way in the "nimble" world of Venice. Thus he had taken upon himself the role of "executioner to vice" (II, 266) in a tone and language indistinguishable from Marston's satires:

> Ile stand as confident as *Hercules*,
> And with a frightlesse resolution,
> Rip up and launce our times impieties. (II, 265)

[6] *The Works of Thomas Nashe,* ed. Ronald B. McKerrow (Oxford, 1958), I, 47.

But by the time Lampatho utters these words, he is really mimicking attitudes he no longer holds. Here he intones them before publicly announcing that he has rejected railing and that his "humor's chang'd" (II, 266).

The change is effected by one of Marston's most interesting characters, Quadratus, a witty Epicure with a bewildering variety of attitudes. In the first scene, for instance, he satirizes an amorist, justly we feel, for his foolish despair, but characteristically he argues his case by developing the paradox that hate is a worthier emotion than love:

> Love? hang love,
> It is the abject out-cast of the world,
> Hate all things, hate the world, thy selfe, all men,
> Hate knowledge . . .
> All thinges are error, durt and nothing,
> Or pant with want or gorg'd to lothing,
> Love onely hate, affect no higher
> Then praise of heaven, wine, a fire. (II, 238–239)

This line of argument is an understandable reaction to the lover Iacomo's romantic outbursts, and it does transform him. After Iacomo is ridiculed by his mistress (Albano's apparent widow), he vows vengeance and invents the plot to disguise the perfumer.

Our next impressions of Quadratus are more complicated. At the home of Laverdure, the foolish French knight whom Albano's "widow" is about to marry, Quadratus observes Lampatho feigning abject admiration for this foolish clothes-horse in order to laugh at his antics. Quadratus indignantly rejects Lampatho's invitation to join the fun, to "shoote him through and through with a jest" (II, 247). Instead, Quadratus mounts a brilliant ironic eulogy of "phantasticknesse." He defends the right to affectations and scorns

> the frownes of a ragg'd *Satyrist,*
> A skrubbing railer whose course harden'd fortune . . .
> Skoules at the fortune of the fairer *Merit.* (II, 249)

He professes to see in "Phantasticknesse,"

> That which the naturall *Sophysters* tearme
> *Phantusia incomplexa* . . . a function
> Even of the bright immortal part of man.

> It is the common passe, the sacred dore,
> Unto the prive chamber of the soule:
> That bar'd: nought passeth past the baser Court
> Of outward scence: by it th'inamorate
> Most lively thinkes he sees the absent beauties
> Of his lov'd mistres.
> By it we shape a new creation
> Of things as yet unborne, by it wee feede
> Our ravenous memory, our intention feast:
> Slid he thats not Phantasticall's a beast. (II, 250)

As the language reveals, Quadratus' defense is not serious. It is, as Lampatho comments, a "Most Phantasticall protection of Phantasticknesse" (II, 250), a piece of "naturall" sophistry in which Quadratus is seeing how far he can develop a paradox. It is not a valid criticism of Lampatho, however much he ought to be chastised. The claim that each of us is different and that satirists want us all to be the same is one thing. But to claim, as Quadratus does in a summary of this argument, *"Tis hell to runne in common base of men"* (II, 250) is to carry the point to absurdity, particularly when Quadratus' defense includes the "inamorates" whom he ridiculed in the first scene.

However extravagant and irresponsible Quadratus' argument, his main purpose is to steer Lampatho away from the fruitless habit of raillery: "pluck out your snarling phanges. When thou hast meanes be Phantasticall and sociable; goe to, heres my hand: and you want fortie shillings I am your *Maecenas*" (II, 251). Quadratus can detect foolishness and absurdity as clearly as Lampatho, but to him it does not seem worth the trouble to rail against it. It is more important to satisfy one's physical needs, as he says in the song which summarizes his brand of Epicureanism: *"Musick, Tobacco, Sack, and Sleepe,/ The tide of Sorrow backward keepe"* (II, 252). The wise man should drink deeply, ignore the claims of glory, fame, and honor, and satisfy his senses:

> *Ile strive to be nor great nor smale,*
> *To live nor die, fate helmeth all,*
> *When I can breath no longer, then,*
> *Heaven take all, there put Amen.* (II, 253)

From his point of view, satiric railing merely hinders one's opportunities to pluck the "lushious vanities" of Venice. Lampatho sees the point and resolves to play the game:

> grumbling hate lye stil
> And turne Phantastique: he that climbes a hill
> Must wheele about: the ladder to account
> Is slie dissemblance, he that meanes to mount,
> Must lye all levell in the prospective
> Of eager sighted greatnesse: thou wouldst thrive,
> The *Venice* state is young, loose, and unknit,
> Can rellish naught, but lushious vanities.
> Goe fit his tooth, O glavering flatterie,
> How potent art thou, front looke briske and sleeke,
> That such base durt as you should dare to reeke
> In Princes nostrils! (II, 259)

The hill he means to climb is not Mount Parnassus or the huge hill where, according to Donne, Truth stands: it is the "ladder" to worldly success. Instead of smashing the world, he will fit the tooth of the age and try to make his way. Quadratus attacks Lampatho's satiric methods not because he wants to teach him a better, more indirect method (as has been claimed), but because he wants him to adopt the life of an Epicurean "temporist," one who plays the game according to society's rules in order to enjoy its luscious sweets.

The last stage in Quadratus' conversion of Lampatho occurs in the fourth act when he introduces him to a group of wealthy young women. Lampatho is shy and inept in their company and realizes that his life of "thin commons" and "foure a clock rising" has made him "a meere Scholler, that is a meere sot" (II, 278). Quadratus resolves to tutor him in the ways of the world:

> Come then Lampe, ile powre fresh Oyle into thee,
> Apply thy spirit that it may nimbly turne,
> Unto the habit, fashion of the age,
> Ile make thee man the Scholler, inable thy behaviour,
> Apt for the intertaine of any presence:
> Ile turne thee gallant, first thou shalt have a Mistresse.
>
> (II, 279)

It is through such means, according to Quadratus' joke, that Lampatho will finally learn the nature of the soul:

> There's more Philosophy, more theoremes,
> More demonstrations, all invincible,
> More cleare divinity drawne on her cheeke,

> Then in all volumes tedious paraphrase
> Of musty eld. O who would staggering doubt
> The soules eternity, seeing it hath
> Of heavenly beauty, but to case it up. (II, 279)

Lampatho proves to be most susceptible to female beauty and instantly catches Meletza's eye. But he nearly ruins his chances of winning her and her ten thousand crowns by falling into the unsophisticated love language of "compliment": "My soul's intranc'd, your favor doth transport/My scence past scence, by your adored graces,/I doat, am rapt" (II, 280). Meletza sends him packing for failing to court her with the fashionable indifference which he initially affected, but by the end of the play they are clearly on the verge of matrimony. Don Kynsayder will become domesticated. According to Quadratus, God made Lampatho "a good foole, and happy and ignorant, and amarous, and riche and fraile, and a Satyrist, and an *Essayest,* and sleepy, and proud, and indeed a foole" (II, 279). Now he can realize all these potentialities and rail no more.[7]

We are left wondering what Marston felt about such a conversion and such a tutor. Clearly he describes Venice in a way that suggests distaste; and there are some hints that as attractive and cultivated as Quadratus appears, Marston disapproved of him, as when he responds to Lampatho's criticism that he is "so square" that he "skorne[s] reproofe":

> No sir should discreete *Mastigophoros*
> Or the deere spirit acute *Canaidus,*
> (That *Aretine;* that most of me belov'd
> Who in the rich esteeme I prize his soule
> I terme my selfe) should these once menace me,
> Or curbe my humors with well-govern'd check,
> I should with most industrious regard,
> Observe, abstaine, and curbe my skipping lightnesse.
> (II, 249–250)

It has often been observed that Marston is alluding here to a speech by Crites in *Cynthia's Revels:*

---

[7] Marston gives us an analogous action, in the conversion of the page Holifernes Pippo, in a subplot. We first see him in the schoolroom on the verge of receiving a beating for doing his Latin poorly. He is rescued from his arid exercises and hired as a page by the fool Simplicius. He becomes a true Venetian through a formal induction into the appallingly sophisticated Court of Pages by their "prince" Bydet (Pippo's equivalent of Quadratus); his initiation requires participation in the successful plot mentioned above (n. 3), to gull his master.

> If good *Chrestus,*
> *Euthus,* or *Phronimus,* had spoke the words,
> They would have moov'd me, and I should have call'd
> My thoughts, and actions, to a stricter accompt
> Upon the hearing.[8]

But it is difficult to see how this echo satirizes Jonson. Instead, it underlines the difference in values between Crites and Quadratus. The unusual name Mastigophoros ("scourge-bearer") must refer to a specific person because Marston also mentions him in his defense of *Pigmalion's Image.*[9] In that context Marston certainly did not regard him as "discreete" or friendly. Marston's attitude toward "Canaidus" is even clearer, for the satires reveal a distinct distaste for Aretino in at least two passages. In one, he speaks of the fact that for "his ranck Fico" Aretino is "surnam'd divine." [10] Quadratus uses the term "fico" twice. Marston makes it clear that despite his pleasant facade Quadratus is an Aretino-like, Epicurean libertine: hence, hardly a model.

But without hints from the actors' tone and manner, it is not until the last scene that we can be certain of the controlling point of view from which the play was written. The scene starts by seeming to demonstrate the ultimate bankruptcy of Epicurean values. A tired sensualist, the Duke, enters, preceded by "as many Pages with Torches as you can" (II, 290). He reveals his boredom with the ordinary run of pleasures:

> Still these same bauling pipes, sound softer straines,
> Slumber our scence, tut these are vulgar straines,
> Cannot your trembling wiers throw a chaine
> Of powerfull rapture bout our mazed scence?
> Why is our chaire thus cushion'd tapistry?
> Why is our bed tired with wanton sportes? (II, 290)

Quadratus offers to provide him with a new kind of excitement:

> and thy scence would banquit in delightes,
> Appropriat to the bloud of Emperors,
> Peculier to the state of Majesty,

[8] *Ben Jonson,* ed. C. H. Herford and Percy and Evelyn Simpson (Oxford, 1932), IV, 87–88, ll. 18–24.
[9] In Marston's "prayse" of *Pigmalion,* he mentions laying open his "faults to *Mastigophoros* eyne" (*Poems of John Marston,* ed. Arnold Davenport [Liverpool, 1961], p. 66, l. 38).
[10] SV, III, 79–80.

> That none can rellish but dilated greatnesse,
> Vouchsafe to view the structure of a sceane
> That stands on tragike sollid passion. (II, 291)

He proceeds to deliver a monologue on Cato's suicide, a favorite topic in the Renaissance, and one which was frequently invoked in discussions of the moral implications of such an act. Quadratus employs it in a very different, Epicurean way:

> Suppose this flowre the *City utica*,
> The time the night that prolong'd *Catos* death:
> Now being plac'd moung his Philosophers,
> These first discourse the soules eternity. (II, 291)

At this point Marston inserts an extradramatic comment which, as much as anything in the play, helps regulate our attitude toward Quadratus. Iacomo suddenly bursts out: "*Cato* grantes that [that is, the "soules eternity"] I am sure, for he was valiant, and honest, which an *Epicure* nere was, and a coward never will be" (II, 291). This harsh, utterly gratuitous judgment tends to undercut the rest of Quadratus' speech:

> Then *Cato* holdes a distinct notion,
> Of individuall actions after death:
> This being argu'd his resolve maintaines
> A true magnanimous spirit should give up durt
> To durt, and with his owne flesh dead his flesh,
> Fore chance should force it crouch unto his foe:
> To kill ones selfe some I, some hold it no:
> O these are pointes would intice away ones soule,
> To break's indenture of base prentisage,
> And run away from's boddy in swift thoughts
> To melt in contemplation — lushious sweetes.
> Now my voluptious Duke Ile feede thy scence,
> Worth his creation. (II, 291–292)

Lampatho wrestled with such "pointes" in order to decide which was true. For an Epicurean who believes that they are ultimately insoluble and that the soul is not immortal, such philosophizing can only be justified as a springboard for aesthetic amusement. Hence, Quadratus' ironic speech amounts to another expression of his "what you will" philosophy. The whole speech is a tour de force: he is saying something out of the ordinary merely to catch the Duke's attention. As with the encomium on behalf of "phantasticknesse," we must take Quadratus' dramatic monologue as an "entertainment."

Quadratus' discourse is interrupted by the urgent matter of validating Albano's identity. He and his double present their cases to the Duke. But nothing less than what Aristotle has called the least artistic kind of recognition scene can prove to the assembled throng that Albano is who he claims to be: he must show the inevitable birthmark in this society where clothes can disguise anything, where, to repeat Albano's words, he could convince only "if *Albanos* name/Were liable to scence" (II, 269). Here, we recall, *"naughtes knowne but by exterior sence"* (II, 252).

Yet finally, Albano, like Lampatho, is drawn into the Venetian world. After having been driven nearly frantic by his plight (compare II, 292), he, too, succumbs with great speed. Once his identity is accepted and he regains his rightful place, he sounds remarkably like Quadratus:

> Wast even so yfaith why then caprichious mirth,
> Skip light moriscoes in our frolick bloud,
> Flaggd veines, sweete, plump with fresh-infused joyes:
> . . . come love daunce,
> Court gallants court, suck amorous dalliance. (II, 294)

Accepted, he becomes accepting, and immediately forgets his idealism. Thus it is in total triumph that Quadratus, now a master of revels, addresses the concluding speech to the audience as well as to the cast:

> Live still springing hopes, still in fresh new joyes,
> May your loves happy hit in faire cheekt wives,
> Your flesh still plumpe with sap'd restoratives,
> That's all my honest frolick heart can wish,
> A Fico for the mew and Envious pish,
> Till night, I wish good food, and pleasing day,
> But then sound rest, so ends our slight writ play.
>
> (II, 295)

The "honest" Epicure thoughtfully prays for restoratives (Eringoes, candied lettuce, etc.: the usual allusion to aphrodisiacs) so that we may find "fresh new joyes." It is a speech altogether in character and it reveals a remarkable unity and clarity of purpose in the play. If the date ascribed to this play is correct (ca. 1601), Marston in *What You Will* made an impressive jump toward dramatic mastery. He produced a nearly objective, detached, and ironic view of the fallen world, the world of the "Cynicke Satyre":

> A Man, a man, a kingdome for a man.
> Why how now currish mad *Athenian?*
> Thou Cynick dogge, see'st not streets do swarme
> With troupes of men? No, no, for *Circes* charme
> Hath turn'd them all to swine.[11]

After the "honest" Epicure has expressed his hope for a mass distribution of "restoratives," it is left to us to recall the prayer with which Marston concluded the satire: "Returne, returne sacred *Synderesis*." [12]

Quadratus' closing speech should remind us how closely this play adheres to the interests of a special audience. "Restoratives" is one hint, but even more revealing is the hope that the audience will gain "faire cheekt wives." Like many of Marston's plays, this one is about and for young men, especially those with a special background. A few references require a close knowledge of Marston's previous work, "Don Kinsayder," "Mastigophoros," "Canaidus": strictly inner circle material for the cognoscenti. Other passages, notably Lampatho's "spaniel" speech and Quadratus' speech on Cato Utican, presume an educated, if not a learned, audience.

Additionally, like many of Marston's plays, *What You Will* has a literary, to some extent, a parasitic, quality by virtue of its relationship to plays that were on the boards elsewhere. Once more, there is a connection with *Hamlet*. There are also many superficial resemblances to *Twelfth Night* — the title, the mistaken identities, the similarity between Simplicius' gulling and Malvolio's, and, especially, the festive atmosphere. But mention of the atmosphere helps to define a fundamental difference between the two plays. Shakespeare uses holiday festivity and revelry as agents of release which lead to a clarification of experience.[13] The special nature of the experience is both refining and purgative so that after the holiday is over a richer view of experience emerges. Marston's use of the festive atmosphere is simpler. It is a metaphor of how the world appears, not only in holiday, but at all times. Venice resembles

---

[11] Ibid., VII, 1–5.

[12] Ibid., VIII, 211.

[13] I am employing the terms which C. L. Barber formulates in Chapter I of *Shakespeare's Festive Comedy* (Princeton, 1959).

Olivia's house during the "uncivil rule" of Sir Toby Belch's drinking party. This is the realization which Lampatho and Albano learn to live with and to which Quadratus has comfortably accommodated himself. It is a world where the Lord of Liberty rules unchecked and where Humanity has no place. Quadratus' advice is only slightly facetious: "Hate knowledge, strive not to be over-wise,/'It drew distruction into Paradise'" (p. 238). Venice resembles Nathanael West's vision of California, a world without a past, lacking connections with any traditional values. There are not even any Malvolios for Sir Toby to flout. But it is not really a tolerant, open society. You must join it on its terms; no plays on Temperance will be allowed. Although the tone of the play is farcical and amused, the implications for the young men in the audience should have been as depressing as anything in the *Parnassus* plays. When in Venice, you must act like the Venetians: "the ladder to account/Is slie dissemblance" (II, 259).

XI *The Malcontent*:
Virtuous Machiavellianism

Marston modestly admits in the preface to one of his later plays that *"above better desert"* he has been *"fortunate in these stage-pleasings."* [1] There is reason to believe that his work was usually well received in the circles I have been describing, but with *The Malcontent* in 1604 he momentarily achieved a wider popularity. [2] Three quartos of this play were required in less

[1] *The Fawne, Plays of John Marston*, ed. H. Harvey Wood (3 vols., Edinburgh, 1934–1939), II, 143.

[2] Nothing has been discovered to dislodge the conclusion of E. K. Chambers, *The Elizabethan Stage* (Oxford, 1923), III, 432, that *The Malcontent* "is Marston's first play for the Queen's Revels after the formation of the syndicate early in 1604." G. K. Hunter in "English Folly and Italian Vice," *Jacobean Theatre*, Stratford-upon-Avon Studies, I (London, 1960), p. 100, mentions that

than six months, and the King's Men judged it to have a broad enough appeal for production at the Globe.[3] The reasons are not hard to discover. It has an exciting plot with a multitude of surprising twists, and in the Hamlet-like title figure Marston created a fascinating role worthy of the actor who played it, Richard Burbage.

But even with Burbage and the other immortals, a production of *The Malcontent* in the vast open spaces of the Globe must have been unsatisfactory. The cramped, claustrophobic setting of a private theater is absolutely essential to Marston's purposes. Using techniques prophetic of German Expressionist drama of the 1920's, the play opens with a barrage of olfactory and aural effects. First, the stage direction tells us, we hear the "vilest out of tune Musicke," after which an opening dialogue between two minor characters establishes the atmosphere:

> BILIOSO: Why how now? are ye mad? or drunke? or both? or what?
>
> PRAEPASSO. Are ye building *Babilon* there?
>
> BILI. Heer's a noyse in Court, you thinke you are in a Taverne, do you not?
>
> PRAEP. You thinke you are in a brothell house doe you not? This roome is ill sented. [*Enter one with a Perfume.*] So; perfume; perfume; some upon me, I pray thee: The Duke is upon instant entrance; so, make place there." (I, 145)

"Heer round about is hell" (I, 204) in a "world . . . turnde upside downe" (I, 177).

In this heightened version of the world of *What You Will,* men are constantly "bewitched" (I, 157) and "beseld" (I, 165)

The Malcontent reflects "much borrowing from Guarini's *Pastor Fido.*" Following Hunter's suggestion, Bernard Harris in his edition of *The Malcontent,* New Mermaid Series (London, 1967), has demonstrated that Marston drew heavily, often nearly verbatim, on an anonymous English translation entitled *Il Pastor Fido or the Faithfull Shepheard* (London, 1602). Perhaps it was awareness of this fact that led Edward Phillips, *Theatrum Poetarum* (London, 1675), p. 113, to ascribe to Marston "the *Faithful Sheapherd* a Pastoral" — although this attribution is almost certainly incorrect. Discovery of this source effectively refutes those who would revive E. E. Stoll's theory that *The Malcontent* dates from 1600 and precedes *Hamlet*; it must postdate the translation of 1602. And in view of Marston's heavy reliance on a notoriously poor translation, this discovery also casts doubt on Marston's mastery of Italian.

[3] After a thorough study of the quartos, M. L. Wine, ed., *The Malcontent,* Regents Renaissance Drama Series (Lincoln, Neb., 1964), p. xv, concluded that since the augmented version "has indications of authorial revision," it was not really pirated.

by their senses. They are helpless before those who would
inflame them:

> in an *Italian* lascivious Pallace, a Lady gardianlesse,
> Left to the push of all allurement,
> The strongest incitements to immodestie,
> To have her bound, incensed with wanton sweetes,
> Her veines fild hie with heating delicates,
> Soft rest, sweete Musick, amorous Masquerers, lascivious
> banquets, sinne it selfe gilt ore, strong phantasie tricking
> up strange delights, presenting it dressed pleasingly to
> sence, sence leading it unto the soule, confirmed with
> potent example, impudent custome inticed by that great
> bawd opportunitie, thus being prepar'd, clap to her easie
> eare, youth in good clothes, well shapt, rich, faire-spoken,
> promising-noble, ardent bloud-full, wittie, flattering:
> *Ulisses* absent, *O Ithaca,* can chastest *Penelope,* hold
> out. (I, 179)[4]

Through such speeches and through symbolic actions, Marston
takes great pains throughout the play to create an atmosphere
of overpowering, nearly irresistible corruption. Life in the palace is imaged by a symbolic dance (IV.ii.) which is far removed
from Davies' heavenly ritual of love and harmony. Instead, it is
a "brawle" — the pun alludes to a complex French dance —
resembling in its meaningless intricacy and confusion a "maze"
where "honor" is lost (I, 188).

Atmosphere and action are inextricably intertwined in this
play; each infects the other. In the second act, for example, the
Duke plans to catch his wife in the arms of her latest lover,
having been informed of the tryst by her former lover. What
could have occupied one scene is broken into three, with each
of these punctuated by scenes in other parts of the palace. First
we see the new lover slip into the duchess' chamber while the old
lover (the worst villain in the play) exults in his imminent
vengeance (II.i.). Then we hear court ladies exchange dirty
jokes about cuckolding and aphrodisiacs with the Malcontent,
Malevole (II.ii.), after which the scene shifts to the last-minute
preparations of the group of courtiers who are to break in upon
the lovers (II.iii.). Once more there is a shift to the ladies, who

---

[4] It has been customary to set this entire passage as poetry although all three
quartos show a portion of it as prose. I prefer to leave it as printed because
Marston appears to have taken some pains with the text and because it is characteristic of Malevole's speeches to hover ambiguously between poetry and
prose. Moreover, some of the lines in this passage resist being chopped into
pentameters.

make amoral comments about the necessity of caring for their beauty as they sip a newly concocted "posset," a beautifier and "restorative" (II.iv.). At the end of the scene we hear music emanating from the duchess' chamber to remind us of what is going on there, and only then do we see the violent scene in which the duchess is publicly disgraced and her lover wounded (II.v.). The cause-effect relationship between these apparently disparate activities is clear. Women who have such matters on their minds will fall into such situations. When the speech about the dangers in an *"Italian* lascivious pallace"* (quoted above) is delivered a few scenes later, its truth has already been demonstrated.

The upshot of the action I have just summarized is that the villainous Mendoza regains his position as the Duchess' lover and as the Duke's favorite and successor. Moreover, his cunning plot, concocted at a moment when he seemed to have been outfoxed, leads to further success. Angered by her public humiliation, the Duchess resolves to revenge herself on her husband. In an instant she invents a plot which reveals her own high competence in the intricacies of *Realpolitik*:

> Ile make thee Duke, we are of *Medices,*
> *Florence* our friend, in court my faction
> Not meanly strength-full; the Duke then dead,
> We well prepar'd for change: the multitude
> Irresolutely reeling: we in force:
> Our partie seconded: the kingdom mazde:
> No doubt of swift successe all shall be grac'd. (I, 171)

The activities just described are normal in the palace. The *"unquiet studies"* of these discontented creatures, in the words of Marston's preface, *"labor innovation, contempt of holy policie, reverent comely superioritie, and establisht unity"* (I, 139). Politically, they engage in usurpations, domestically, in cuckolding. In the Duke's palace the two activities are connected. To gratify these linked appetites, one must be able to plot. The Duchess Aurelia's mastery of this art comes to her naturally because she is a Medici, but there are other great technicians of plotting. The form of the play can be described as a structure of progressively cunning plots; through them, the usurping Duke Pietro is usurped, and the successful usurper, Mendoza, is in turn usurped by the rightful Duke, Altofronto, who has been masking as the Malcontent, Malevole. In this atmosphere plotting is as natural as breathing.

In addition to linking atmosphere and action more profoundly than in his previous plays, Marston has also inhabited the palace with a more fully realized set of characters. The villainous Mendoza is a satiric portrait, but Marston endows him with the ability to express his physical pleasure at being a prince's favorite in remarkably vivid images: "to have a generall timerous respect, observe a man, a statefull scilence in his presence: solitarinesse in his absence, a confused hum and busie murmure of obsequious suters trayning him; the cloth held up, and waye proclaimed before him; Petitionary vassailes licking the pavement with their slavish knees, whilst some odde pallace *Lampreel's* that ingender with Snakes, and are full of eyes on both sides with a kinde of insinuated humblenesse fixe all their delightes upon his browe" (I, 154). In addition to reaching "the *Olympus* of favor" (I, 154), he is ravished by his role as the Duchess' lover. When his ideal situation is threatened, he defends himself with great cunning because he remembers precisely what it feels like to be a menial:

> Shall I whose very humme, strooke all heads bare,
> Whose face made scilence: creaking of whose shooe
> Forc'd the most private passages flie ope,
> Scrape like a servile dog at some latch'd doore?
> Learne now to make a leg? and cry beseech ye,
> Pray yee, is such a Lord within? be aw'd
> At some odde ushers scoft formality?
> First seare my braines: *Unde cadis non quo refert.*
>
> (I, 163)

The Senecan tag is not a revenge play cliché. It is an association which naturally springs to the mind of a Machiavellian. Mendoza is frequently a comic figure, but he is fully imagined and credible.

The Duchess Aurelia is a much slighter portrait, but Marston successfully captures the image of a haughty, passionate aristocrat. She reacts with defiance and extravagant indifference to the public exposure of her immoral conduct and with equally extravagant contrition after she is betrayed by her lover. She dances defiantly when her husband's death is announced, but after her conversion she wears a "mourning habit" and interrupts courtly revels by reciting pious poetry (I, 211).[5]

[5] As Arthur H. Bullen discovered, this poem is by Thomas Bastard, the schoolmate of Hoskins, Davies, and Wotton mentioned in Chapter IV (see also Appendix A). Thus the insertion of this passage is an inner circle allusion, which, through Marston's designation of the author as an "honest Priest" (p. 211),

The weak usurper, Duke Pietro, is also conceived with some psychological subtlety. He is a puppet set up by an outside power and manipulated by Mendoza. Inept at politics, he is, fittingly, also a cuckold. It is this predicament which troubles him most, for his repentant wife's words at the end of the play confirm what we have already seen: "As the soule lov'd the body, so lov'd he" (I, 195). When Pietro is finally compelled to take vengeance, Marston does not use the situation as a pretext for stale jokes about cuckoldry. He makes him into a pitiable and sympathetic figure:

> I strike but yet like him that gainst stone walles
> Directs his shafts, reboundes in his owne face,
> My Ladies shame is mine, O God tis mine.
> Therefore I doe conjure all secrecie,
> Let it be as very little as may be; pray yee, as may be?
> Make frightlesse entrance, salute her with soft eyes,
> Staine nought with blood — onely *Ferneze* dies,
> But not before her browes: O Gentlemen
> God knowes I love her, nothing els, but this,
> I am not well. (I, 166–167)

The request to "salute her with soft eyes" is a delicate touch; it prepares us for Pietro's eventual moral regeneration. He has been living in a fool's paradise, and he eloquently attests to the pain of learning the truth:

> I am not unlike to some sickman,
> That long desired hurtfull drinke; at last
> Swilles in and drinkes his last, ending at once
> Both life and thirst: O would I nere had knowne
> My owne dishonour: good God, that men should
> Desire to search out that, which being found kils all
> Their joye of life: to taste the tree of Knowledge,
> And then be driven out of Paradice. (I, 174)

Pietro is a convincing combination of sensitivity and weakness. He provides a subtle contrast to the two other figures who take their turns as Duke. He lacks the passionate intensity of the one and the moral stature of the other.

---

constitutes a compliment to a friend of several important Middle Templars. Marston's joke on p. 150 about the disappearance of simony in the next age may also have been derived from Bastard's epigram "Ad Thymum," *Chrestoleros* (London, 1598), p. 113.

These are the main ingredients of the world which the hero must set right. Dispossessed of his kingdom and sentenced to exile, the rightful Duke of Genoa, Altofronto, remains at court in the disguise of a "malcontent." This term, which seems to have entered the language in the 1580's, denotes a clearly defined type. A man of some parts, developed by education and foreign travel, the malcontent was poor, usually unemployed, and obsessed by a sense of unrewarded merit; often he was melancholic. Thus he was a prime source of danger to the kingdom since he was readily available for schemes against the established order. In these, he could be relied on to employ special skills acquired in Italy for plotting and murder. As many scholars have pointed out, the malcontent was only in part a literary construction. Economic and political conditions fostered his appearance late in Elizabeth's reign, and, in fact, such men did sow some discord, as Henry Cuffe's role in the Earl of Essex's uprising illustrates. By the time of this play, the malcontent had become a stock figure on the stage. Nevertheless, there must have been special interest attached to a play with this title, written by an author with a reputation for "malcontentedness." [6] The evidence of the preface, the "Prologus," and the Induction indicates that some members of the audience interpreted the play *"with subtilitie (as deepe as hell)"* (I, 139). Marston claimed that it was *"over-cunning"* (I, 139) to ferret out contemporary allusions, but, as we shall see, a few clear examples have survived.

Even if Marston did not conceive the play as having a specific contemporary application, this play, with its suggestively political title, is primarily about the conduct of politics in a world "turnde upside downe" (I, 177). From the first moments it is apparent that the Malcontent is an agent of discord. It is he who produces the "vilest out of tune Musicke" offstage, and his first speech, blurted from the same place, is the verbal equivalent of this discord: "Yaugh, godaman, what do'st thou there: Dukes *Ganimed Junoes* jealous of thy long stockings: shadowe of a woman, what wouldst Weesell? thou lambe a Court: what doost thou bleat for? a you smooth chind Catamite!" (I, 145). This clash of obscene discords seems to mirror a "soule . . . at variance (within her selfe)" (I, 146), as the Duke says in his character sketch of the Malcontent. Although "his speach is halterworthy at all howers," the Duke has licensed him to speak freely in order to help him to "understand those weakenesses which others flattery palliates" (I, 146). Thus the title figure

[6] See the epigram by John Davies of Hereford, quoted below, Chapter XV.

with the name that means "ill will" appears to be a domesticated
malcontent, a Lord of Misrule authorized to castigate the Duke
and his courtiers. He goes at it with wild abandon, changing
his direction at every moment:

> PIETRO. But what's the common newes abroade *Male-*
> *vole,* thou dogst rumor still.
> MALEVOLE. Common newes? why common wordes are,
> God save yee, Fare yee well: common actions, Flattery
> and Cosenage: common things, Women and Cuckolds:
> and how do's my little *Ferrard:* a yee lecherous Animal,
> my little Ferret, he goes sucking up & downe the Pallace
> into every Hens nest like a Weesell: & to what doost
> thou addict thy time to now, more then to those Antique
> painted drabs that are still affected of yong Courtiers,
> Flattery, Pride, & Venery. (I, 147)

This passage has elements of traditional Tudor satire: the
abstractions of the Ship of Fools, the use of the beast fable, and
moral commonplaces. But the rapid shifts and the colloquial
style charge Malevole's satiric prose with a vitality Marston
rarely achieved in his verse satires. In these passages, he adopts
the manner of a vaudeville entertainer, stringing together a
seemingly random series of jests suitable for preservation in a
"table-booke," as the character Sly mentions in the Induction
(I, 141). But the role of entertainer which Altofronto adopts is
part of a more complicated disguise. In an original variation,
Marston's figure is a true malcontent posing as a malcontent.
As a dispossessed duke, Altofronto has a perfect right to the
character of a malcontent. When he describes his malcontented
state without his verbal disguise, there is none of Malevole's
broad, gross-jawed style:

> in night all creatures sleepe,
> Onely the Malecontent that gainst his fate,
> Repines and quarrels, alas hees goodman tell-clocke;
> His sallow jaw-bones sincke with wasting mone,
> Whilst others beds are downe, his pillowes stone. (I, 178)

To regain his kingdom he adopts as his disguise an "affected
straine" which allows him to indulge in *"Free speach":*

> I may speake foolishly, I knavishly,
> Alwaies carelesly, yet no one thinkes it fashion

To poize my breath, "for he that laughs and strikes,
Is lightly felt, or seldome strucke againe." (I, 150–151)

The special quality to Malevole's manner springs from the fact that he is acting: Marston makes us hear the effort it requires for him to sustain his wild and whirling words: "Sir *Tristram Trimtram* come aloft, Jacke-a-napes with a whim wham, heres a Knight of the lande of *Catito* shall play at trap with any Page in Europe; doe the sword daunce, with any Morris-dauncer in Christendome; ride at the Ring till the finne of his eyes looke as blew as the welkin, and runne the wilde-goose chase even with *Pompey* the huge" (I, 148). Through Pietro's comment, "You runne — " (I, 148), Marston suggests his own attitude toward Malevole's style. It is not the idiosyncratic manner of an amusing character like Tucca, nor the acerb commentary of a "pure" malcontent like Bosola, nor a stage version of madness. It is designed to convey a sense of the pressure on someone who is acting a part which is not natural to him and which he occasionally finds odious: "O God, how loathsome this toying is to mee, that a Duke should be forc'd to foole it: well, *Stultorum plena sunt omnia,* better play the foole Lord, then be the foole Lord" (I, 204). He resembles the court fool Passarello, a professional comedian who finds his job a "drudgery" (I, 160) in a world of "loose vanities" (I, 162). "Stultorum plena sunt omnia" is a true saying because if you are not a fool naturally, the world will force you to become one.

The strain and wildness of Malevole's language are justified by his personal plight and by his need for a disguise. The language has the further value of providing an ideal medium in which to express a special view of the world. Malevole is a kind of visionary who sees the waking world as a perpetual nightmare. His "dreams" are the reality which others cannot see:

PIETRO. Dreame, what dreamst?
MALEVOLE. Why me thinkes I see that Signior pawn his footcloth: that *Metreza* her Plate: this madam takes phisick: that that tother *Mounsieur* may minister to her: here is a Pander Jeweld: there is a fellow in shift of Satten this day, that could not shift a shirt tother night: here a *Paris* supports that *Hellen:* theres a Ladie *Guinever* bears up that sir *Lancelot.* Dreames, dreames, visions, fantasies, *Chimeras,* imaginations, trickes, conceits. (I, 147–148)

Throughout the play, Malevole's goal is to make people see the world as his "dreams" have revealed it to him, to make them see how "strange" (to use his recurrent phrase) and vile and unnatural it is. He wants to convert them to his "faith" that, as Pietro comes to realize, "All is damnation, wickedness extreame, there is no faith in man" (I, 193). Sometimes he shows them the invisible truth by inventing an appropriate visual metaphor: "Muckhill overspread with fresh snow" (I, 147), "pigeon house . . . smooth, round, and white without, and full of holes and stinke within" (I, 153). Sometimes he makes people "see" by the detailed evocation of a vivid, concrete picture, as when he describes Aurelia's adultery to Pietro. To excerpt one example from a long speech, he says that even when she does yield *"Hymeneall* sweetes,"

> the thaw of her delight
> Flowes from lewde heate of apprehension,
> Onely from strange imaginations rankenes,
> That formes the adulterers presence in her soule,
> And makes her thinke she clips the foule knaves loines.
> (I, 149)

Pietro reels before Malevole's "Hydeous imagination" (I, 150), but Malevole, in a speech that constitutes one of the most famous expressions of "Jacobean melancholy," forces him to see more and greater horrors:

> th' art but in danger to loose a Dukedome, thinke this: this earth is the only grave and *Golgotha* wherein all thinges that live must rotte: tis but the draught wherein the heavenly bodies discharge their corruption, the very muckhill on which the sublunarie orbes cast their excrement: man is the slime of this dongue-pit, and Princes are the governours of these men: for, for our soules, they are as free as Emperoures, all of one peece, there goes but a paire of sheeres betwixt an Emperoure and the sonne of a bagpiper: only the dying, dressing, pressing, glossing, makes the difference: now, what art thou like to lose?
> *A jaylers office to keepe men in bonds,*
> *Whilst toyle and treason, all lifes good confounds.* (I, 197)

This is the generality to which every detail in the play has been contributing; it is a moving elaboration of Antonio's realization in *Antonio's Revenge* that men are "vermine bred of putrifacted slime" (I, 118). Nor do any subsequent events in the play, not even the "happy" ending, modify its force. Nevertheless, for Malevole, the "Golgotha" speech is also a piece of rhetoric designed to induce Pietro to give up his claim to the dukedom. He responds correctly: "I heere renounce for ever Regency: O *Altofront,* I wrong thee to supplant thy right" (I, 197). Step by step, the Malcontent has educated the usurper to recognize the worthlessness of his office in order that he, Altofronto, may regain it. The only difference between an emperor and a bagpiper is "a paire of sheeres," but Altofronto prefers his own clothes.

Thus the "Golgotha" speech is true, but it is also cunning. It illustrates an art which Altofronto has acquired and mastered. He had lost his dukedom, he explains, because

> I wanted those old instruments of state,
> Dissemblance and suspect: I could not time it *Celso,*
> My throane stood like a point in midd'st of a circle,
> To all of equall neerenesse, bore with none:
> Raind all alike, so slept in fearlesse vertue,
> Suspectles, too suspectles: till the crowde:
> (Still liquerous of untried novelties)
> Impatient with severer government:
> Made strong with *Florence:* banisht *Altofront.* (I, 151)

Since then he has learned to "time it" by waiting for his chance and by prodding his enemies toward their ruin. The experience has taught him that "we are all Philosophicall Monarkes or naturall fooles" (I, 152). Either you stand stiffly aloof from the world, a Stoic sage, speaking sententiously like Altofronto and his impregnable, virtuous wife while your kingdom is stolen away, or you immerse yourself in the world with all its degradation and horror and become nature's fool. To paraphrase, "the Emperor Aurelius may be a model for a Philosophicall Monarke, but don't live in an *Italian* lascivious pallace without Machiavelli."

Thus it is that Malevole can improve on one of Mendoza's plots so impressively that he inspires the unabashed compliment: "ô unpeerable invention, rare, Thou God of pollicie! it hunnies me" (I, 183). Malevole has indeed become the "unpeerable" god of policy in a contest with masters. He can exchange aphrodisiac recipes with court ladies and Machiavellian aphorisms with Mendoza, he can convert Pietro and Aurelia, insult

Bilioso with obscene jokes, and, most importantly, he can fool
Mendoza "most powerfully" (I, 180) with his disguise. But after
bragging about this last accomplishment, he betrays an interesting confusion (whether in Marston or in Altofronto, it is impossible to say). He says caustically that Mendoza

> faine would claspe with me: he is the true slave,
> That will put on the most affected grace,
> For some vilde second cause. (I, 181)

Obviously Altofronto is doing the same thing. He is putting
on an affected "gracelessness" for a "second cause" which he
has shown to be "vilde": the regaining of his "jaylers office" as
duke.

Whether or not Marston intended Altofronto's remark to
be an unwitting partial self-condemnation, other passages suggest that Altofronto's left hand has different values from his
right.[7] After Pietro has relinquished the dukedom, Altofronto
comments on his act in a speech which begins with pious platitudes and ends with a Machiavellian *sententia*:

> Who doubts of providence,
> That sees this change, a heartie faith to all:
> *He needes must rise, who can no lower fall,*
> *For still impetuous* Vicissitude
> *Towzeth the world, then let no maze intrude*
> Upon your spirits: wonder not I rise,
> *For who can sincke, that close can temporize?*
> The time growes ripe for action, Ile detect
> My privat'st plot, lest ignorance feare suspect:
> Let's cloase to counsell, leave the rest to fate,
> *Mature discretion is the life of state.* (I, 198)

Altofronto's position shifts with each sentence. He first claims
that Pietro's conversion should buttress faith in a presiding
moral order, but then uses his own rise to demonstrate Fortune's continuing influence on events in this world; he was so
low that vicissitude had no direction in which to push him but

---

[7] Even the name "Altofronto" has equivocal implications. According to the
most famous book of physiognomy of the period, Joannis Baptista Porta's *De
humana physiognomonia* (Ursel, 1601), p. 127, an "alta frons" signifies firm-
ness and bravery: "Qui frontem altam habent, pertinaces vel audaces sunt." On
the other hand, Malevole says to the cuckold Bilioso, "you have a passing high
forehead" (I, 152). As a duke who has been usurped, having a name associated
with cuckoldom would not be out of place for Altofronto.

upward! Earlier in the play, speaking in the guise of an amoral malcontent, he had said to Mendoza, "only busie fortune towses, and the provident chaunces blends them together; Ile give you a symilie: did you ere see a Well with 2. buckets, whilst one comes up full to be emptied, another goes downe emptie to be filled; such is the state of all humanitie" (I, 181). One man rises at the expense of another: Pietro up, Altofronto down; Mendoza up, Pietro down; Altofronto up, Mendoza down. "This *Genoas* last yeares Duke" (I, 151) gets another turn. But more important than the power of Fortune is his own recent acquisition of "mature discretion." He has learned how to "time it."

The morality which Altofronto is forced to adopt sounds like Mendoza's, but the parallel Marston develops more fully is that between Malevole and the most immoral figure in the play, the bawd Maquerelle. After Mendoza has gained power in Act V, Malevole asks her what she thinks of "this transformation of state now" (I, 201). Her reply is the sexual equivalent of his political metaphor of the two buckets: "wee women always note, the falling of the one, is the rising of the other: . . . as for example, I have two court dogges, the most fawning curres . . . now I, like lady Fortune, sometimes love this dog, sometimes raise that dog" (I, 201–202). She plays Lady Fortune in sexual matters, having brought an uncountable number of "maidenheads . . . to the blocke" (I, 203), just as Malevole manipulates political fortunes. She is the "God of pollicie" in her realm, with her cunning advances in the technology of adultery (I, 161), her possets and resoratives, her tricks for seduction. She is a Machiavelli of the bedchamber who constantly counsels "discretion" (for example, I, 186) and mastery of the art of "timing it" (for example, I, 202). As early as the first act, Malevole hints at some kind of relationship between himself and Maquerelle (I, 148), and in the last act he excuses an action by saying that he did it "as baudes go to Church, for fashion sake" (I, 197). A successful politician, Marston shows, must be something of a bawd.

This parallel makes it clear that the Malcontent is a more complicated figure than he is often thought to be. He is not merely an upholder of virtue whose disguise allows him to satirize everyone at will in an extension of the author's manner. Despite his high moral standards, he has learned the black arts required to manipulate men, as his final plot demonstrates. In an original variant on the formulaic concluding masque of the revenge play, all but one of the masquers whom Malevole employs are apparent murder victims of Mendoza. The villain's response, consistent with the theme Marston has been developing, emphasizes that Altofronto has succeeded in turning dreams into reality:

> Are we surprizde? What strange delusions mocke
> Our sences, do I dreame? or have I dreamt
> This two daies space? where am I? (I, 213)

The reign of the devil has been overthrown, the good are redeemed, the bad are punished. But it is important to notice that Marston does not make extravagant claims for the effect of the experience on the lascivious palace creatures. The courtier Ferneze had been the first of Mendoza's victims after having succeeded him as the Duchess' lover. Rescued by Malevole, he was treated to a moral sermon on the evil effects of lust. During the masque of the revengers he dances with the dissolute Bianca, and his first act on returning to the court is to try to seduce her. With Maquerelle instantly involving herself in the transaction as she had in his earlier effort at seduction, Ferneze's regeneration is not a conspicous success.

Nevertheless, we are back in the virtuous and rational reign of Duke Altofronto, as we see from his just but merciful meting out of punishment. Turning to the arch-villain, Mendoza, he refuses to kill him, explaining that a true monarch, someone with a *"glorious soule,"* disdains to hurt a peasant "prostrat at my feete" (I, 214). Aside from a few hasty lines to tuck in loose ends, the private theater text concludes on this note of self-satisfied grandeur. However, when Marston lengthened the play for public theater performance, he added thirteen lines to Altofronto's speech. These lines are important because they discuss directly the central political problem of the play, how to be both "good" and a "king." Altofronto begins by moralizing about the action of the play:

> O, I have seen strange accidents of state! —
> The flatterer like the Ivy clip the Oke,
> And wast it to the hart: lust so confirm'd
> That the black act of sinne it selfe not shamd
> To be termde Courtship. (I, 214)

Mendoza had made his way by a combination of flattery and lust, as had the courtier Bilioso. But since such activity was not unknown in courts closer than Genoa, Altofronto aims the rest of his oracular speech at the great and sinful rulers of the world:

> O they that are as great as be their sinnes,
> Let them remember that th' inconstant people,
> Love many Princes meerely for their faces,
> And outward shewes: and they do covet more
> To have a sight of these men then of their vertues,
> Yet thus much let the great ones still conceale,
> When they observe not Heavens imposd conditions,
> They are no Kings, but forfeit their commissions. (I, 214)

The people are not loyal to a prince because he is virtuous. As Altofronto has learned to his cost, they are "Impatient with severer government" (I, 151) and want "outward shewes," impressive appearances. But a king cannot commit immoral acts with impunity. He must be a moral ruler, or Heaven will see to his fall. The problem is how to square the requirements of Heaven with those of politics. Altofronto's answer is centered on the word "conceale," the crucial importance of which is often obscured by an emendation (to "conceive") for which there is no textual justification. Altofronto has learned that however virtuous you are, you must conceal it. You can be a philosophical monarch only if you act like a natural fool. You must temporize and pretend to play the game even if it means becoming something of a bawd.

In addition to its general political relevance, this passage was apparently understood to have a contemporary political meaning. In the corrected version of the third quarto, the words "Princes" and "Kings" were changed to "men," the censor suppressing what must have been interpreted as a blow at King James. The claim that kings forfeit their commissions when they fail to observe Heaven's conditions would have sounded like a clear rejection of James's cherished doctrine of Divine Right. Marston's attitude must have been nurtured in the nursery of liberty where he was residing; certainly it would have been approved by many in his audience. With this play Marston began to skirmish in very dangerous territory, as a brief passage from the first quarto demonstrates:

> BEAN[CHA]. And is not sinnior S. *Andrew Iaques* a gallant fellow now.
>
> MAQUERELLE. By my maiden-head la, honour and hee agrees aswell together, as a satten sute and wollen stockings.[8]

---

[8] First quarto, *The Malcontent* (London, 1604), sig. H2v.

That this was a hit at James, and a brutal one at that, is confirmed by the elimination of *"Iaques"* in the second quarto, which thus changed the passage to a general indictment of the Scots. At the same time that *"Iaques"* was eliminated, Marston inserted verses (after the "Epilogus" in the second quarto and designated as the "Prologue" in the third quarto) which attack *"too nice-brained cunning"* for wresting *"each hurtlesse thought to private sence"* (p. 216). These two revisions of the first quarto suggest that *The Malcontent* has a place in the series of politically indiscreet plays for which the Children of the Queen's Revels became notorious.

This is not to suggest that *The Malcontent* was in any important way an attack on the monarch, but its political theme does constitute advice in the "Mirror for Magistrates" tradition to which so many Inns of Court writers had contributed. This political theme did not require the overt statement of the added lines; it is visible in the shorter, private theater version. Early in the first act Malevole mentions the importance of temporizing, and in the world which Marston depicts, only cunning and concealed virtue can survive. Malevole's disguise guards him from real danger, but this does not diminish the insidious nature of the atmosphere he is combating. His role is exemplary. As a satirist and teacher, he shows what the world is; as a god of policy, he shows how to cope with it. It is a joke on the world that an outsider has mastered its tricks, but he can do nothing to eliminate the atmosphere or to regenerate the vermin who pollute it and are in turn polluted by it.

I have been discussing the political and moral implications of *The Malcontent,* but it was through a theatrical innovation that Marston made these moral complexities appear convincing and relevant. He transformed the convention of the disguised revenger by endowing its separate halves with essentially distinct personalities; Malevole-Altofronto has many of the characteristics of a "double" figure. I do not know how much is gained by describing these two halves as the "superego" and the "id"; nonetheless, some signs of that eternal struggle are perceptible, indeed are exploited as part of the total pattern of the play. Thus Malevole-Altofronto impinges on our consciousness at a deeper level than most of Marston's intellectually conceived characters. A further contribution to the richness of the theatrical experience — particularly apparent with the addition of John Webster's Induction in the third quarto, where Burbage appears onstage before the play begins — results from the employment of Malevole as an actor playing the role of an actor. There is no Pirandello-like metaphysics in this device. Role-playing is shown to be a physical necessity for moral man in an immoral society. The pestilential atmosphere communicated through the charged rhetoric and the "Expressionist" stage techniques constitutes Marston's most successful representation of a morally debilitated world. He had shown a comic version of it in *What You Will,* but there the characters tend to be mouthpieces of simple ideas. In the *Antonio* plays, the satiric background is very imperfectly linked to the concerns of the main characters. *The Malcontent* achieves a meaningful union of these components. It possesses the immediacy and credibility of a nightmare.

Because of the play's symbolic and dreamlike atmosphere, its relationship to Marston's audience is not as clear as usual. For example, his protagonist, for the first time, is not a young man. But its ultimate relevance to this audience is of the same order as in most of his plays because its substructure is that of the initiation ritual. It is a demonstration of what it must cost the morally innocent to participate in a degraded society. In this play, Marston's terms are political, but with some exceptions he confines his treatment to general matters of conduct and ethics. In contrast, when he next wrote a play with a disguised duke in an Italian palace, *The Fawne* (1606), his aims were far more immediate and specific. As he learned more about "S. Andrew Iaques," his speech became like Malevole's, "halter-worthy at al howers."

XII *The Dutch Curtezan*:
"Rich Sence" and "Bad Language"

Marston's next dramatic work appears to have been his collaboration with Jonson and Chapman on *Eastward Hoe* (1604–05).[1] It is not possible to isolate the specific contribution of each writer in this remarkably homogeneous and consistent work; hence, it would serve no useful purpose to discuss it here. However, it is noteworthy that the play appeared at the moment when the extravagant, meretricious court of James was having its first impact on Londoners. It was almost inevitable

[1] As its prologue indicates, *Eastward Hoe* was written in response to *Westward Hoe* of 1604. Since *The Malcontent* appears to have been produced earlier in the year, a date in late 1604 or early 1605 appears likely. Chambers' date (1605) refers to the quarto.

that these collaborators would include some direct political satire of the Court and the Scots, particularly since the play was designed for the daring acting company which specialized in such matter, the Children of the Queen's Revels. When King James heard about it from a Scotch courtier, Jonson and Chapman, and perhaps also Marston, were imprisoned. Chapman strongly implies in a letter that it was Marston who wrote the offensive passages, and there is no reason to doubt it. Perhaps it was his superior financial position which led him to take great chances; or perhaps, as the chambermate of the Treasurer of the Middle Temple, he felt that he was operating from a privileged sanctuary.

The impression that Marston somehow felt immune to punishment is increased by his next play, *The Dutch Curtezan* (1605). Although his colleagues in *Eastward Hoe* nearly had their ears and noses cut, Marston once more satirized the Scots. It is almost as though he was testing the patience of the authorities, for he also criticized the censorship of books and advocated attitudes toward sexual behavior which were far from orthodox. The passage of satire against the Scots requires some attention because it has been overlooked by previous commentators; its identification has the further value of helping to date the play with some precision. I refer to the scene in Act II in which a witty knave named Cocledemoy masquerades as a barber in order to steal money from a dishonest vintner named Mulligrub. In addition to his barber's paraphernalia, he announces that his disguise will include the adoption of the accent of "a Northern Barbar" (II, 87).[2] When Cocledemoy appears before his adversary, he says that his name is "Andrew Sharke" (II, 94). The implications of his surname are clear; as for the Christian name, we saw a similar employment of the name of the patron saint of Scotland in *The Malcontent* in the barb against the honor of "S. *Andrew Iaques*" (modified to "S. *Andrew*" in later quartos). The ensuing dialogue confirms one's suspicions concerning the name and accent. When "Andrew" reveals that he has been in his trade for "this two yeare," Mulligrub suggests that this is not long enough to make him a "good worke man." Andrew's response is the first of the anti-Scots jokes: "O feare not, we ha polde better men then you, we learn the trade very quickly" (II, 94). That "we" includes his "countrimen" is clear from his next speech: "I was a Pedler in Germany, but

---

[2] Similar mockery of the Scots accent is preserved by the phonetic spelling of one passage in *Eastward Hoe, Ben Jonson,* ed. C. H. Herford and Percy and Evelyn Simpson (Oxford, 1932), IV, 582, l. 178.

my countrimen thrive better by this trade" [that is, by polling and shaving Englishmen] (II, 94). Finally, the barber is linked with the Court, where, he concedes, he "Sometimes pole[s] a Page or so" (II, 94).[3] When Mulligrub, blinded by suds, eventually realizes that he has been robbed, he exclaims, "plague of all *Andrewes*" (II, 96).[4] In a passage with such clear contemporary relevance, the mention of two years of polling and shaving would have to be a fairly accurate figure. This suggests a date for *The Dutch Curtezan* around 1605 because James and his retinue arrived in London in May of 1603.[5]

If *Eastward Hoe* did not get Marston into trouble, *The Dutch Curtezan* did. The cause may have been this slight piece of gratuitous political satire, but his plight may just as well have been occasioned by the morality of the play. This seems to be the implication of Anthony Nixon's attack on Marston in *The Blacke Yeare* (1606) "for bringing in the *Dutch Courtezan* to corrupt English conditions, and sent away *Westward* for carping both at Court, Cittie, and countrie." [6] While he exaggerates the harm which a play can cause, Nixon does describe accurately the fundamental action within the play. It shows the corrupting effect of an alien force, a Dutch prostitute, on the life of a young Englishman living in London. Malheureux, as he is called, is a youth "of faire bloud, well meand, of good breeding,/Best fam'd, of sweet acquaintance, and true friends"

---

[3] In addition to its usual significance, "page," according to the *NED,* may also refer to an officer in the king's household.

[4] There may also be some kind of political satire in the passage about "Spanish Jennetes" and "Flaunders Mares" on p. 95. It may involve a hit at the Scots since Marston's colleague at the Middle Temple, Edward Sharpham, makes the connection in speaking about court ladies in *The Fleire,* ed. H. Nibbe, *Materialien zur Kunde des alteren Englischen Dramas,* XXXVI (Louvain, 1912), p. 23, ll. 169–170: "they love the fine little Scottes Spurre, it makes the Court Gennet curvet, curvet gallantly."

[5] This date, somewhat later than Chambers' claim of 1603–1604, has recently been suggested by Anthony Caputi, *John Marston, Satirist* (Ithaca, 1961), pp. 217–240. His method is to demonstrate the priority of *Eastward Hoe* and hence a date for *The Dutch Curtezan* later than 1604. Caputi claims that the plot structure of the collaborative play influenced Marston's double plot. I would suggest that *Eastward Hoe* is built on a structure of contrasts similar to that which Marston had already employed in *Jack Drum's Entertainment*: Brabant Jr. vs. Brabant Sr., Camelia vs. Katherine, Pasquill vs. Mamon, etc. These are similarities and differences within one world. *The Dutch Curtezan,* on the other hand, employs a "pastoral" subplot. There are two different social and economic levels; the contrasts are vertical.

[6] Sig. B2r. Some scholars detect an allusion to the *Eastward Hoe* troubles in the italicized *"Westward"* and assume that whatever punishment Marston incurred or fled "westward" to avoid was precipitated by his part in the collaboration. But since *The Dutch Curtezan,* as we now know, also contains political "carping," it is possible that the passage refers only to one play.

(II, 133). He is well educated, and his social circle includes knights and substantial members of the gentry. Thus, for the first time since *Jack Drum*, Marston set a play precisely in his audience's world. We can be sure that an audience of *"Heliconian* Gallantes," as Marston describes them (II, 136),[7] would have taken more than a casual interest in a play about a young man trying to cope with newly discovered sexual desires. Once again, the pattern of Marston's play is that of initiation.

All these elements we have come to expect in Marston; what surprises us is that some of his basic attitudes appear to have changed radically in this play. After a casual opening in which a group of gallants in a tavern exchange witticisms, two of the group begin a friendly argument. It appears that Freevill plans to visit his mistress, the "Dutch Curtezan," while his friend, the aforementioned Malheureux, wants to see him home safely and chastely. Malheureux, a moralist with a narrowly prescriptive code, offers harsh judgments against the use "of a money Creature,/One that sels humane flesh: a Mangonist" (II, 73). Freevill defends prostitutes in a jocular "paradox" reminiscent of similar performances in the Inns' revels, as an excerpt reveals: "Alas good creatures, what would you have them doe? would you have them get their living by the curse of man, the sweat of their browes? so they doe, everie man must follow his trade, and everie woman her occupation . . . You will say beasts take no money for their fleshly entertainment: true, because they are beasts, therefore beastly; onely men give to loose, because they are men, therefore manly: and indeede, wherein should they bestow their money better?" (II, 73–74). In *The Scourge* Marston excoriated the casual, laissez-faire morality of the gallants as the product of "humors that are borne/In slime of filthy sensualitie" (SV, XI, 206–207), but here Freevill's morality is shown to be preferable to Malheureux's inhumane rigidity and, as we shall see, even to possess a degree of wisdom.

The reason for Marston's change in attitude is not hard to find. Sometime after writing *The Malcontent*, he discovered Montaigne's essays in the translation by John Florio published

[7] He also addresses the audience as "Worship[ful] friends in the middle Region" (II, 136). There has been some mystification about this phrase, although it has been assumed that it refers to a section of the theater auditorium. As far as I know, the phrase is not used elsewhere as a theatrical term. "Region" can mean a part of the body. Lust is described as "one of the middle sinnes" on p. 73, and a similar use of "middle" is implied on p. 101: *"Crisp.* I am as many are, peec'd above and peec'd beneath./*Tisefew.* Still the best part in the ———." To ascribe a sexual interest to the audience would be consistent with the theme of the play; the significance of the phrase could easily have been clarified by a gesture.

in 1603. Marston had conducted large-scale raids on authors before, especially on the Roman satirists, on Seneca, and on Guarini, but Montaigne was far more to Marston than a quarry for sententious or witty passages, although the *Essayes* also served that purpose. For instance, Marston included no less than forty-five passages from the *Essayes* in *The Dutch Curtezan,* of which twenty-three came from a single essay, "Upon Some Verses of Virgil." [8] For Marston, reading Montaigne was not a matter of discovering a whole new world. Instead, as is frequently the case when one author has an immense impact on another, Montaigne expressed memorably certain ideas and attitudes which Marston had held at one time or another, and he suggested relationships among these ideas which Marston had not previously perceived. For example, Marston learned from Montaigne how to reconcile his feeling, expressed in *Pigmalions Image,* that sex is a powerful and pleasurable force in human life with his conviction that the casual lust of young gallants was brutish. In the essay "Upon Some Verses of Virgil," Montaigne treats these subjects with incomparable candor. Speaking as an old man looking back on the role which sexual activity has played in his life, he views it quite simply as "a Centre whereto all lines come, all things looke." [9] It is a natural force which none can escape; it can only be conquered by accepting it: *"Belike we must be incontinent that we may be continent, burning is quenched by fire."* [10] After reading this essay, Marston could even view whoring as a natural, if regrettable, response to a very human need.

Further, Montaigne's naturalism confirmed Marston's prejudice against ethical codes with impossible or even harmful standards of conduct. As we saw in *Antonio's Revenge,* the Stoic Pandulpho Feliche spoke like "more then a god," but he realized that he was "lesse then a man." [11] It was one of Montaigne's recurrent themes (expressed in the essay on Virgil's verses but most impressively in "Of Experience") that a man

[8] First noticed by Charles Crawford, *Collectanea, Second Series* (Stratford-on-Avon, 1907). Further parallels to Montaigne were noted by H. Harvey Wood, ed., *Plays of John Marston* (3 vols., Edinburgh, 1934–1939), II, 310–326 passim, and by M. L. Wine, ed., *The Dutch Courtesan,* Regents Renaissance Drama Series (Lincoln, Neb., 1965), pp. 112–120 (which collects all of the parallels). I should mention that an essay by Gustav Cross, "Marston, Montaigne, and Morality: *The Dutch Courtezan* Reconsidered," *ELH,* 27 (1960), 30–43, treats the subject in some detail and arrives at different conclusions.

[9] *Essayes of Michael Lord of Montaigne Done into English by John Florio,* ed. Thomas Seccombe (London, 1908), III, 96.

[10] Ibid., 97.

[11] *Plays,* I, 121.

should be "pittyed . . . who outwent others, and would not bee contented with the state and condition of mortall man." [12] Moreover, "Super-celestiall opinions, and under-terrestriall manners, are things, that amongst us, I have ever seene to bee of singular accord." [13] This disparity, which Montaigne discerned, between the observable primacy of sexual passion in man's makeup and the ideal abstractions of philosophy supplied Marston with the theme for *The Dutch Curtezan*. In Malheureux he shows a man whose supercelestial opinions are translated into underterrestrial manners when he first feels sexual passion.

What this would-be wise man is ignorant of, according to Montaigne, is the subject he ought to know best: "I had rather understand my selfe well in my selfe, then in *Cicero*." [14] But self-knowledge is not easy to obtain for someone whose mind (in Montaigne's words) is besotted with many a "scrupulous and verball superstition." Marston shows that Malheureux can only gain such knowledge through the harsh lessons of experience. Here it is possible that Montaigne served as an influence on a philosophic theme of *The Dutch Curtezan* and caused a basic shift in Marston's thinking. It will be recalled that in the satires Marston had flatly dismissed the possibility of moral reformation; only God's grace could produce change. This view led to the extreme pessimism of *Antonio's Revenge* and the cynicism of *What You Will* and *The Malcontent*. In Montaigne's most pessimistic essay, the "Apology for Raymond Sebond," he concedes that, untrustworthy though the senses are, "all knowledge is addressed unto us by the senses, they are our maisters." [15] By the time he wrote "Of Experience," he had moved a little farther: "In this universality I suffer my selfe ignorantly and negligently to be managed by the generall law of the world. I shall sufficiently know it when I shall feele it." [16] Experience, he maintains, is the best teacher, far superior to books. It is not possible to prove that Marston adopted from Montaigne a view which is hardly distinguished for its novelty. But when so much else in the play springs from that source and considering that Marston had not previously expressed it, the likelihood is high.

I have been stressing the influence of Montaigne on this

[12] *Essayes*, III, 482.
[13] Ibid., 481.
[14] Ibid., 414.
[15] Ibid., II, 378.
[16] Ibid., III, 413. The notion of learning by experience is not in Marston's narrative source.

play, but it is a mistake, which vitiates at least one study of this subject, to assume that Marston followed Montaigne totally or that he structured his play to demonstrate the validity of Montaigne's philosophical positions. As I shall try to show, the relationship is more complicated. Most obviously, Marston did not accept Montaigne's views on love and marriage. Montaigne felt that love was neither possible nor desirable in marriage; Marston, on the other hand, saw married love as the fulfillment of what was only imperfectly embodied in illicit sexual relationships. It follows that Marston did not accept Montaigne's rather mechanistic definition of love: "I finde that *love is nothing else but an insatiate thirst of enjoying a greedily desired subject*." [17] This is only one example of Marston's divergence from or modification of Montaigne's views. Sometimes he transplants passages from Montaigne to new contexts, where their meaning is quite different from the original author's intention; occasionally he puts Montaigne's serious statements into the mouths of unsympathetic figures or even villains.[18]

Nonetheless, the influence of Montaigne on Marston constitutes an excellent example of how one Elizabethan dramatist's mode of feeling was directly and freshly altered by his reading (to wrench T. S. Eliot's famous critical formulation from its context). Before Montaigne, Marston's world was suffused with Italianate darkness. *The Dutch Curtezan* is also a tragicomedy with a full complement of fools and knaves, but in this play most of them are shown to be (in Swift's term) "docible" through the harsh ministrations of experience. In the process, Marston's attitude toward his own world seems to undergo a change. Whether consciously or not, he manages in this play to make sense of what I have been calling the morality of the revels, the gallants' confused combination of tolerance for the pursuit of "low-prized venery" and admiration for the "honorable course of love."

2

The Dutch Curtezan contains two plots which derive from separate sources.[19] For the subplot, Marston pieced together

---

[17] Ibid., 125.

[18] To take a few obvious examples, see Marston's use of Montaigne in M. L. Wine's third and fourth examples on p. 112 and the sixth example on p. 113 in the complete list of parallels appended to his edition of *The Dutch Courtesan*.

[19] For the main plot, see John J. O'Connor, "The Chief Source of Marston's *Dutch Courtezan*," *Studies in Philology*, 54 (1957), 509–515. For the subplot, see James J. Jackson, "Sources of the Subplot of Marston's *The Dutch Courtezan*," *Philological Quarterly*, 31 (1952), 223–224.

comic episodes from various authors. The main plot retains almost all the narrative material from one French story, although Marston did make significant changes in emphasis; a story about love and friendship becomes one about guilt and redemption. What is most illuminating, however, is his transformation of the characters and language from a relatively realistic to a relatively abstract level of representation. Marston's "Argumentum" suggests that he is writing a play about an idea; it is to be a contrast between *"the love of a Curtezan, & a wife"* (II, 69). The Prologue implies a similarly generalized conception of the action as "Nothing but passionate man in his slight play" (II, 69). If "Young Freevils unhappie friend," as the Dramatis Personae describes Malheureux, represents "passionate man," Freevill is plainly someone who possesses free will. It was Marston's usual practice to label his characters with significant names, but in this play the allegorical element is maintained in the main plot by means of the characters speaking to an unusual degree in the generalized language of moral sententiae, faculty psychology, and philosophy. This is true not only of the learned and philosophical Malheureux. Even the Dutch courtesan uses psychological terms and in her Dutch accent utters generalities taken from Montaigne: " 'De more degrees and steps, de more delight,/De more endeered is de pleasure hight' " (II, 126).

Thus the main plot has something of the character of an exemplum or, as someone has suggested, of a morality play.[20] More precisely, it is a rigorously objective case history with philosophical and psychological implications. Even when we hear intimate revelations of suffering from the "passionate man," we are prevented from feeling sympathy by a variety of dramatic devices. An eavesdropper may ridicule his behavior, or it may be undercut by an analogous action in the subplot, or something in his expression may alienate us. Indeed, it is not easy to sympathize with this unhappy and unpleasant figure. The plot is triggered by Malheureux's officious assumption of the role of Freevill's moral mentor: "I dare not give you up to your owne companie, I feare the warmth of wine and youth, will draw you to some Common house of lascivious entertaine-

[20] See Robert Presson, "Marston's *Dutch Courtezan*: the Study of an Attitude in Adaptation," *Journal of English and Germanic Philology*, 55 (1956), 406–413. He implies that the play possesses this general quality by relating it to morality plays. However, most of his study is devoted to the citation of parallels in such plays. The main thesis about adaptation is undermined by comparisons to what had been thought to be the source of the play before the discovery by O'Connor (see n. 19).

ment" (II, 72). He tends to deliver advice with the patient condescension of a scholar who has surveyed all the arguments on a subject:

> Deere my lov'd friend, let mee bee full with you,
> Know Sir, the strongest argument that speakes
> Against the soules eternitie is lust,
> That Wisemans folly, and the fooles wisedome. (II, 73)

But his next words give us a hint of the true grounds for his own chastity:

> But to grow wild in loose lasciviousnesse,
> Given up to heat, and sensuall Appetite:
> Nay to expose your health, and strength, and name,
> Your precious time, and with that time the hope
> Of due preferment, advantageous meanes
> Of any worthy end. (II, 73)

His code, it appears, is connected with a desire to keep up appearances. He is proud of his reputation as a man of "a professed abstinence" (II, 78); his supercelestial ambition is to be revered as a Stoic "wise man," someone who acts rightly without the aid of sympathy or any other feeling. As "wise man" he frequently delivers sanctimonious sententiae: "for know this ever:/Tis no such sinne to erre, but to persever" (II, 74). Or again, "The sight of vice augments the hate of sinne" (II, 75).

To this, the nettled Freevill responds prophetically, "The sight of vice augments the hate of sinne, very fine perdy" (II, 75), and almost immediately vice appears in an unexpected shape. Freevill's courtesan comes from outside Malheureux's world, as her accent emphasizes, and she does not look like a conventional prostitute. She is "a pretty nimble eyd Dutch Tanakin; an honest soft-harted impropriation, a soft plumpe, round cheekt froe" (II, 75). It takes only one glance to puncture Malheureux's self-assigned moral pre-eminence and to reveal the flimsy nature of his defenses. Through a series of monologues and soliloquies, Marston shows that Malheureux is as ill equipped for this challenge as a person starting out on a Polar expedition with summer clothes and maps of the Italian lakes (as Freud said in a similar context). These speeches are crucial to the success of the play; we must derive from them a sense of spiritual deterioration and of a helplessness which can only be cured by radical means. Marston communicates this by employing his special talent, one we saw in the characterizations of Antonio and Lampatho, for showing how people are trapped and deceived by their own language. As I shall show, Malheureux's speeches will "boldly abide the most curious perusall" (II, 144): proud words which Marston threw to the world about *Sophonisba,* but which are more appropriate here.

The first of these speeches shows Malheureux's immediate reaction to Franceschina's appearance. It is a desperate attempt to rationalize his passion; it would be pitiable if the arguments were not so specious:

> Is she unchast, can such a one be damde?
> O love and beautie, yee two eldest seedes
> Of the vast Chaos, what strong right you have,
> Even in thinges divine, our very soules . . .
> Are strumpets then such things, so delicate,
> Can custome spoile, what nature made so good?
> Or is their Custome bad? Beauti's for use,
> I never saw a sweet face vitious,
> It might be proud, inconstant, wanton, nice,
> But never tainted with unnaturall vice.
> Their worst is, their best art is love to winne,
> "O that to love should be or shame, or sinne!" (II, 79)

This is the reason-hunting of reasonless passion. His mélange of Neoplatonism and naturalism even contains a maxim from the Machiavelli of the bedchamber, Maquerelle, who used to advise her circle of court ladies in *The Malcontent* to "use your beauty." [21] "I never saw a sweet face vitious" is a perversion of such Neoplatonic sentiments as Spenser's "all that faire is, is by nature good";[22] its main effect is to impress upon us Malheureux's almost hopeless naïveté. The best comment on Malheureux's haphazard and casuistical argument is offered by Freevill, who has been overhearing it with barely suppressed glee. After jokingly throwing some of Malheureux's platitudes back at him, he concludes: " 'Of all the fooles that would all man outthrust,/He that 'gainst Nature would seeme wise is worst' " (II, 80). Malheureux's disordered monologue represents the first stages of the revenge that Nature takes upon a "wise man" who has denied her power.

[21] *Plays,* I, 168.
[22] "An Hymne in Honour of Beautie," *Complete Poetical Works of Edmund Spenser* (Boston, 1908), p. 748, l. 139.

In the second act, Marston probes deeper into Malheureux's troubled and confused state of mind. He prepares for his appearance by showing Freevill, now freed from "base affections, and unfruitfull heates" (II, 81), exchanging vows of affection with his beloved Beatrice. Then Malheureux comes onstage, with Freevill again eavesdropping. His speech is one of Marston's most impressive pieces of dramatic poetry. While it remains objective and ironic, it is also a convincing expression of the struggle between Malheureux's conscience and his passion:

> The studious morne with paler cheeke drawes on
> The dayes bold light. harke how the free-borne birdes
> Carroll their unaffected passions, [*The Nitingalls sing.*]
> Now sing they sonnets, thus they crye, we love.
> O breath of heaven! thus they harmles soules
> Give intertaine to mutuall affects.
> They have no Baudes: no mercenary bedds
> No politike restraints: no artificiall heats
> No faint dissemblings, no custome makes them blush,
> No shame afflicts their name, O you happy beastes
> In whome an inborne heat is not held sinne,
> How far transcend you wretched, wretched man
> Whom nationall custome, Tyrannous respects
> Of slavish order, fetters, lames his power
> Calling that sinne in us, which in all things els
> Is natures highest virtue.
> (*O miseri quorum gaudia crimen habent.*)
> Sure nature against vertue crosse doth fall
> Or vertues selfe is oft unnaturall,
> That I should love a strumpet, I a man of Snowe
> Now shame forsake me whether am I fallen!
> A creature of a publique use, my frendes love too,
> To live to be a talke to men, a shame
> To my professed vertue. "O accursed reason,
> How many eyes hast thou to see thy shame
> And yet how blind once to prevent defame!" (II, 83)[23]

[23] Wood, *Plays*, II, 314, proposes Ovid's *Amores*, I.x, as the source for this speech. But in addition to a lack of verbal echoes, Marston's argument here is very different from Ovid's. Ovid is berating a woman for asking for rewards for love and uses the example of beasts to show the perversity of her request. He finds Nature superior to Civilization because there love is not connected with pay. But Malheureux prefers the beasts' condition because they can love without shame or inhibition or unnatural intermediaries. While such sentiments are not unique, I would suggest as a more likely source some lines from the translation of *Il Pastor Fido* which Marston used frequently in *The Malcontent*:

We may note first that most of the speech is an amplification
of the line with which he concluded his previous monologue:
" 'O that to love should be or shame, or sinne' " (II, 79). The
expansion of this one line into nineteen and the shift from
neat aphorisms to disordered catalogues mirror his heightened
unhappiness. Composed at about the same time as Fulke Greville's famous "Chorus" on the "wearisome condition of humanity," Malheureux's speech has been read as a similar expression of man's divided nature. In fact, its dramatic context
endows it with a very different meaning; every sentiment is
rendered ironic by what surrounds it. The placement of the
speech just after the ardent avowals of Freevill and Beatrice
suggests that Malheureux has exaggerated the distinction between Nature and Man, that humans, too, can feel "unaffected
passions." The fact that the birds are specifically identified as
"nitingalls" links them to Franceschina, who sang a song comparing herself to that bird when Malheureux first saw her (II,
79).[24] The love of bird for bird is one thing; the entanglement
of a human with a birdlike creature is not natural and may not
be "harmles." Only a wise man of professed abstinence could
claim that "an inborne heat" is considered a "sinne" or that
Nature and Virtue are in direct opposition. It may be added
that Malheureux's views do not represent the naturalism of
Montaigne, who was far from advocating the unbridled satisfaction of every wayward impulse; for him, the ideal life accommodated the claims both of body and soul.

Most of Malheureux's speech is general and philosophical.
He seems to avoid direct statements about his own situation
until the last lines. Then he reveals that it is not really sin
and virtue which concern him; it is his cherished reputation
for virtue. In his final sentence, characteristically impersonal
in expression, he realizes that all his moralizing will not deter
him for pursuing Franceschina. We now see that he has become
a creature of pure will like the birds he has been envying and,

---

> Oh happie savadge beasts whom nature gives
> No lawes in love, save verie love it selfe.
> Inhumane humane lawe, that punish'st
> This love with death, if't be so sweet to sin,
> And not to sin so necessary bee,
> Imperfect nature that repugneth law,
> Or law too hard that nature doth offend. (Sig. H3r-v)

[24] This is not an unworkable association on stage if the music played at this
moment is that of Franceschina's song. The tune for this has recently been discovered by Andrew J. Sabol, "Two Unpublished Stage Songs for the 'Aery of
Children,' " *Renaissance News*, 13 (Autumn, 1960), 222–232.

it may be added, like the Dutch "nightingale" for whom he lusts.

As I said earlier, Marston maintains a consistently comic stance toward Malheureux's suffering. For the second time, Freevill has been overhearing his private thoughts and he instantly explains the true motivating force behind his high-sounding lamentation: *"Diaboli virtus in Lumbis est,* morrow my frend: come, I could make a tedious scene of this now but, what, pah, thou art in love with a Courtezan, why sir, should we loath all strumpets sume men should hate their owne mothers or sisters, a sinne against kinde I can tell you" (II, 83). He proposes that Malheureux solve his self-created problem simply by buying the "pleasure" it is Franceschina's "occupation" (II, 74) to sell. As we saw, Montaigne is the source for Freevill's rationale of this procedure:

> "Incontinence will force a Continence,
> Heate wasteth heate, light defaceth light,
> Nothing is spoyled but by his proper might." (II, 84)

But the "wise man," as he once again describes himself (II, 83), falters. He wants to save his reputation for purity and to enjoy Franceschina as well. Freevill then adopts the tactic of indirect moral suasion. He reminds him that loving a prostitute is like making

> use of a Statue,
> A body without a soule, a carkasse three monethes dead,
> Yet since thou art in love —
>   MAL. Death man, my destiny I cannot choose.
>   FREE. Nay I hope so, againe they sell but onely flesh,
> No jot affection, so that even in the enjoying,
> *Absentem marmoreamque putes,* yet since you needs
>   must love —
>   MAL. Unavoidable though folly, worse then madnes. (II, 84–85)

Marston drew Freevill's series of metaphors for a prostitute's love from Montaigne, who expressed abhorrence for sexual intercourse in which mutual affection was lacking. Through this conversation it is now clear that Malheureux's long pent-up lust has assumed a depraved, unnatural character. Thus far, Freevill's response to the disclosure of his friend's fallibility has been jaunty, and he is not totally displeased; his standards are those of an experienced Heliconian gallant. Being onstage during Malheureux's struggles with his conscience, he learns of his friend's gradual deterioration at the same moment the audience does. Along with them he comes to perceive the compulsive and uncontrolled form Malheureux's lust is taking. His ironic comment at the end of this scene does not register serious concern yet, but its tone is perceptibly deeper: "since you needs *must* love, you *must* know this,/He that *must* love, a foole, and he *must* kisse" (II, 85, italics mine).

The unusual nature of Malheureux's desire also becomes apparent to Franceschina when he finally discloses his love to her. She has just been abandoned by Freevill after a ferocious argument in which she screams out in Malheureux's presence, "Gods Sacrament, ick could scratch out her [Beatrice's] eyes, and sucke the holes" (II, 89). Thus he sees exactly what he is dealing with, but nothing can dull his passion. Before he begins his proposal, he is able to allude to the *locus classicus* for describing his moral state; then, typically, he excuses himself by citing the fallibility, not of man, but of the gods:

> I am no whit my selfe, *Video meliora proboque,*
> But raging lust my fate all strong doth move:
> "The Gods themselves cannot be wise and love." (II, 90)

His declaration begins ineptly with the ardor of an amorist, after which he bluntly blurts out his proposal:

> MAL. Will you lie with me?
> FRANC. Lie with you, O no, you men will out-lie any woman, fait me no more can love.
> MAL. No matter, let me enjoy your bed. (II, 90)

Franceschina has craftily assessed his character and quickly gains a moral ascendency over him by the nature of her rejection:

> FRANC. O vile man, vat do you tinck on me, doe you take mee to be a beast, a creature that for sence onely will entertaine love, and not onely for love, love? O brutish abhomination! (II, 90)

This ethical retort in a Dutch accent serves to parody Malheureux's former pretentious moralizing. It also describes his moral degradation quite accurately. Franceschina perceives his utter subjugation and is able to maneuver him to his lowest point:

> FRANC. So long as *Freevil* lives, I must not love.
> MAL. Then he —
> FRANC. Must —
> MAL. Die. (II, 91–92)

Malheureux means what he says, and after Franceschina departs, he begins a soliloquy with the same argument which Antonio used to justify his murder of Julio:

> To kill my friend! O tis to kill my selfe,
> Yet mans but mans excrement, man breeding man,
> As he do's wormes — or this,
>   [*He spits.*] to spoile this nothing:
> The body of a man is of the selfe-same soule,
> As Oxe or horse, no murther to kill these,
> As for that onely part, which makes us man,
> Murther wants power to toucht. (II, 92–93)

At this moment in the play, there is no way of knowing how far Malheureux's madness will take him. But this is a comedy, and therefore Marston shows one barely perceptible spark of "synderesis" smoldering in the husk of Malheureux's body. It is ignited by the mention of Freevill's soul. He sees that his "hellish" wit has raised his "nature/Gainst sacred faith" (II, 93). Once again, it is worth noting that the Nature which he opposes to "sacred faith" is not Montaigne's variety but the kind which is described in the "homo homini lupus" formula; it is akin to Machiavelli's.[25] As he describes the difference between the pure love of a friend and that of a low woman, he seems at last to have regained control of himself:

> whose very having,
> Looseth all appetite, and gives satietie;
> That corporall end, remorse and inward blushinges,
> Forcing us loath the steame of our owne heates. (II, 93)

Having realized this much, it is only a step to a series of generalizations which sound like the triumphant awakening in a fifth act:

---

[25] Marston presents this position sympathetically in one of Antonio's soliloquies in the *Revenge, Plays,* I, 101.

> Lord, how was I misgone, how easie ti's to erre,
> When passion will not give us leave to thinke!
> "A learn'd that is an honest man may feare,
> And lust, and rage, and malice, and any thing,
> When he is taken uncollected suddenly:
> Ti's sinne of colde blood; mischiefe with wak'd eyes;
> That is the damned and the truest vice,
> Not he that's passionles but he 'bove passion's wise,"
> My friend shall know it all. (II, 93)

In a mood of relief and self-congratulation he utters a series of comfortable moral generalities. To sin when inflamed, he realizes, is easy; it is cold-blooded sin which cannot be excused. He also sees that his orthodox Stoicism did not make due allowance for the power of passion. Now he knows that passion must be accepted as a fundamental part of the human makeup before it can be conquered. But this moment is one of the subtlest touches in Marston's characterization because the "enlightenment" is almost entirely factitious. All Malheureux has really learned is how to say the right words. It is true that he has gained control of himself sufficiently to refrain from murdering his friend, but his references to himself as learned, honest, and wise suggest that he has not really changed. His subsequent actions reveal the total compartmentalization of his feelings. He praises himself for having mastered the passion which made him promise to murder his friend. Meanwhile he fails to mention his passion for Franceschina which, as we soon discover, continues unchecked.

He returns to Freevill to inform him of his temptation by Franceschina. He sounds totally cured as he somberly concedes that "The eldest child of nature nere beheld/So dam'd a Creature" (II, 103). He also feels pleasure and self-satisfaction for having resisted the temptation to commit murder: "Deare loved Sir, I finde a minde courageously vitious, may put on a desperate securitie, but can never bee blessed with a firme injoying and selfe satisfaction" (II, 104). Nonetheless, he admits in his usual prideful way that his appetite is as strong as ever: "yet I must use her, that I a man of sense should conceive endelesse pleasure in a body whose soule I know to be so hideously blacke . . . I doe malign my creation that I am subject to passion" (II, 104). Once again Malheureux demonstrates how "sensible" he is, this time by maligning creation for something which it is in his power to control. Marston employs the word "sense" in the same complex way Shakespeare does in *Measure for Measure*.[26] Malheureux thinks that he is sensible (rational) and is unaware that he has become sensual. Freevill finally perceives that none of the normal aids to moral reformation,

> no requests,
> No arguments of reason, no knowne danger,
> No assured wicked bloodines (II, 133)

can bring him to his senses. He has become the worst of all kinds of fools, " 'Who with a willing eie, do seeing fall' " (II, 115). Therefore he must be reached through the senses:

> Now repentance the fooles whip seize thee,
> Nay if there be no meanes Ile be thy friend,
> But not thy Vices; and with greatest sence
> Ile force thee feele thy errors. (II, 115)

Freevill has hit upon a method of education particularly appropriate for a Stoic to whom it was a fundamental tenet that the senses cannot furnish any useful knowledge.

When Malheureux finally feels his errors at the foot of the gallows, he acknowledges that Freevill's severe methods were necessary and efficacious, that, as he puts it, "Rich sence makes good bad language" (II, 134). In the portion of the play I have been examining, Marston has exhibited Malheureux's "bad language" in exhaustive detail. The language is bad in ways which Marston's audience, trained in logic, disputation, and moral philosophy, would have been quick to detect. But the author does not leave it solely to the audience or to Freevill to analyze its defects. At the beginning of Act III, by which point he has essentially completed his exposure of Malheureux's character, Marston introduces a figure to relate at great length, often nearly verbatim, Montaigne's views on candor of expression. Placed in the center of the play, these speeches constitute a definite interruption which is barely justified dramatically; this is a measure of Marston's interest in the ideas per se. In order to attract the attention of the audience, he adopted the unusual idea of putting these speeches, containing language extremely

---

[26] William Empson, *The Structure of Complex Words* (Norfolk, Conn., n.d.), p. 270, says that the "word then covered (1) 'sensuality' and (2) 'sensibility,' and I maintain that it also covered (3) 'sensibleness,' though in a less direct way, through the ideas of 'a truth-giving feeling,' and 'a reasonable meaning.' " In the passage quoted above, the meaning is clearly Empson's "(3)."

coarse even for him, into the mouth of Beatrice's sister, the young, virginal Crispinella. To extract the most important of her extensive remarks:

> lets neere be ashamed to speake what we be not ashamd to thinke, I dare as boldly speake venery, as think venery . . . we pronounce boldly Robbery, Murder, treason, which deedes must needes be far more lothsome then an act which is so naturall, just and necessary, as that of procreation. You shall have an hipocriticall vestall virgin speake that with close teeth publikely, which she will receive with open mouth privately, for my owne part I consider nature without apparell, without disguising of custome or complement, I give thoughts wordes, and wordes truth, and truth boldnes; she whose honest freenes make it her vertue, to speake what she thinks, will make it her necessity to thinke what is good, I love no prohibited things, and yet I would have nothing prohibited by policy but by vertue, for as in the fashion of time, those bookes that are cald in, are most in sale and request, so in nature those actions that are most prohibited, are most desired . . . vertue is a free pleasant buxom qualitie: I love a constant countenance well, but this froward ignorant coynes, sower austere lumpish uncivill privatenes, that promises nothing but rough skins, and hard stooles, ha, fy ont good for nothing but for nothing. (II, 98–99 *passim*)

From the earthy realism of the diction as well as from the sentiments expressed, we can see that every word of this can be construed as a criticism of Malheureux. His character exhibits precisely the opposite traits; he was formed by shame and custom, not by nature. Even when he is trying to gain Franceschina's consent, he murmurs to himself, "I must not rave, Scilence and modesty two customarie vertues" (II, 90). His "bad language" clothes rather than expresses; it leads to lying and hypocrisy. "Good language," according to Crispinella, is naked and natural; it speaks openly about feelings. Malheureux thought "vertues selfe . . . unnaturall" (II, 83). Crispinella shows how easily nature and virtue can be joined: if you say what you think, you will think what is good. She speaks freely, but her actions conform naturally to the traditional values of Elizabethan society. It is Freevill's task to teach Malheureux the same sense of the natural.

3

Marston describes the main plot as being *"intermixed with the deceits of a wittie Citie Jester"* (II, 69). He is referring to the series of ingenious tricks which Cocledemoy[27] plays on the vintner Mulligrub and his wife. The "polling and shaving" episode in the second act is the first to appear onstage, although we hear a description of an earlier robbery at the very beginning of the play. Thereafter Cocledemoy plays one such trick in each act, but "trick" becomes a euphemism as he pushes Mulligrub to the brink of madness and nearly to the gallows. Nevertheless Marston manages to keep the tone comic, in fact uproariously funny, through the inventiveness and ingenuity of Cocledemoy's attacks against victims who richly deserve their fate.

The Mulligrubs are stage Puritans, endowed with all the traditional vices. They cheat by overcharging and by substituting *"Popish* wines" for the "true auntient *British* and *Troyan* drinks" (II, 135). They are gluttonous, particularly when the food is provided by others, and sexually loose, as befits members of the often maligned sect, "The Family of Love." They also have pretensions to gentility. What most qualifies them as objects of satire is their absolute self-righteousness and hypocrisy, including their use of a special pharisaical jargon to cloak their actions:

> MRS. MULLIGRUB. Come spread these Table Diaper Napkins, and do you heare, perfume: this Parlour do's so smell of prophane Tabacco, I could never endure this ungodly Tabacco, since one of our Elders, assured me upon his knowledge Tabacco was not used in the Congregation of the family of love: spread, spread handsomely, Lord these boyes doe things arsie, varsie, you shew your bringing up, I was a Gentlewoman by my sisters side. I can tell yee so methodically: methodically, I wonder where I got that word. O sir *Aminadab Ruth* bad me kisse him methodically, I had it somewhere, and I had it indeede. (II, 108)

[27] Thomas Parrott and Robert Ball, *A Short View of Elizabethan Drama* (New York, 1958), p. 157, describe him as a "debauched scholar in the familiar tradition of George Peele." However Cocledemoy's Latin and pseudo-Greek are too defective and primitive for him to fit that description. A comment on the play by John Selden, *Table-Talk,* Temple Classics (London, 1898), p. 146, suggests a more accurate social category. Not recalling Cocledemoy's name, Selden describes him by the generic name "John O Powls." In other words, he considers Cocledemoy a "Paul's Man," one of those idlers who lounged around St. Paul's looking for news, work, or trouble.

Mrs. Mulligrub's speeches smack of free association; otherwise, her vulgar, realistic language is typical of the subplot. It should be clear from my description of the main plot that it requires some ballast to specify and authenticate its higher philosophical concerns. This the subplot does. It makes it clear that the action is occurring now and in London.

For Cocledemoy, the persecution of these people is his reason for existence, his mission in life: "Ile gargalise my throate with this Vintner, and when I have don with him, spit him out, Ile shark, conscience does not repine; . . . to wring the whythers of my gowtie barmd spiggod-frigging-jumbler of elements, *Mulligrub*, I hold it as lawfull as sheepe-shearing, taking egges from hens, caudels from Asses, or butterd shrimps from horses, they make no use of them, were not provided for them. And therefore worshipfull *Cocledemoy*, hang toasts, on, in grace and vertue to proceed, onely beware beware degrees, there be rounds in a ladder, and knots in a halter" (II, 106). He has been provoked to this affirmation of purpose by the half-crazed manner in which Mulligrub reacted to his "polling and shaving": "I will hang the knave, no, first he shall halfe rot in fetters in the Dungeon, his conscience made despairfull, ile hyre a Knave a purpose, shall assure him he is damn'd, and after see him with mine own eyes, hanged without singing any Psalme. Lord that hee has but one necke" (II, 105). The sheer excess of this is comic. Nonetheless, Mulligrub's passionate response is, as one onlooker remarks, "too tyrannous" (II, 105). His ruthless urge for revenge resembles that of the "Punck rampant," Franceschina, to whom he is linked through her special malediction of "1000 divells" (II, 106).

In his chastisement of the passionate, hypocritical, dishonest, and antisocial Puritan, Cocledemoy — the foulmouthed companion to whores and bawds whose very name sounds like an obscene pun — seems to be righting the balance of nature. Freevill's function in the main plot is similar. Unlike many double plots in Elizabethan drama, this one scarcely requires the ingenuity of an Empson to notice the high degree of similarity between the two stories. In each, a wit plays tricks on a self-righteous victim; in each, the antagonist humbles his victim's pride by subjecting him to a bitter experience. Careful planning of the parallel is apparent in small as well as in large matters. Thus Cocledemoy and Freevill make the same unusual sound for a laugh ("Wa, ha, ho": the falconer's cry), and Mulligrub's name means the same thing as Malheureux's. (The "mulligrubs" are a griping of the intestines; hence, the term signifies a sulky, unhappy mood.) Even before we see how Freevill and Cocledemoy function in the play, we notice the similarity of their long, witty "defenses" of whores and bawds in successive scenes in the first act. Their casual, worldly acceptance of the role of sex appears to be the outgrowth of their personal experience; yet the paradox of Marston's play is that they both display pre-eminently that "free pleasant buxom qualitie" which Crispinella ascribed to true virtue. In brief, they are qualified by character and training for their self-imposed roles as scourges of bad conduct and false morals.

The similarity between their victims is equally clear. Most obviously, both have pretensions to "purity." Malheureux's rigid insistence on a narrow moral standard testifies to a "hard hart" (II, 136) as much as Mulligrub's curses do. His hypocritical concern for reputation resembles the pretensions of the "spiggod-frigging" innkeeper. His unhumorous pursuit of a prostitute is essentially the same as his counterpart's passionate thirst for vengeance.

There is very little interaction between the plots, but we are constantly reminded of the parallelism of the experience. For instance, just after Malheureux inveighs against "mischiefe with wak'd eyes" while continuing to pursue it (II, 93), Mulligrub hears his wife expressing qualms of conscience about their dishonest practices but urges her to "skore false with a vengeance" (II, 94). Or again, just after Malheureux has shown himself in the third act to be utterly helpless before his lust, Mulligrub, totally out of control, curses Cocledemoy. In the fourth act, Malheureux thinks himself on the verge of finally catching Franceschina just as Mulligrub thinks he has Cocledemoy. But Mulligrub ends the act in the stocks, and Malheureux is imprisoned a moment later. The plots are finally joined at the moment when both are sentenced to be executed. After spending most of the play stealing everything Mulligrub owns, Cocledemoy now steals Malheureux's purse as he awaits execution. This incursion by Cocledemoy into the main plot is a good illustration of William Empson's point that the "power of suggestion is the strength of the double plot; once you take the two parts to correspond, any character may take on *mana* because he seems to cause what he corresponds to or be Logos of what he symbolises." [28] Just as Cocledemoy becomes an antagonist of Malheureux, we feel that Freevill is also Mulligrub's opponent. The play is not merely a satire of Stoicism or Puritanism; it shows the defects of moral absolutism in any of its

[28] *Some Versions of Pastoral* (London, 1950), p. 34.

forms. The double plot also has another function. It helps preserve the comic tone by suggesting the similarities between Malheureux and Mulligrub. A man who acts like a hypocritical Puritan vintner so often and in such a variety of ways cannot be regarded as a tragic figure.

Eventually Cocledemoy's tortures produce results. At the foot of the scaffold Mulligrub has a sudden, yet somehow believable, conversion; he confesses that it is his "hard hart" that "has procurd all this, but I forgive as I would be forgiven" (II, 136). The unusual knave, Cocledemoy, as if to clarify the nature of his motives in this project of moral reformation, proves that he is "no knave" by restoring his loot and stressing that "whatsoere he has don, has bin only *Euphoniae gratia*, for Wits sake: I acquit this Vintner as he has acquitted me, all has bin done for *Emphises* of wit my fine boie, my worshipfull friends" (II, 136). Cocledemoy is frequently described by bird images, and his life displays the moral irresponsibility for which Malheureux envied the "free-borne birdes." He justifies his persecution of Mulligrub by reference to the laws of nature. To take his possessions is as "lawfull as sheepe-shearing, taking egges from hens." It is natural to punish a "jumbler of elements" (II, 106).

Cocledemoy's actions may be natural, but are they virtuous? This is the question Freevill ponders after he decides that he must frighten Malheureux into virtue by an elaborate, potentially dangerous trick:

> But is this vertue in me? No, not pure,
> Nothing extreamely best with us endures,
> No use in simple purities, the elementes
> Are mixt for use, Silver without alay
> Is all to eager to be wrought for use:
> Nor precise vertues ever purely good
> Holdes usefull size with temper of weake bloud:
> Then let my course be borne, tho: with side-wind,
> The end being good, the meanes are well assignd.
>
> (II, 115–116)

This passage is largely derived from Montaigne, although Altofronto had already discovered that "pure" virtues are not useful to a mixed creature like man. Stoicism was designed for gods, not men; it did not prepare Malheureux for the impurity of his nature. As Montaigne said in the essay from which Marston derived much of this passage, simple virtue "which *Ariston,*

Pirrho, and the Stoikes, made the end of their life, hath been able to doe no good without composition." [29]

With Freevill's determination to act, the main plot takes on something of the character of the subplot, with the pyschological and philosophical interest now necessarily subordinate to elaborate intrigue. The virtuous Machiavel, Freevill, reveals that he too can be a god of policy, and concocts an elaborate plot involving a trick within a trick. The action now moves swiftly. First, he instructs Malheureux to deceive Franceschina into believing that he has performed the murder. Then, unknown to anyone, he gains employment with the prostitute in the disguise of a pander, which thus permits him to oversee and manipulate the action. Franceschina responds to Malheureux's deception as a "punk rampant" and creature of pure will should. She informs the world that Malheureux has killed Freevill and tells Beatrice that her fiancé had never loved her. While his friend Malheureux is placed in prison and his beloved suffers extreme anguish at the news of her lover's death and infidelity, Freevill maintains his disguise. Only after Malheureux has endured public infamy and stands on the brink of execution does he reveal himself. He is instantly defensive about his tactics, reminding Malheureux, in a passage quoted earlier, that he had tried gentle methods and that nothing less severe could have cured his madness. Malheureux concurs and announces that the treatment has been effective:

> I am myselfe, how long wast ere I could
> Perswade my passion to grow calme to you?
> Rich sence makes good bad language, and a friend
> Should waigh no action, but the actions end.
> I am now worthie yours, when before
> The beast of man, loose bloud distemperd us,
> "He that lust rules cannot be vertuous." (II, 134)

Thus his last utterance in the play is a sententia exactly like those he recited in the first act. The difference, obviously, is that this last maxim has been authenticated by experience.

Nonetheless, it is interesting to note that *The Dutch Curtezan* does not end as a modern reader might expect. Rather than offering a Jacobean version of a D. H. Lawrence-style panegyric on the new powers now happily unlocked in Malheureux, Marston concentrates in the latter part of the play on the value

[29] *Essayes,* II, 498.

of education by experience. This involves a detailed demonstration of the *"difference betwixt the love of a Curtezan, & a
wife"* (II, 69). Indeed, Marston contrasts Franceschina's deviltry
and Beatrice's saintliness to the point of tedium. To underline
their differences, he nearly turns Freevill into a sadist whose
love is fed by watching the beauty of his beloved's grief.[30] Freevill is given no fewer than three soliloquies (II, 120, 127, 128)
to comment on the difference, his sentiments always being the
same:

> O heaven: what difference is in women, and their life?
> What man, but worthie name of Man:
> Would leave the modest pleasures of a lawfull bed, . . .
> To twine the unhealthfull loynes of common Loves,
> The prostituted impudence of things,
> Sencelesse like those by *Cataracks* of Nyle. (II, 127)

These are the words of the man who had defended the "good
creatures" so jovially at the beginning of the play. Although
his defense of prostitution was joking and equivocal in the
first place, his tone has darkened measurably. "Rich sence" has
also affected Freevill's language.

On the surface, Marston would seem to be advocating two
contradictory attitudes toward illicit sexual activity. With the
help of Montaigne, he shows that whoring is not as harmful
to a young man as denying his humanity is. It is the mark of
the fool to ignore the importance of his passions; it is a sign
of wisdom to accept the alloy in man's makeup. At the same
time, he makes it clear that whoring is a dirty, dangerous
business and that the love of a whore differs from that of a
wife. Freevill's course is not the best, but since "Nothing ex-
treamely best with us endures," the path from Franceschina to
Beatrice, from "heart" to "soule" (II, 78), is at least natural. It
is this realistic view of man's development which justifies the
"revels' morality" of the gallants in the audience. Anthony
Nixon was only half wrong in attacking Marston "for bringing
in the *Dutch Courtezan* to corrupt English conditions." A narrow moralist might well read the play as a sanction for sowing
wild oats, but Marston does not minimize the dangers or exag-
gerate the joys of Freevill's path. It should not send the *"Heli-*

---

[30] After Franceschina has taunted Beatrice cruelly, Freevill says, "I will goe
and reveale my selfe: staie: no, no,/Greefe endeeres Love" (II, 120). He delays
revealing himself until nearly the end, by which time Beatrice's beautiful suffering is so severe that Crispinella reproaches him for subjecting her sister to
such a trial (II, 130).

conian Gallantes" pouring out of Blackfriars to the stews; on the other hand, the personal dangers from a "purity" not tempered by experience and humanity are very great.

Much of the play — I am tempted to say precisely three quarters of it — must be judged, along with *The Malcontent,* as Marston's best work. In the subplot he sustains one idea with fertile inventions and variations; its enlightening relationship to the main plot is contrived with thought and skill. The ironic presentation of the suffering Malheureux is Marston's outstanding achievement in character portrayal. He enriches the intellectual fabric of the play by his use of Montaigne and in most cases incorporates his borrowings unobtrusively. Unfortunately, the latter half of the main plot is not as impressive. Once there is no more need to study Malheureux intensively, he becomes a flat character in an intrigue, and the concentration on the contrast between Beatrice and Franceschina produces simplifications in language and attitude. From Crispinella's speeches onward, the didacticism is often heavy. It was a danger Marston had to risk in a play that attempted to mold the confused moral values of his audience and of his colleagues into a humane but responsible pattern.

XIII *Parasitaster or The Fawne*:
King James and the Prince D'Amour

The joy at James' accession to Elizabeth's throne was compounded of relief at its peaceful passage and high hopes for
England's future under the rule of a poet, philosopher, and
scholar. As Richard Martin, the sometime "Prince d'Amour,"
said in a speech delivered to the King on his arrival in London,
"Your majesty's government shall make us partakers of that
felicity which divine Plato did only apprehend but never see
(whose king is a philosopher) a philosopher being our king." [1]

[1] *A Speech Delivered, to the Kings Most Excellent Majestie in the Name of
the Sheriffes of London and Middlesex* (London, 1603), sig. B2v. John Davies,
Complete Poems, ed. Alexander Grosart (London, 1876), II, 229–236, greeted him
with a poem claiming that one might recognize the King in a group by look-

It is almost incredible how quickly admiration and high hopes changed to disgust and disillusionment. Elizabeth died in March of 1603, and James arrived from Scotland in May. "Before the summer was over," according to G. B. Harrison, "the old Queen was very generally regretted, for those very qualities which had seemed irksome were soon magnified into virtues." [2] Elizabeth had been genuinely interested in her people and in governing well. She worked hard and was aware of her kingdom's day-to-day problems. On the whole, James preferred hunting to governing. For various well-known reasons — his tragic childhood and difficult years in Scotland, his new wealth and his natural sloth, among others — he took only an intermittent interest in affairs of state.

This soon became clear to his subjects, so that at one and the same time he let the reins of government go slack and lost the hearts of his people. One clear sign of this is the sudden appearance on the London stage of direct satire against the King and his court. To anyone familiar with the rigorous control of the stage in Tudor times, Chambers' account of the new laxity would sound extravagant if his evidence were not so overwhelming:

> For some years after the coming of James, the freedom of speech adopted by the stage, in a London much inclined to be critical of the alien King and his retinue of hungry Scots, was far beyond anything which could have been tolerated by Elizabeth. The uncouth speech of the Sovereign, his intemperance, his gusts of passion, his inordinate devotion to the chase, were caricatured with what appears incredible audacity, before audiences of his new subjects. "Consider for pity's sake," writes Beaumont, the French ambassador, on 14 June 1604, "what must be the state and condition of a prince, whom the preachers publicly from the pulpit assail, whom the comedians of the metropolis bring upon the stage, whose wife attends these representations in order to enjoy the

---

ing for someone "more than other clearly wise,/Or wisely just, or justly valiant." Davies mastered the proper mode of address early, for, as D. H. Willson says in his authoritative study, *King James VI and I* (London, 1956), p. 168, "Courtiers discovered that no adulation was too gross, no praise too strained or fulsome for the taste of their new monarch. Eventually, it was said, he ignored words spoken to him unless they were prefaced by titles such as most sacred, pleasefull, wise, or learned."

[2] *A Companion to Shakespeare Studies*, ed. H. Granville-Barker and G. B. Harrison (New York, 1960), p. 181. For a possible expression of such regret in this play, see n. 15 below.

laugh against her husband." Beaumont's evidence is confirmed by a letter of 28 March 1605 from Samuel Calvert to Ralph Winwood, in which he writes that "the play[er]s do not forbear to represent upon their stage the whole course of this present time, not sparing either King, state, or religion, in so great absurdity, and with such liberty, that any would be afraid to hear them." [3]

Chambers goes on to mention that the prime offender in these political satires was the company which had been taken under the protection of the Queen with the title "Children of the Queen's Revels." Among other plays, they produced Samuel Daniel's *Philotas* (1605), for which the author was called before the Privy Council for supposed allusions to the Earl of Essex; the aforementioned *Eastward Hoe,* for which at least two of its authors were imprisoned; and John Day's *The Isle of Gulls* (1606), for which "sundry were committed to Bridewell." The reader may note that the relaxation in control was only relative.[4]

It was during this free-spoken period that Marston wrote *Parasitaster, or The Fawne* (1604–1606), for the Queen's Revels. The action occurs in the court of Duke Gonzago of Urbino, who is described in the list of "interlocutores" as a "weake Lord of a selfe admiring wisedome" (II, 146). In his own words, he is as "wise . . . As mortall man may be" (II, 172). He claims, according to his daughter, to be able to "interpret eies, understand the language of birds, interpret the grumbling of dogs & the conference of cats, . . . [he] can read even silence" (II, 183). He also prides himself on his learning:

> you must know my age
> Hath seene the beings and the quide of things,
> I know *Dimensions* and *termini*
> Of all *existens*. (II, 153)

In addition to being a philosopher (II, 154) and a poet (II, 173 and 215), he is a self-conscious rhetorician (cf. II, 187 and 188) who considers himself the master of a "most pathetique piercing Oratorie" (II, 183). He surrounds himself with flatterers, de-

---

[3] E. K. Chambers, *The Elizabethan Stage* (Oxford, 1923), I, 325.

[4] See Harold N. Hillebrand, *The Child Actors,* University of Illinois Studies in Language and Literature, vol. XI, nos. 1 and 2 (Urbana, 1926), pp. 171–206, for a similar account of the troubles which the Queen's Revels brought on themselves.

lights in being addressed as "royally wise, and wisely royall" (II, 185), and is eventually exposed as "an egregious Asse" (II, 222), an utterly witless, credulous fool. Given the uninhibited type of satire practiced by this acting company and by this author, it is natural to notice the many ways in which Gonzago resembles King James. This identification was first hesitantly proposed by A. H. Bullen in his edition of Marston's works in 1887, and it was supported by Alexander Upton in a modest and sensible article in 1929.[5] Upton's method was simply to compare the outstanding traits and actions of Marston's Duke with those of James, as described by contemporary observers. Very few scholars have bothered to discuss this theory, although no one has attempted to refute it. Yet this is not merely another effort to identify someone in a subplot as Dekker or the Earl of Essex. If the Duke is a caricature of James, this would be the only full-length portrait of the ruling sovereign in Elizabethan drama. Moreover, we know from the French ambassador's letter that some such portrait existed.

It is possible (although I have no evidence of this) that scholars have ignored Upton's identification because the apparent date of the play seems to make it impossible. Upton puts much stress on several allusions to the Gunpowder Plot of November 1605. This seems too close to the Stationers' Register entry for *The Fawne* (March 12, 1606) to allow time for the writing of the play. On the other hand, some have argued for production of the play as early as 1604, a date which seems too early for a caricature of James.[6] I happen to believe that the text of the quarto does contain allusions to the Gunpowder Plot and even to the quartering of Sir Everard Digby on January 30, 1606; Chambers has supplied a perfectly feasible explanation of how this could have occurred.[7] But I would stress that Upton's basic

[5] Bullen, *Works,* I, xliii, and Alexander W. Upton, "Allusions to James I and His Court in *The Fawne,*" *Publications of the Modern Language Association of America,* 44 (1929), 1048–1065. H. Harvey Wood, ed., *Plays of John Marston* (3 vols., Edinburgh, 1934–1939), II, xix, has suggested that Gonzago is modeled on Polonius. I can only discern their common tendency to be "tedious old fools." Polonius is educated, but he has none of Gonzago's intellectual pretensions, and he is almost free of self-praise and the need for flattery. Since Marston does quote *Hamlet* frequently, it is worth mentioning that there are no verbal echoes in Gonzago.

[6] Anthony Caputi, *John Marston, Satirist* (Ithaca, 1961), pp. 266–268.

[7] The title page says that the play was presented by the Queen's Revels and later at Paul's. Chambers says, "As a Queen's Revels play, this must date from 1604 or 1605; presumably it was transferred to Paul's by Edward Kirkham, when he took charge of them for Christmas of 1605–6" (III, 432). Nevertheless, Chambers finds that the "cumulative effect of the quadruple allusions here, in Day's *Isle of Gulls,* in Sharpham's *Fleir,* and in Middleton's *Michaelmas Term,*" to

argument depends not at all upon allusions to events in late 1605 and early 1606. There is very little in the portrait that was not standard gossip within a few months of James' arrival in London.

My only reservation about Upon's article is that he under-states the degree to which Marston copied specific mannerisms and habits of expression from James. For example, Gonzago's unending praise of his own eloquence can be matched by James' elaborate justification of his "Eloquence" — he uses the term three times in a paragraph — at the conclusion of his well-known first speech to Parliament:

> My conclusion shall onely now be to excuse my selfe, in case you have not found such Eloquence in my Speech, as peradventure you might have looked for at my hands. I might, if I list, alledge the great weight of my Affaires and my continuall businesse and distraction, that I could never have leasure to thinke upon what I was to speake, before I came to the place where I was to speak: And I might also alledge that my first sight of this so famous and Honourable an Assembly, might likewise breede some impediment. But leaving these excuses, I will plainely and freely in my maner tell you the trew cause of it, which is; That it becommeth a King, in my opinion, to use no other Eloquence then plainnesse and sinceritie. By plainenesse I meane, that his Speeches should be so cleare and voyd of all ambiguitie, that they may not be throwne, nor rent asunder in contrary sences like the old Oracles of the Pagan gods. And by sinceritie, I understand that uprightn[e]sse and honestie which ought to be in a Kings whole Speeches and actions: That as farre as a King is in Honour erected above any of his Subjects, so farre should he strive in sinceritie to be above them all, and that his tongue should be ever the trew Mes-

---

Sir Everard Digby's execution by quartering on Jan. 30, 1606, "is pretty strong. . . . I do not like explaining discrepancies by the hypothesis of a revision, but if Kirkham revived the *Fawn* at Paul's in 1606, he is not unlikely to have had it written up a bit" (III, 433). As for Caputi's claim that Marston could have been referring to an earlier quartering, I would point out that Digby's was a cause célèbre and that many considered the punishment unjustly harsh (hence the ironic reference to its being "most just" [II, 199]). Marston's description of the victim as a "goodlie man" (II, 199) is consistent with the judgment by a contemporary that Digby was the "goodliest man in the whole court" (quoted in G. P. J. Akrigg, *Jacobean Pageant, or the Court of King James I* [Cambridge, Mass., 1962], p. 74). My conclusion is that the text, at least as we have it in what may be an augmented form, dates from 1606.

senger of his heart: and this sort of Eloquence may you
ever assuredly looke for at my hands.[8]

The similarity of this device to Duke Gonzago's manner of
concluding his first long speech is striking:

> wise heads use but few words.
> In short breath, know the Court of *Urbin* holds
> Your presence and your embassage so deere,
> That wee want meanes once to expresse our heart
> But with our heart: plaine meaning shunneth art.
> You are most welcome (Lord *Granuff* a tricke,
> A figure, note) we use no *Rethorick*. (II, 154)

In several passages (see II, 209 and 174), Marston shows the
contradiction between Gonzago's self-conscious and overelab-
orate rhetoric, on the one hand, and his pretensions to a
natural, plain style, on the other. King James' speeches seemed
as long-winded and pedantic to his contemporaries as they do to
us; yet he praises sententious brevity and a plain style again
and again in works like the *Basilikon Doron,* to which Marston
would have had ready access.[9] An edition was published in London at the time of James' accession, and, according to Bacon, it
fell "into every man's hands." [10]

This is not the only indication that Marston was familiar
with James' speeches and writings. At one spot in the play Gonzago admires "Cupid's" opening remarks to his "Parliament":
"Since multitude of lawes are signes either of much tirannie
in the prince, or much rebellious disobedience in the subject,
we rather thinke it fit to study, how to have our old lawes
thorowly executed, then to have new statutes comborously in-
vented" (II, 216). While this is not a unique opinion about law-
making, it amounted almost to an obsession with James. As
early as the *Basilikon Doron,* he expressed it, and he reiterated
it whenever he spoke to Parliament, as in his speech of 1603:
"beware to seeke the making of too many Lawes, for two espe-
ciall reasons: First, because *In corruptissima Republica pluri-
mae leges;* and the execution of good Lawes is farre more
profitable in a Common-wealth, then to burden mens memories

---

[8] *The Political Works of James I,* ed. Charles H. McIlwain (Cambridge, Mass.,
1918), pp. 279–280.

[9] See esp. ibid., pp. 46–47.

[10] Quoted by James Craigie, ed., *Basilikon Doron,* Scottish Text Society, 3rd
ser., no. 18 (Edinburgh, 1950), II, 18, n. 1. *The Diary of John Manningham,* ed.
John Bruce, Camden Society Publication 99 (London, 1868), p. 155, mentions the
Basilikon two days after publication, March 30, 1603.

with the making of too many of them. And next, because the making of too many Lawes in one Parliament, will bring in confusion, for lacke of leisure wisely to deliberate before you conclude." [11] Gonzago's one piece of unstinting praise is reserved for an opinion by the wisest fool in Christendom.

Even in small details Marston seems to have been attentive to James' tastes and utterances. He has Gonzago describe himself as one of the "men of discerning wit/That have read *Plinie*" (II, 153). Pliny was one of James' favorite authors,[12] and Marston may have been referring specifically to the very curious, naively pedantic way in which James uses Pliny in his book of poems, *Essayes of a Prentice* (1585). At the end of the volume, he reprints Pliny's well-known passage from the *Naturalis Historia* about the Phoenix (which he had used in one of the poems) and explains, "I have insert for the filling out of thir vacand pageis, the verie wordis of *Plinius* upon the *Phoenix* as followis." [13] Clearly, he had read Pliny.

To take two final examples, Upton notes that Marston seems to be alluding to James' notorious drinking habits, but he fails to cite the lines which make the clearest hit: "Drunkennes . . . makes the king and the peasant equall, for if they are both drunke alike, they are both beastes alike" (II, 216). I point out this fairly direct gibe because Upton omitted it, and it may also be noted that Marston could have derived the particular formulation from James' warning against drunkenness in the *Basilikon Doron*: "beware of drunkennesse, which is a beastlie vice, namely in a king." [14] Similarly, the Fawne tells a wife that since her husband "takes Tobacco, therefore with great authority you may cuckolde him" (II, 191). I suggest that the "great authority" is James, who had just published his *Counter Blaste to Tobacco* (1604).

I conclude that the closer one looks at the play, the more likely Upton's identification appears. In small matters as well as in large,[15] everything tends to confirm it. It is almost equally

---

[11] *Political Works*, p. 277. Cf. also pp. 19–20 and 288.

[12] Allan Westcott, ed., *New Poems of James I of England* (New York, 1911), p. xxii.

[13] (Edinburgh, 1585), sig. P4r. Marston also has Gonzago brag of having "reade *Cicero de Oratore*" (II, 208). According to Craigie, *Basilikon Doron*, II, 333, James cited *De Oratore* four times in the *Basilikon*, but his prime authority was *De Officiis*, cited twenty-seven times.

[14] *Political Works*, p. 44.

[15] In a play satirizing James, it would be natural to regret the loss of the old Queen. This, I suggest, is what Dondolo is doing as he looks into an "Almanacke" for "this yeare": "Let mee see the moone, fore pity, tis in the wayne, what griefe is this? that so great a planet should ever decline or loose splendore" (II, 212).

significant for a play of this nature and of this time that nothing in it resists the most obvious conclusions by the sort of *"malignus interpres"* (II, 143) about whom Marston complains in his preface. Nonetheless, the fact remains that *The Fawne* is Marston's first play in the Jacobean period which did not involve him in some trouble,[16] probably because it is the first one in which he did not inject any overt gibes at the Scotch. John Day's portrait of Duke Basilius in *The Isle of Gulls* also shows a duke who prides himself on his wit, but it is a slighter sketch with far fewer correspondences to James. Nevertheless everyone connected with the production landed in Bridewell because it clearly refers to friction between the Scotch and the English. Apparently the authorities at this time were willing to ignore almost anything so long as the insults were not specific.

I have offered additional reasons for accepting Upton's theory because its validity radically affects the aesthetic experience of this play, as the discovery that Shakespeare modeled Hamlet on Prince Henry would not. *The Fawne* is not simply a topical satire, but it is very strongly tied to a certain time and place. Its parochial roots are further accentuated by the fact that Marston drew on the Middle Temple's "Prince d'Amour" revels for a substantial portion of the fifth act.[17] It will be recalled that "arraignments" were a standard element in the Christmas revels and that in 1597–98 the revelers conducted a mock trial of a discontented lover and of a jealous lover, judging them by a set of laws which were read out as part of the festivities. A similar arraignment occurs in *The Fawne*. In the last act a "Parliament of Cupid" is organized as a courtly entertainment. In it, the vices of various "enemies" of love are exposed and judged by reference to certain "laws of love." These laws strongly resemble the ones recited at the Prince d'Amour's

[16] I am referring to the censorship apparent in the second quarto and in the corrected third quarto of *The Malcontent* as well as to its reputation as a "bitter play," to the trouble with *Eastward Hoe*, and to the trouble Nixon mentions concerning *The Dutch Curtezan*.

[17] See my detailed discussion of this relationship, "The Use of the Middle Temple's Christmas Revels in Marston's *The Fawne*," *Studies in Philology*, 44 (1967), pp. 199–209. William A. Neilson, *The Origins and Sources of the "Courts of Love,"* Harvard Studies in Philology and Literature, VI (Boston, 1898), p. 267, claims that the Parliament of Cupid in *The Fawne* derives from the medieval "courts of love." But the "laws" in *The Fawne* resemble those in the *Prince d'Amour* more than any which Neilson cites. Moreover, the "Court of Love" tradition had long been dormant in England, whereas Marston lived in an institution which continually conducted such arraignments. And most important, the connection between Marston's play and the Middle Temple's revels is not confined to the arraignment since the Prognostication and the recitation of paradoxes were also part of the entertainment.

revels. Thus, the first criminal violated an "Act against the plurality of Mistresses" (II, 217). Several statutes in the *Prince d'Amour* deal with this practice; for example, "If any man be retained with two Mistrisses at one time, concealing the one from the other, he is to pay double dammages to the party grieved." [18] In all, there are six criminals, one of whom is the Duke Gonzago, and each is judged by a law which has one or more parallels in the Middle Temple's revels.

Marston also appropriated material from other portions of the revels. One evening in the entertainments of 1597–98 was occupied with "The Prognostication," which "with great skill foretold things that were past." To give one example: "Some Revellers shall receive great down-falls, for presuming to imitate the heavens in their circular motions." [19] A "prognostication" is also provided in *The Fawne*. Significantly, it is placed after the Parliament of Cupid has been convened but just before the scene of judgment, so that the two events appear to be part of the same entertainment — as indeed they were. The series of jokes from the "Almanacke or prognostication" in *The Fawne* is similar to those in the revels: "heeres likewise prophesied a great skarsitie of Gentrie to ensue, and that some Bores shall be dubbed Sir *Amoroso*. A great scarsitie of Lawyers is likewise this yeare to ensue, so that some one of them shall be entreated to take fees a both sides" (II, 213).

At the Temple's revels of 1597–98 a "Defense of Woman's Inconstancy" was scheduled for January 3, but it was not delivered. However, a "defenc of womens inconstancye" was delivered at a later revel at the Temple; that the same topic should appear in two unrelated revels suggests that such an oration was a standard item.[20] Marston's "Fawne" delivers a set piece on exactly the same topic (II, 169); the crux of his argument (that inconstancy, being a sign of perfection in all natural objects, should also be considered so for women) is the same as that in the revels' oration. Such paradoxes were quite modish at the Inns of Court at that time; a character named Paradox was a leading figure in the Gray's Inn's revels of 1617–18. The Fawne might also have been called by that name, for he utters no less than ten paradoxes of various lengths in this play.

Although there is no evidence that Marston wrote this play

---

[18] *Prince d'Amour* (London, 1660), p. 65.

[19] Ibid., pp. 83 and 35, respectively.

[20] The unfulfilled plan to have a commendation of women's inconstancy is mentioned in *Prince d'Amour*, p. 85. The text of the later commendation appears in Edward Pudsey's commonplace book (Bodleian MS. Eng. Poet. d.3), fol. 87r.

for the Middle Temple's revels, it certainly would have possessed a special appeal for those able to recognize how cunningly Marston wove standard ingredients from the revels into the fabric of his play. His employment of this material is one more piece of evidence suggesting the degree to which a writer like Marston conceived of the audiences at the private theaters and at the Inns as essentially identical. The "laws of love" would evoke the same responses and have the same appeal at the one place as at the other; so, apparently, would the political attitudes.

2

Marston's basic artistic task in *The Fawne* was fairly simple. He had to find a plot that would permit him to display Duke Gonzago at length, and he had to place him in an atmosphere that would reflect the Duke's character. For the background he again used an Italian palace, while for the plot he employed once more the device of a disguised duke acting as a commentator; but, in keeping with Marston' requirements, this duke disguises himself as a smooth-tongued flatterer rather than as a gross-jawed railer. At the conclusion of *The Malcontent*, Altofronto placed flattery above even lust in his recital of the evils which can undermine a state: "The flatterer like the Ivy clip the Oke,/And wast it to the hart." [21] This passage was one of the additions to *The Malcontent* for the King's Men; it reflects the slight change in emphasis which results from the expansion of the role of the courtier Bilioso. His prime activity is flattery, by which he is specifically linked to the new Scotch favorites:

> BILIOSO. . . . I am in wondrous credite Lady.
>
> BIANCA. See the use of flattery, I did ever counsell you to flatter greatnes, and you have profited well: any man that will doe so shal be sure to be like your Scotch Barnacle, now a blocke, instantly a worme, and presently a great goose: this it is to rot and putrifie in the bosome of greatnes.[22]

It is a fair guess that Marston's decision to expand *The Malcontent* by showing the activities of a flatterer was based on a growing awareness of the prime importance of this activity in the new court. The dominance of this motif in *The Fawne* is additional evidence of Marston's political purpose.

[21] *Plays*, I, 214.
[22] Ibid., 175.

In this play Duke Hercules of Ferrara comes to the Court of Urbino to observe and, if possible, to influence the conduct of his son Tiberio. The sixty-four-year-old Duke has sent Tiberio as his emissary to negotiate his marriage to Duke Gonzago's fifteen-year-old daughter Dulcimel, but he hopes to trick his shy son into falling in love with her himself. The Duke's assumed name, "Fawnus," describes his role, the nearly allegorical nature of which is suggested in a remark by Duke Gonzago: "this *Fawnus* is a very worthy fellow, and an excellent Courtier, and belov'd of most of the princes of Christendome" (II, 184). Marston devotes almost half the play to the activities of this archetype of a flatterer. Through the highly unrealistic, procession-like plot of a "comical satire," he provides a series of occasions for the Fawne to exhibit the art of flattery.

Marston makes the subplot entertaining and surprisingly complex by the variety of ways in which he employs flattery. His flatterer is infinitely agreeable, capable of finding a favorable aspect to every vice, humiliation, or misfortune:

> HERCULES. I perceive Knight you have children, oh tis a blessed assurance of heavens favour, and long lasting name to have many children.
> SIR AMOROSO. But I ha none, *Fawne,* now;
> HER. O that's most excellent, a right special happinesse, hee shall not bee a Drudge to his cradle, a slave to his childe, hee shall be sure not to cherish anothers blood, nor toyle to advance paradventure some Rascals lust; without children a man is unclog'd, his wife almost a Maide: *Messalina,* thou cryedst out, O blessed barrennesse! why once with child the verie *Venus* of a Ladies entertainment hath lost all pleasure.
> SIR AMOR. By this ring *Fawnus* I doe hugge thee with most passionate affection, and shall make my wife thanke thee. (II, 162–163)

Arguing mainly by means of proverbs and commonplaces, the Fawne can prove that it is "blessed" to have children and, without blinking, that it is "blessed" not to have them; like a lawyer, he can comfortably take either side of any question.

As I suggested above, Marston cast much of the Fawne's flattery into the forms of the paradox and the mock encomium, those exercises in witty ingenuity which were so popular with an Inns of Court audience. The phrase "And indeede" usually signals the start of one of these outrageous set pieces, as in the

Fawne's encouragement of a wife in her special brand of adultery: "And indeede since the vertue of procreation growed hopeless in your husband, to whome should you rather commit your love and honour to, then him that is most like and neere your husband, his brother" (p. 191). These orations — there are at least thirteen of various lengths, including some by other characters — resemble the disconnected, witty displays of the revels; through their tonal similarity to such festal occasions they prepare the way for the similar wit of the Parliament of Love in the last act.

The Fawne's speeches expose the total moral vacuum in which a flatterer operates. Marston also employs flattery as disguised satire. Thus the Fawne's justification of lying points covertly to its prevalence at court: "as for thy lying, as long as theres policie int, it is very passable, wherefore haz heaven given man tong but to speake to a mans owne glory? hee that cannot swell bigger then his naturall skinne nor seeme to bee in more grace then hee is, has not learn'd the very rudiments or A.B.C. of courtshippe" (II, 196). The "Faun" (as it is intermittently spelled in the quartos) is really a satyr-satirist in another guise.

The Fawne's flattery also serves an important function in the development of the plot. Through flattery he so ingratiates himself with his victims that he manages to extract from them their deepest secrets. As one of them complains at the Parliament of Love after the Fawne has publicly humiliated him, "By the hart of dissemblance, this *Fawne* has wrought with us as strange Taylors work in corporate cities . . . all inward, inward, he lurkt in the bosome of us, & yet wee know not his profession" (II, 219). The Fawne acts deceitfully because he has discovered how to use flattery as an instrument for moral reformation. When he first arrives at Gonzago's court, he is shocked to discover how differently courtiers talk about a prince when he is absent. He realizes that flattery has lulled him into a "dreamefull slumber" and recognizes the value of an atmosphere

> Where what is honest, you may freely thinke,
> Speake what you thinke, and write what you doe speake,
> Not bound to servile soothings. (II, 158)

Unfortunately, as Marston had discovered, no one listens to a scourger of villainy; direct satire has lost its potency:

> all knowes the sharpenesse
> Of reprehensive language is even blunted
> To full contempt. (II, 158)

At the same time, Hercules (repeating almost verbatim one of Freevill's Montaigne-inspired sentences) realizes that some new moral agent must be found since "vice is now term'd fashion" (II, 158). Thus he resolves to be a "parasitaster," just as Altofronto was a "malcontentaster." Malevole's method was to "afflict al in that to which they are most affected." [23] Hercules plans to try precisely the opposite tactic:

> flattering all
> In all of their extreamest vitiousnesse,
> Till in their owne lov'd race they fall most lame,
> And meet full butte, the close of Vices shame. (II, 158)

One act later Hercules realizes that his experiment has been successful. The scourging of villainy, he sees, merely invites "legge-ringes," the "turnd key," and enmity. Flattery is a "gratefull venome," and he prays that his injections will make the "impostumbd members" swell until they "burst" (II, 175). This is essentially Freevill's technique with Malheureux, but Hercules has transformed it into a medical "cure" for vice.

Hercules' methods lead him to discover that Gonzago's court is far from the "patterne of godlinesse and all honest vertues, to all the rest of the people" which King James tells his son in the *Basilikon* a court ought to be.[24] He finds a collection of courtiers — all of them highly simplified, nearly allegorical figures — who suffer from the perversion of some natural instinct, most often their sexual instinct. Nimphadoro vows eternal and undeviating affection to all women from lowest to highest while loving none. Herod cuckolds his older brother for money and thereby loses his inheritance when he gets his sister-in-law with child.[25] And in the most fully developed of these small plots, Don Zuccone is psychopathically jealous of a wife who, everyone agrees, is "the musik of sweetly agreeing perfection, more clearely chast then ice or frozen raine" (II, 202). The Fawne's flattery accentuates the natural inability of these courtiers to see the absurdity of their conduct: "The eye sees all thinges but his proper selfe" (II, 206).

---

[23] Ibid., 146.

[24] *Political Works*, p. 33.

[25] This seems to be alluding to a contemporary scandal. See Arnold Davenport, ed., *Poems of John Marston* (Liverpool, 1961), pp. 353–354.

The extended subplot in which the Fawne is the unifying
figure satirizes the practice of flattery while employing flattery
as a form of satire. It also displays the sickness of the court over
which Duke Gonzago presides. This is clearly why Marston
devotes so much time to sketching in the background, for a
court mirrors its prince. A king, according to James, should be
"a daily watch-man" [26] over his court, but Gonzago is the
blindest person there, slumbering in an atmosphere of unending flattery. Although he surrounds himself with toadies and
fawns, it is his own injections of the "gratefull poyson" of flattery which lull him into a "dreamefull slumber" (II, 158).

Marston satirizes Gonzago's self-love and vanity through a
plot which permits him to exhibit a few traits again and again.
In one of Boccaccio's stories a young wife tricks her confessor
into acting as her pander. In Marston's adaptation it is Gonzago's daughter Dulcimel who ingeniously maneuvers her father
into wooing Duke Hercules' son Tiberio for her. As with Cocledemoy's attacks on Mulligrub, Marston shows Dulcimel repeatedly gulling Gonzago at approximately the same point in
each act. Each time she uses the same trick. Pretending that
Tiberio has been wooing her, she asks her father to dissuade
him, thereby informing Tiberio of her interest. Dulcimel continues this Machiavellian exploitation of her father's blindness with an absolute purity of method: "I will so stalke on
the blind side of my all knowing fathers wit, that do what his
wisedome can, he shall be my onely mediatour, my onely mes-
senger, my onely honourable spokesman, hee shall carrie my
favours, he shall amplifie my affection, nay hee shall direct the
Prince the meanes the very way to my bed, hee and onely he,
when hee onely can doe this, and onely would not doe this, hee
onely shall doe this" (II, 183). This leads to much slapstick
hilarity, and Marston ingeniously elaborates on Boccaccio's
plot. For instance, in Boccaccio's story the confessor unwittingly
tells the gallant precisely how to get into the witty lady's room.
Gonzago gives Tiberio most of this information but neglects to
communicate all of the relevant details. Tiberio is in anguish
about how to accomplish his assignment until Gonzago "hastily" reappears:

> Sir sir this plaine tree was not planted here
> To get into my daughters chamber: and so she praide
>   me tell you.
> What though the maine armes spreade into her window?

[26] *Political Works,* p. 33.

> And easie labour climes it: Sir know
> She has a voice to speake, and bid you welcome,
> With so full breast that both your eares shall heare ant,
> And so she praide me tell you: ha wee no braine;
> Youth thinkes that age, Age knowes that youth is vaine.
>
> (II, 210)

In reading this passage — and there are many similar ones in this play — it is well to recall Marston's urgent addition to his prefatory epistle: "*Comedies* are writ to be spoken, not read: Remember the life of these things consists in action" (II, 144). Much of this play is based on the most primitive comic formulas which "action" can make entertaining. There is no such "foolish animal in *rerum natura*" (II, 222) as the Duke Gonzago, but the exaggeration of his portrait in *The Fawne* suggests that he serves a very different purpose from that served by the Duke in *The Malcontent*. By this time in his career, Marston had shown himself capable of designing a play with complex twists in plot and subtle shadings in character. In *The Fawne* everything is simplified and, while frequently amusing, highly repetitive. This is precisely what is required for political caricature; it must be reductive and denigrate by simplification and repetition. The more complex the portrait (for example, Duke Pietro in *The Malcontent*), the more likely we are to take the object of attack seriously or to feel some degree of sympathy. Our sense of superiority and our contempt toward Gonzago remain undisturbed.

For four acts Marston conducts two separate but highly similar actions. Like Freevill and Cocledemoy, the Fawne and Dulcimel have analogous functions in their respective plots. Dulcimel is not conducting an experiment in moral reformation through her flattery, but in the fifth act the Fawne exploits her work and draws the Duke into the web in which he has trapped the rest of his victims. At the same time, all the thematic polarities, youth and age, vision and blindness, wit and stupidity, the natural and unnatural, which have been more or less implicit thus far, are brought to the surface while the action moves closer to allegory. The aim, as Marston's mouthpiece announces at the beginning of the fifth act, is "morall learning" (II, 211).

The final act begins with an unusual use of the two-level stage: "Whilst the Act is playing, *Hercules* and *Tiberio* enter, *Tiberio* climes the tree, and is received above by *Dulcimel*, *Philocalia* and a Preist: *Hercules* staies beneath" (II, 211).

Thus we are to understand that the judgment scene is occurring at the same time the marriage is being consummated. In a very literal sense the spirit of healthy and natural love presides over the scene. Hercules makes this explicit in a long prayer to the "Genitall,/You fruitefull well mixt heates" (II, 211). He conceives the union of Tiberio and Dulcimel in the most fundamental terms, connecting it to fertility and the future:

> O blesse the sheetes
> Of yonder chamber, that *Ferraraes* Dukedome,
> The race of princely issue be not cursde,
> And ended in abhorred barrennes. (II, 211)

With this vision of the importance of the "right true end of love" and healthy marriage, the action shifts to the trial and condemnation of those who have violated the sacred and fundamental laws of life. The Parliament is conducted with the "solemn foolery" which we saw in the arraignment at the Inns' revels, but the solemnity is at least as insistent as the foolery. Each courtier is condemned for having violated one of Cupid's laws: Nimphadoro for having a "plurality of Mistresses" (II, 217); Sir Amaroso for "counterfeiting of *Cupids* royall coine, & abusing his subjectes with false money" (II, 218); Herod for violating the law against "forgers of love letters, false braggarts of ladies favours, and vaine boasters of counterfeit tokens" (II, 219); and Don Zuccone for being one of the "slanderers of *Cupids* liege ladies names, and lewde defamers of their honors" (II, 219). In all these cases, of course, it is upon the evidence of the Fawne that they are condemned, so that his method has succeeded in showing "how/Vice may be cur'de" (II, 175). Some of his victims are incurable and are released without punishment because they are harmless: this is Sir Amoroso's case. Some are genuinely repentant, and the Fawne has helped to effect a cure: this seems to be the case of Don Zuccone. Nimphadoro and Herod are apparently exiled to the Land of Cockayne.

Finally, the Duke himself is brought before the bar, and the link between his acts and those of the other fools is made definite. He, too, it appears, has violated Cupid's laws:

> HERCULES. An act against privie conspiracies, by which if any with ambitious wisedome, shall hope and strive to outstrippe love to crosse his wordes, and make frustrate his sweete pleasures, if such a presumptious wisedome fall to nothing, & die in laughter, the wizard so trans-

gressing is *ipso facto* adjudged to offend in most deepe treason, to forfeite all his witt at the will of the Lord, and be instantly committed to the shippe of fooles for ever. (II, 221–222)

The tone of the accusation is mock-serious, but the charge goes to the core of what a Gonzago can mean. Not only does it chastise his pretensions to wisdom; it suggests the harm such pretensions can inflict on others. Like the sterile husband and the oversuspicious one, Gonzago's "crime" is ultimately the obstruction of the natural course of life. The comic battle between youth and age is really a series of connected battles between nature and artifice, knowledge and ignorance, life and death. In the ritual expulsion of the dangerous elements from the kingdom, the open, healthy society is assured.

The play ends on a note which seems to ask for just such a definite formulation. One does not feel much need to verbalize the implicit vision of the ideal society after Shakespeare's comic endings of reconciliation, marriage, and music. A masque of Jonson's like *Hymenaei,* in which the Four Affections and Four Humors attempt to interrupt a marriage and are expelled by Reason, states the matter explicitly. *The Fawne,* with its characters who are nearly affections and humors, its highly simplified Youth-Age battle, and its mock-ritual ending, concludes in a manner much closer to this more abstractly conceived image.

The incorporation of the ritual of the Inns' revel adds an extra dimension to the judgment scene. It arraigns Gonzago and his courtiers in a tribunal of the young and judges the conduct of the court by the standards of the Inns. In this sense, we can, without straining the fabric of the play, see *The Fawne* as a latter-day, comic, more sophisticated descendant of *Gorboduc,* trying to warn the King about matters as important as those which the earnest Templars brought to the attention of the young Queen. By displaying the harmful effects of flattery, the play makes a point very similar to Sackville and Norton's:

This is the end when in fonde princes hartes
Flattery prevailes and sage rede hath no place.[27]

In *The Fawne* Duke Gonzago finally realizes "wherefore this Parliament was: what a slumber have I been in" (II, 224).

[27] *Chief Pre-Shakespearian Dramas,* ed. Joseph Quincy Adams (Cambridge, Mass., 1924), p. 534, ll. 237–238.

There is nothing to indicate that the Fawne's methods had an equivalent impact on the outside world. The King was probably hunting in Royston while his Queen was "enjoy[ing] the laugh" at representations of her spouse on the stage at Blackfriars. *The Fawne* may have been ineffectual, but in it Marston demonstrated that a play that was primarily personal political satire could also be civilized and witty.

XIV *Sophonisba*:
Wonder and Shame

Marston's last complete play, *The Wonder of Women, or The Tragedie of Sophonisba* (1606), has provoked more difference of opinion as to quality and basic characteristics than any of his other plays. T. S. Eliot professed to hear in it a tone unique not only in Marston but in all Elizabethan drama.[1] For him it was Marston's best play, as it was for Peter Ure, who felt that in writing a Roman play Marston had found the proper setting for his Stoical views.[2] For Anthony Caputi, on

[1] *Essays on Elizabethan Drama* (New York, 1960), p. 177.
[2] "John Marston's *Sophonisba*: a Reconsideration," *Durham University Journal*, 41, n.s., 10 (1949–1950), 81–90.

the other hand, *Sophonisba* "reflects a complete, if temporary, abandonment of the satiric attitude . . . and a neglect, at least, of those refinements on classical Stoicism characteristic of his personal version of Neo-Stoicism." [3]

Clearly Marston had special feelings about this play. He announced in the preface to *The Fawne* that he was taking unusual pains with it (II, 144). In an appendage to the epilogue of *Sophonisba* he expressed nervous concern that the reader not hold against him "the fashion of the Entrances and Musique of this Tragidy" (II, 64). He revealed in a prefatory letter that his aim in this play was to provide more than mere pleasure. Finally, in the Epilogue, his tone approaches Jonson's aggressive "By God, 'tis good," as he claims that the play ought to gain a favorable reception if *"wordes well senc'd, best suting subject grave"* (II, 64) are deserving of praise.

Why this special concern on the part of Marston, who usually affected Persius' role of the disengaged amateur: "Ipse semi-paganus/Ad sacra vatum affero nostrum"? In part, I think, Marston was trying to prove that he was capable of producing high art. I shall return to this point, but there is a deeper reason. In the figure of the heroine of this play, Sophonisba, Marston directly and without any protective irony tried to express an ideal of human perfection about which he had a nearly obsessional preoccupation. One remembers vividly his portraits of inconstant and lascivious females, particularly the Duchess Aurelia and Franceschina. But from the time of his earliest plays, and in all but one of them,[4] Marston had also invoked the notion of a woman of ideal virtue, beauty, and goodness who struck wonder and amazement in all who saw her. Moreover, the language of this quasi-Mariolatry was nearly identical in each case.

Its first expression in *Histriomastix* is not at all remarkable since it appears to be a piece of conventional praise for Queen Elizabeth, perhaps slightly more extravagant than some:

> Heere comes *Amazements* object, wonders height,
> *Peaces* patronesse, *Heavens* miracle,
> *Vertues* honour, *Earths* admiration,
> *Chastities* Crowne, Justice perfection,
> Whose traine is unpolute *Virginity.*[5]

---

[3] *John Marston, Satirist* (Ithaca, 1961), p. 241.

[4] The one exception is *What You Will*, a fact which confirms my view of the play as the most ironic and objective in Marston's oeuvre.

[5] *Plays of John Marston*, ed. H. Harvey Wood (3 vols., Edinburgh, 1934–1939), III, 301.

Formulaic though it may be, this list of abstract absolutes establishes the terms in which Marston praises a succession of female paragons. We may recall Pasquil on Katherine in *Jack Drum*:

> Amazement, wonder, stiffe astonishment,
> Stare and stand gazing on this miracle,
> Perfection, of what e're a humane thought
> Can reach with his discoursive faculties.[6]

Antonio's description of Mellida in *Antonio and Mellida*[7] makes use of the same language, as does his mother's lamentation for Mellida on her death in the *Revenge*:

> The beautie of admir'd creation,
> The life of modest unmixt puritie,
> Our sexes glorie, *Mellida*.[8]

At about the time Marston wrote the *Antonio* plays (1601), he was invited to contribute verses to Robert Chester's strange volume, *Love's Martyr*. In his four connected poems, Marston wrote "*A narration and description of a* most exact wondrous creature, arising *out of the Phoenix and Turtle Doves ashes.*" Whatever this creature was, it evoked the same "wonder" and "amazement" for "this measureles pure Raritie" for which "No speech is Hyperbolicall." The speaker is in doubt whether to call it "Perfection," "Heavens mirror," "Beauties resistlesse thunder," or "Deepe Contemplations wonder." [9] Clearly, when Marston wanted to describe absolute perfection of whatever kind, he lapsed into nearly identical locutions.

He is even capable of mocking this habit, as when he has Mendoza in *The Malcontent* write a "sonnet" of "passionate flashes" to the Duchess:

> *Beauties life, Heavens modell, Loves Queene,*
> *Natures Triumph, best on Earth,*
> *Thou onely wonder that the world hath seene.*[10]

These lines are directly traceable to Mucedorus' description of Philoclea in Sidney's *Arcadia*: "the ornament of the Earth, the

---

[6] Ibid., 236.

[7] Ibid., I, 48.

[8] Ibid., 117.

[9] *Poems of John Marston,* ed. Arnold Davenport (Liverpool, 1961), pp. 177–179 passim.

[10] *Plays,* I, 157. I have arranged this as a continuous poem by omitting Maquerelle's interruptions.

modell of heaven, the Triumphe of Nature, the light of beauty, Queene of Love." [11] Perhaps Sidney's passage crystallized Marston's feeling on this subject; at least it provided the model for his expression of it.

In each of the later plays Marston has one or more objects of wonder, each described in the same language: for example, Beatrice in *The Dutch Curtezan*[12] and Donna Zoya and Philocalia in *The Fawne.*[13] The character of the language is so invariable that it can even serve as an aid in the attribution of passages about which the authorship is in dispute, as in a love letter in *The Insatiate Countess: "Astonishment of nature, unparaleld excelency, and most unequal raritie of creation."* [14] Marston may laugh at the high-flown quality of his own rhetoric, he can see that this language may be debased into a formula as it is by Mendoza, or that it can sound silly as it occasionally does with Pasquil. But its recurrence in play after play suggests that he held an unexamined hope or dream that unsullied purity and perfection still existed or might exist in this fallen world.

2

The Wonder of Women is an attempt to embody in a character and an action Marston's vision of perfection. It is not primarily a play about the virtues of Stoicism, or an attempt to rival *Sejanus* as a Roman history, or a play about the power of Fate. It is a play about perfection and what happens to it in this world. The Sophonisba story was as good a vehicle as any for Marston's nearly impossible task. This story of female heroism told by Livy and Appian had been used by Trissino in the first "regular" tragedy of the Renaissance; it was a vehicle for high and noble sentiments throughout the seventeenth century. Marston announced that he was not primarily interested in the historical aspects of his subject: *"I have not labored in this poeme, to tie my selfe to relate any thing as an historian but to inlarge every thing as a Poet, To transcribe Authors, quote authorities, & translate Latin prose orations into English blank-verse, hath in this subject beene the least aime of my studies"* (II, 5). This statement probably involves an unfair slap at *Sejanus,* but it also describes quite accurately Marston's treatment of his sources in the construction of the play. He changes and

[11] *The Countesse of Pembrokes Arcadia,* ed. A. Feuillerat (Cambridge, Eng., 1912), p. 90.
[12] *Plays,* II, 130.
[13] Ibid., 202–203.
[14] Ibid., III, 27.

expands Appian and invents and incorporates material for which there is no authority in the histories. Thus he first shows us Sophonisba just before her marriage to Massinissa in order to demonstrate how a wonder of women should act at such a time:

> I wonder *Zanthia* why the custome is
> To use such *Ceremonie*, such strict shape
> About us women: forsooth the Bride must steale
> Before her Lord to bed: and then delaies,
> Long expectations, all against knowne wishes.
> I hate these figures in locution,
> These about phrases forc'd by *ceremonie*. (II, 11)

Obviously Marston had no historical authority for Sophonisba's frank avowal of female desire: this she acquired from Montaigne by way of Crispinella. The attack on hypocrisy makes Marston's rarefied image of perfection credible by endowing her with some earthly attributes; in the light of subsequent events, it also strengthens her right to be revered as a wonder.

A moment later her marriage ceremonies are interrupted by the announcement that Carthage has been invaded. Her husband Massinissa must leave before the marriage is consummated. Since we have been informed of Sophonisba's sexual desire, we can admire all the more her instant abdication of her womanly rights:

> I will not stay my Lord.
> Fight for our country, vent thy youthfull heate
> In field not beds. (II, 17)

Not until he hears these words of self-abnegation does Massinissa appreciate the full stature of the woman he has married. It inspires the first of his many expressions of wonder at her character:

> Wondrous creature, even fit for Gods, not men,
> Nature made all the rest of thy faire sex
> As weake essaies, to make thee a patterne
> Of what can be in woman. (II, 18)

Marston enlarged on history to allow Sophonisba to represent "what can be in woman."

Another principle influenced Marston's arrangement of his-

torical material. He wished to show as strikingly as possible
the world in which this wondrous creature had to live. Thus, as
Peter Ure points out, the play does not open with the scene of
the aborted wedding. Instead, we see Sophonisba's disappointed
suitor, King Syphax, vowing revenge against all who have
frustrated his marital plans. He justifies his course of action in
the language of "policy":

> knowe while Kings are stronge
> What thei'le but thinke and not what is, is wrong . . .
> *Passion* is *Reason* when it speakes from Might. (II, 11)

Since the scene immediately shifts to Sophonisba's pre-marriage
speech, we hear her express her normal, healthy aspirations
with an ironic awareness of the black world in which she lives.
This principle of construction is confirmed by the events which
occur after the noble Massinissa unhesitatingly leaves his bride
to fight for his beloved country. In the next scene the senators
of Carthage engage in a debate in which they agree to betray
Massinissa and Sophonisba in order to gain the support of the
more powerful Syphax. Marston makes an evil senator justify
the politic decision by means of a notable paradox:

> Nothing in Nature is unservisable,
> No, not even *Inutility* it selfe,
> Is then for nought dishonesty in beeing? (II, 20)

A noble senator Gelosso (one of Marston's inventions) attacks
the senate's policy:

> If treachery in state be serviceable,
> Let hangmen doe it: I am bound to loose
> My life but not my honour for my country;
> Our vow, our faith, our oath, why th'are our selves,
> And he thats faithlesse to his proper selfe
> May be excusd if he breake faith with princes. (II, 21)

Thus the fundamental conflict in the play is between those
who have personal integrity and honor, and those who follow
policy and utility. Though we ultimately see the politic creatures punished, evil is certainly shown to be the dominant force
in this world. The good retreat from one defense position to
the next; their integrity is constantly assaulted; they are hopelessly outnumbered. Gelosso is in a normal situation when

he alone argues against "policy." He must therefore betray his city for a higher good. Massinissa must become a traitor for a similar reason. Even Sophonisba must use some guile to defend her honor against Syphax. This world involves such horror that the mere fact of living has no meaning to people like her:

> what power can make me wretched? what evill
> Is there in life to him, that knowes lifes losse
> To be no evill. (II, 23)

The best that life can offer is happiness, but this is a corrupting state because, as Sophonisba declares, it makes one a slave to fortune:

> How neere was I unto the curse of man, Joye,
> How like was I yet once to have beene glad:
> He that neere laught may with a constant face
> Contemne *Joves* frowne. Happinesse makes us base.
>
> (II, 60)

But there is nothing for weeping or lamentation in Sophonisba's suicide. It is not tragedy, but a positive and triumphant act to leave such a world.

This attitude is emphasized by the strange episode involving the witch Erictho which Marston felt the need to insert in the play. It is, in effect, a small morality play exhibiting the "folly to inforce free love" (II, 6 and cf. II, 51). During one of Sophonisba's encounters with Syphax, he threatens to violate her, even if she first commits suicide (II, 45). Later he calls on the witch Erictho (a figure from Lucan's *Pharsalia* who feeds off corpses) to help him satisfy his desire for Sophonisba. The witch disguises herself as the queen and by means of this trick fills her "longing armes with *Syphax*" (II, 51). Thus he becomes a hellish creature while still alive, as he learns from the ghost of Asdruball (II, 53). But it is important to note that the evil and now hellish Syphax does not die but in fact causes the dilemma which provokes Sophonisba's suicide. Through his contact with Erictho, Syphax becomes a gigantically magnified and distorted symbol of the overpowering, destructive evil of this world, because of which the purely good cannot survive. The incident is grotesque; artistically, the language and action here are totally unrelated to anything else in the play. But it makes Sophonisba's gesture even more justifiable and triumphant: to leave a world in which Syphax survives is not even regrettable.

The battle lines between the characters are clearly drawn, and yet every commentator of whom I am aware, notably Peter Ure in the best essay on this play, has missed an important point in describing it as a black and white contrast between the values of Stoicism and Machiavellianism. It is certainly true that the "good" try to act according to the Stoic code and profess Stoic sentiments. But a close look at the character of Massinissa will reveal Marston's usual reservations about Stoicism: that however admirable it may be as an abstract doctrine, it has distinct limitations as a code of conduct for ordinary mortals.

Massinissa is a magnanimous figure, perhaps a little naive in his trustfulness and patriotism, but capable of amazing gestures and noble sentiments. He is at his height when refusing to kill the hired poisoner, Gisco (II, 26), and he is similarly "God-like" (II, 26) in disdaining to kill Syphax after defeating him in single combat. But while he is a worthy mate for Sophonisba, he is clearly her moral inferior. This is suggested by showing in consecutive scenes their distinctly dissimilar responses to adversity. In Act II, scene 1, Sophonisba is informed by the Carthaginian senators of their treacherous decision to transfer her to Syphax. She refutes the logic of their arguments most cogently, but when nothing will dissuade them, she obeys, saying:

> I goe: what power can make me wretched? what evill
> Is there in life to him, that knowes lifes losse
> To be no evill . . . .
> Tearlesse O see a miracle of life—
> A maide, a widdow, yet a haplesse wife. (II, 23)

When Massinissa learns in the next scene that he has been betrayed, his response verges on disorderly rant and "stagelike passion":

> Why wast thou born at *Carthage,* O my fate.
> Divinest *Sophonisba!* I am full
> Of much complaint, and many passions,
> The least of which expresd would sad the Gods
> And strike compassion in most ruthless hell.
> . . . O you Gods,
> Revenge worthy your anger, your anger, O,
> Downe man, up hart. (II, 27)

Massinissa is struggling with the classic Stoic problem: in order to be true to his creed, he must repress his natural responses.

The "man" in him must be kept "downe," but man will out despite philosophy.

When we see him next, he labors to retain his self-control although he is being goaded into passion by Scipio, the Roman general to whom he has defected. Reminding him of the many grounds he has for "passion," Scipio brands him a "statue, not [a] man" (II, 40). Massinissa grieves inwardly but remains firm until he finally breaks out:

> Scipio he that can weepe,
> Greeves not like me, private deepe inward drops
> Of bloud: my heart—for Gods rights give me leave
> To be a short time Man.
> SCIPIO. Stay prince.
> MAS. I cease;
> Forgive if I forget thy presence: Scipio
> Thy face makes Massinissa more then man. (II, 40)

Once again Massinissa comes perilously close to acting like a man instead of a statue. (He is not the only Stoic with this problem. Earlier, the good senator Gelosso had said, "O let me slake a little/Austere discourse, and feele Humanitie" [II, 21]). As the dialogue with Scipio continues, Massinissa breaks out once again into an immoderate and passionate speech for which he must apologize. Clearly Marston wants to show that Massinissa's passion is part of his noble nature; an emotional concern with the blows of fortune makes it impossible for him to act with Stoic constancy. But more important than his violation of "manners" is the question of whether his actions conform to the standards of Stoic conduct. Certainly the events of the play are arranged so that Massinissa has almost no choice, and yet one wonders whether a true Stoic should have defected to Scipio. In contrast, the option of the asp, the knife, or poison always presents itself to Sophonisba as it never does to Massinissa. Acts III and IV are largely devoted to a series of unsuccessful assaults on her person, but she remains unassailable and almost unmoved. She is capable of resourcefulness when she tricks Syphax, but never of capitalizing on the weakness of her sex.

The concluding events of the play clarify the significance of the contrast between Sophonisba and Massinissa. After Massinissa has defeated Syphax, he appears before Sophonisba, disguised by his closed helmet. Thinking him a soldier, she implores him either to save her from humiliating captivity by the Romans or to kill her. As Massinissa "disarmes his head," he utters Marston's supreme compliment: "Rarity" (II, 58). Now that she is reunited with her husband, Sophonisba exhibits her only sign of weakness by sinking faintly into his arms, overcome with joy. Under these circumstances Massinissa is notably controlled and even urges Sophonisba not to be too effusive in her happiness: "Peace,/A silent thinking makes full joyes increase" (II, 58). But almost immediately their positions are reversed. Under Syphax's baleful influence, Scipio demands that Massinissa remain true to his vow of loyalty and deliver up Sophonisba to Roman captivity and public humiliation. Faced with the dilemma of treachery either to Rome or to his wife, Massinissa, true to character, collapses completely: "Right which way/ Runne mad impossible distraction" (II, 60). For a true Stoic there should be no dilemma. Certainly there is none for Sophonisba, who, after calming her passionate husband, instantly decides to commit suicide so that he can keep his "faith upright" (II, 60). It is impossible to determine exactly what Marston is trying to convey at the next moment, but Massinissa's response to her offer can scarcely be called a refusal: "Thou darst not die, some wine, thou darst not die" (II, 60). Not only does she dare, her last request (characteristically a "command") emphasizes their temperamental difference: it is that he "not weepe" (II, 61). Sophonisba does not allow him to miss the significance of her gesture. As she drinks the wine, hastily and wordlessly mixed with poison by her solicitous husband, she reminds him that she is giving up "An abhord life" to "save *You, you* [italics not mine], (for honor and just faith/Are most true Gods, which we should much adore)" (II, 61). She has successfully passed her last trial and can view her life with some objectivity and complacency in her last words: "a Virgin wife, try'de to my glory,/I die, of female faith, the long liv'de story" (II, 61).

Massinissa's eulogy is accurate and at the same time revealing:

> Covetous
> Fame-greedy Lady, could no scope of glory,
> No reasonable proportion of goodnes
> Fill thy great breast, but thou must prove immense
> Incomprehence in vertue, what, wouldst thou
> Not onely be admirde, but even adorde?
> O glory ripe for heaven? (II, 61)

Despite his godlike stance, Massinissa is a reasonable man who observes limits and degrees, but her aspirations were immeasurable, disproportionate, her virtues boundless. Hence she could not continue to live on this earth because, as Freevill said in *The Dutch Curtezan,* "Nothing extremely best with us endures" (II, 115). Marston's one authentic Stoic was a virgin martyr.

The distinction between Sophonisba and Massinissa is emphasized further when he delivers her corpse to Scipio. The Roman does ample justice to the "glory of [her] vertue," and "adornes *Massinissa*" with symbols of conquest, saying:

> for ever breath[e]
> *Romes* very minion: Live worth thy fame
> As far from faintings as from now base name. (II, 63)

It is impossible not to hear some contempt mixed with Scipio's praise, for no matter how favorable the connotations of "minion," it defines a relationship which Sophonisba scorned: "Let me not kneele to Rome" (II, 58).[15] The "worth" of Massinissa's "fame" seems to be severely limited by its connection with "faintings," to which, as we have seen, he has been prone, and also by the phrase "now base name." Perhaps Marston meant that Massinissa would henceforth be far from a "base name," but the last words in the play, Massinissa's own, tend to confirm the less favorable implication. In a final paean to Sophonisba, he compares her to hardened steel and to fire. Rightly, he "adornes" her corpse with the honors he has received from Scipio because his honor derives from her action. Now he has regained his Stoic composure and concludes by calling her "Womens right wonder, and just shame of men" (II, 63). The implication is clear: the transaction by which she has kept his honor clean has brought shame upon him. But the word is "men": Massinissa is a man, not a god; he has acted as men do and his fame is in "proportion." Thus, I suppose, one could call *Sophonisba* a "Stoic" play, but only with some complicated reservations. At the same time that Marston shows the glory of acting in strict accordance with Stoicism's doctrines, he suggests, as he has before, that it is constricting and inhumane for most men. It requires utter indifference to one's fortunes in this world; only an amazing rarity, a wonder, can do this with serenity.

[15] It is a fair assumption that the audience would have known that historically Massinissa remained a minion, even to the extent of helping Scipio to defeat the greatest of all Carthaginian soldiers, Hannibal.

3

In the comedies just before *Sophonisba,* Marston had been mixing copious, realistic prose with a relaxed dramatic poetry which observed speech mannerisms and character differences. Such a style is consonant with the notion, ultimately derived from Cicero, that the *"nymble forme of commody"* was a *"spectacle of life, and publique manners."* [16] The language of this tragedy, on the other hand, is a remarkably homogeneous medium, most of the characters speaking in stiff, sententious verse, often in rhymed couplets, and with no intermission from a tone of high-minded moral instruction. (The "exceptional consistency of texture" seems to have been one of the main attractions of this play for T. S. Eliot.) Marston's clearly different use of language in tragedy, as opposed to comedy, proceeds from a fundamental distinction formulated by him in the preface to *The Fawne*: "*Comedies* are writ to be spoken, not read: Remember the life of these things consists in action; and for your such courteous survey of my pen, I will present a Tragedy [*Sophonisba*] to you which shall boldly abide the most curious perusall." [17] Comedies are to be observed; tragedies may also be read. In reading, a comedy *"presents"* an *"unhansome shape"* because it appears without *"the soule of lively action,"* as he says about *The Malcontent*.[18] He describes *Sophonisba* not as a play but, for the only time in his work, as a *"poeme"* (II, 5).

Sophonisba was performed on the stage, and yet it is hard to imagine that even the most select auditors could have comprehended many of the speeches unless they had first given the quarto a most "curious perusall." Regardless of the speaker, the language tends to be elliptical, condensed, and sententious. The diction is plain and the members are brief, but connectives and articles are frequently omitted. The effect can be grave and sententious, but it is always more or less obscure. Such a style has obvious affinities with the sententious, "short-breathed" [19] Senecan style in prose which, as Hoskins' remarks in *Directions* indicate, was in vogue in London at this time. I find it impossible to place Marston's language precisely in any of the anti-Ciceronian subcategories proposed by Morris Croll and elaborated by George Williamson, more especially because it is a poetic version. But it cannot be fortuitous that Marston

[16] Prologue to *The Fawne, Plays,* II, 145.
[17] "To my equall Reader," *Plays,* II, 144.
[18] *Plays,* I, 139.
[19] *Directions for Speech and Style by John Hoskins,* ed. Hoyt Hudson (Princeton, 1935), p. 39.

suddenly adopted a style which resembles the Senecan for a play which portrays the apotheosis of a Stoic saint. Marston was not the first to write a Senecan play in the new Senecan manner. As Geoffrey Bullough points out, Fulke Greville's poetic plays also have many of the characteristics of the new prose.[20] The crucial difference from Marston's effort is that Greville's plays were designed for the closet, not the stage. It was Cicero's opinion that "Stoic oratory is too close knit and too compact for a popular audience." [21] This is even truer for the drama. Most obviously, it would be tedious to listen to for a long period of time. As Hoskins says about the sententious style, "If it be a matter of short direction for life and action, or notes for memory, I intend not to discredit this new trick. But otherwise, he that hath a long journey to walk in that pace is like a horse that overreacheth and yet goes slow." [22] There are further objections to this style as a medium for dramatic poetry, perhaps the most important of which is the unwitting absurdity which results when everything is said sententiously, for example, "a naked man is soone undrest" (II, 37) and "Syphax has no knees" (II, 32). Without pursuing this point further, I would only add that no one who thinks highly of this play has seen fit to justify all that is patently undramatic and absurd in its language.

The dramaturgy also diverges from Marston's previous practice. Marston employs an unusual amount of ceremony and music; in addition, he frequently inserts a shocking, unexpected event on stage, primarily a visual experience, as the following stage directions will indicate: "Enter Carthalon his sword drawne, his body wounded, his shield strucke full of darts: Massin. being reddy for bedde" (II, 13); "Syphax with his dagger twound about her haire drags in Sophonisba in hir nightgowne petticoate" (II, 32); "Enter Erictho in the shape of Sophonisba, her face vailed and hasteth in the bed of Syphax . . . Syphax hasteneth within the Canopy as to Sophonisbas bed" (II, 50). Such moments are not outrageous coups de théâtre, as one critic asserts. Marston uses them as stimuli for new actions which illustrate the basic Stoic theme of indifference to the blows of fortune. The alternation between static and dynamic action, the three elaborate ceremonies, the nearly total opposition of the characters into clearly defined camps combine to give a distanced, abstracted quality to the play

[20] The Poems and Plays of Fulke Greville (New York, 1945), I, 20.
[21] Quoted by George Williamson, The Senecan Amble (Chicago, 1951), p. 128.
[22] Directions, p. 40.

which is not inharmonious with the frigid, sententious language. Indeed, the play is nearer to some kind of quasi-religious spectacle than to conventional tragedy. With its coronation of the dead Sophonisba and the implication that she has entered the realm of fire, the play can be seen as showing the assumption of a Virgin into her proper sphere. We should not feel woe because, to her, "lifes loss . . . [is] no evill" (II, 23). We are to feel shame and wonder.

There is much that is unusual in Marston's treatment of the Sophonisba story. Nevertheless, it is surprising to find an author with some degree of general popularity writing a play in 1606 which has more affinities with *Gorboduc* than with the nearly simultaneous *King Lear*. This choice of form reveals once again Marston's adherence to the standards and tastes of his immediate milieu. In the epilogue to *Sophonisba* he implies that he has conformed to the requirements of tragic decorum by choosing *"wordes well senc'd, best suting subject grave"* and a *"Noble true story"* (II, 64). Behind these terms we can hear quite clearly Jonson's prescription for tragedy in the preface to *Sejanus,* a play to which Marston wrote commendatory lines but which, we may gather from his ironic remarks in the preface about the use of historical sources, he was trying to surpass. Jonson lists the "offices of a *Tragick* writer" which he had "discharg'd": "truth of Argument, dignity of Persons, gravity and height of Elocution, fulnesse and frequencie of Sentence." [23] This formulation, in turn, is remarkably similar to Sir Philip Sidney's terms of admiration for *Gorboduc*: "which notwithstanding, as it is full of stately speeches and well sounding Phrases, clyming to the height of *Seneca* his stile, and as full of notable moralitie, which it doth most delightfully teach, and so obtayne the very end of Poesie." [24] As late as 1612 we find John Webster lamenting the fact that the *"uncapable multitude"* lack the taste to appreciate *"the most sententious* Tragedy . . . *ever written."* He describes Tragedy in terms essentially identical to those used by Sidney and Jonson: *"heighth of stile; and gravety of person; . . . sententious* Chorus, *and as it were life'n* Death, *in the passionate and waighty* Nuntius." [25]

The aesthetic behind *Gorboduc* and behind the statements by Sidney, Jonson, and Webster was not based on a pious

[23] *Ben Jonson,* ed. C. H. Herford and Percy and Evelyn Simpson (Oxford, 1932), IV, 350.
[24] *Elizabethan Critical Essays,* ed. G. Gregory Smith (Oxford, 1904), I, 196–197.
[25] *The Works of John Webster,* ed. F. L. Lucas (London, 1927), I, 107.

veneration of the classics but (as Tillyard suggested in the comment about *Gorboduc* quoted earlier) on an essentially avant-garde taste for an abstract, stylized drama like that of France and Italy. Writers like Jonson and Webster could not pursue this ideal because they were forced to concern themselves with "popular delight," but Marston had a more sympathetic audience for this sort of thing at the Blackfriars. All the evidence suggests that *Sophonisba* was Marston's attempt at a masterpiece. We have seen his pretentious announcement that it was in preparation, his nervous concern that the reader not judge the play by its accidentals, his implicit condemnation of Jonson's similar effort, his warning that giving pleasure was not his only purpose, his carefully conceived and unusual style, and his choice of a grandiose subject. It was in this, his most serious, carefully contrived work that Marston chose to conform to the aesthetic which Sidney first expressed in English. Nothing that Shakespeare had done could expunge from some writers this image of an ideal dramatic form. More than one scholar has suggested that had Sidney lived, his prestige and patronage might well have inspired much similar drama. This would have created a split between popular and "educated" drama of vastly greater significance than that between the dramas of the public and private stages. But as matters developed, the aristocratic and pedantic writers were mostly confined to their closets, and Marston attempted only one masterpiece.

The result in *Sophonisba* was a thoughtful, earnest, high-minded, tedious production. Marston's major mistake was to attempt to embody in a drama, hence in physical form, an idea which can only be expressed by the most elaborate indirections. Curiously enough, in one of Marston's contributions to the *Love's Martyr* anthology, he had already achieved a minor success in a lyric poem on this same subject. (I hasten to add that he set himself a problem which only Dante could master.) Marston's method was to describe the futility of the effort to verbalize an absolute ideal. The language is technical and abstract, but feeling is expressed through the speaker's sense of the inadequacy of any of his categories:

Perfectioni Hymnus

What should I call this creature,
    Which now is growne unto maturitie?
How should I blase this feature
    As firme and constant as Eternitie?

Call it Perfection? Fie!
    Tis perfecter then brightest names can light it:
Call it Heavens mirror? I.
    Alas, best attributes can never right it.
Beauties resistlesse thunder?
    All nomination is too straight of sence:
Deepe Contemplations wonder?
    That appellation give this excellence.
Within all best confin'd,
    (Now feebler *Genius* end thy slighter riming)
No Suburbes all is *Mind*
    As farre from spot, as possible defining.[26]

The studied gracelessness and unembarrassed awe are blended in the last line. By means of the off rhyme, antithetical structure, metrical regularity, and internal sound linkages, Marston conveys a sense of wonder while he confesses intellectual defeat. In a brief epigram of praise for Jonson's *Sejanus,* he asserts that he "could say much, not more." [27] *Sophonisba* says much but not more than the *"Perfectioni Hymnus."*

[26] *Poems,* p. 179.
[27] Ibid., p. 181.

XV Conclusion:
A "Timely Change"

Had *Sophonisba* been Marston's last work, we could take his heroine's willing withdrawal from the world as a sign of the author's state of mind and as a presage of his imminent retirement. But another, later play, at least partly by Marston, has no similar theme, and there are reasons for believing that his departure from London and the stage was not entirely voluntary.

A tragedy called *The Insatiate Countess*, first printed in 1613, designates Marston as the author. A later edition assigns the play to William Barksted, and verbatim repetitions from Barksted's poems make it certain that he had some share in the play.

Chambers conjectures that while Marston was writing the play he got into serious trouble and that he left the play unfinished.[1] Barksted, according to this theory, completed it, probably long after Marston stopped writing inasmuch as it contains a quotation from a poem which Barksted published in 1611. The evidence for Marston's having left an incomplete fragment is strengthened by the fact that even in its finished form one of the plots is left unresolved and the other two are almost totally without relationship to each other.

Yet I must concur with H. Harvey Wood when he insists that Marston's hand is evident throughout the play.[2] As I said in the previous chapter, the love letter in the subplot must be Marston's, and there are equally clear signs that he was involved in the main plot. In effect, the play is a companion piece to *Sophonisba,* the contrast between the Countess and Sophonisba being of the same order as that between Franceschina and Beatrice in *The Dutch Curtezan.* The Countess' lovers learn that "Women were made/Of blood, without soules" (III, 51), although to new lovers she looks like a Sophonisba:

> What rarietie of women feeds my sight,
> And leades my sences in a maze of wonder? (III, 61)

The clearest signs of Marston's involvement in the main plot occur in the scenes depicting the Duke Gniaca. He is a kind of Malheureux who justifies his love by saying " 'Tis custome, and not reason makes love sinne" and "Why should heaven frowne on joyes that doe us good?" (III, 48). The Countess tempts him to murder his good friend whom he has supplanted as her lover, but as happens frequently in Marston's plays, he thinks better of his passionate decision after he has left his temptress.

While Marston's hand is similarly visible in all parts of the play, Barksted's more romantic, Shakespeare-permeated verse is also sprinkled throughout the text. There is no point in attempting to assign lines to each author on the basis of subjective feelings about the style, because nothing is particularly noteworthy or valuable in the play as it stands. Marston was apparently trying to contrast three ways of loving: the Countess' psychopathic lust, the comic husbands' psychopathic hate, jealousy, and shame, and the altruistic and civilized devotion

[1] *The Elizabethan Stage* (Oxford, 1923), III, 434.
[2] *Plays of John Marston* (3 vols., Edinburgh, 1934–1939), III, xxviii.

of the Count Mendoza and the Lady Lentulus. But we are rarely aware of relationships among the plots because Barksted (apparently) failed to see what Marston had been trying to do. On the basis of Marston's previous practice, one would suppose that all three groups were to meet in the final execution scene, a mixed comic and tragic affair. Perhaps at that point he would have compared the bloody, insatiate Isabella's fierce desire to live, the comic desire of the husbands to be executed out of simple stubbornness, and the innocent Count Mendoza's noble willingness to be a martyr for his loved one's honor. However, Barksted forgot about the Mendoza-Lentulus plot, and he showed the other execution scenes separately. In the form in which it has survived, *The Insatiate Countess* does not reveal any new energy or inventiveness; it is a reworking of the sort of thing Marston had already done and been applauded for. The fact that the language is very similar to that of *The Dutch Curtezan* confirms the view that *Sophonisba* was an experiment or, at any rate, a special case. For that evidence, at least, the survival of the play is useful, but beyond that it is not possible to speak critically because Barksted's contribution bulks too large to permit any meaningful statements.

Although the ensuing events in Marston's dramatic career are uncertain, Chambers' suggestion is most persuasive: "on 29 March 1608 the French ambassador . . . reported that all the London theatres had been closed, and were now threatened by the King with a permanent inhibition on account of two plays which had given the greatest offence." [3] One was about the French king, apparently Chapman's *Tragedy of Byron*. The other was a personal attack on James himself, satirizing his scheme for mines in Scotland and showing him as drunk and bad tempered. Needless to say, the offending company was once more the Children of the Blackfriars, as the Queen's Revels were now called. According to a letter from Sir Thomas Lake to Lord Salisbury on March 11, 1608, the King "had vowed they should never play more, but should first begg their bred and he wold have his vow performed, And therefore my lo. chamberlain by himselfe on your 11. at the table should take order to dissolve them, and to punish the maker besides." [4] Chambers comments, "I feel very little doubt that the maker of the play on the mines was once more Marston, who was certainly summoned before the Privy Council and committed to Newgate, on some offence not specified in the extant record,

[3] *The Elizabethan Stage*, II, 53.
[4] Quoted by E. K. Chambers, *The Elizabethan Stage*, II, 54.

on 8 June 1608. And this was probably the end of his stormy connexion with the stage. He disappeared from the Blackfriars and from literary life, leaving *The Insatiate Countess* unfinished, and selling the share in the syndicate which he had acquired from Evans in 1603 to Robert Keysar for £100." [5]

The triple coincidence of the scandalous satiric play, Marston's imprisonment by order of the Privy Council, and his abandonment of the stage makes Chambers' theory a virtual certainty. I would suggest that another piece of evidence confirms this hypothesis about Marston's retirement. I refer to John Davies of Hereford's epigram to Marston published in 1610 in *The Scourge of Folly*:

> Thy *Male-content,* or, *Malecontentednesse*
> Hath made thee change thy *Muse* as some do gesse.
> If Time mispent, made her a *Male-content;*
> Thou needst not then her timely change repent.
> The end will shew it: meane while do but please
> With vertuous paines, as erst thou didst with ease:
>   *Thou shalt be prais'd; and kept from want and wo;*
>   *So, blest are* Crosses, *that do blesse us so.*[6]

From comments on this poem I have seen, I suspect that its significance has been obscured by a failure to consider when it was written. The references in Davies' volume are almost exclusively to events and persons in London in the period from 1608 to 1610, and this is consistent with the fact that Davies took up residence in London in 1608.[7] The epigram does not refer, as some have assumed, to some imagined change in Marston's style or morality after the War of the Theaters. It describes a rumor around town about the reasons for his recent switch in muses. The key word, I suggest, is "Crosses," too strong a word to apply to aesthetic disagreements with Ben Jonson. Davies is saying that Marston had been in some trouble because of his malcontentedness and had made a "timely change" of muses. The sanctimonious tone of the conclusion is further evidence that he was referring to a religious occupation.

By December of 1609 Marston was ordained and after this he never wrote again.[8] He observed his pledge or someone else's

---

[5] Ibid.

[6] (London, 1610), p. 105.

[7] See C. D. Murphy, "John Davies of Hereford" (*Cornell Abstracts of Theses,* 1940), p. 40.

[8] That is, unless R. E. Brettle, "John Marston and the Duke of Buckingham, 1627–1628," *Notes and Queries,* 212 (1967), 326–330, is correct in attributing to Marston certain satires against Buckingham.

command or his own urge to keep silent so rigorously that when his collected works were printed in 1633, he took steps to have his name removed from a reissue later in the year. Marston died in 1634; he renewed his connection with the Middle Temple by choosing the Temple Church for his interment.

This explanation of the sudden close of Marston's writing career is rendered all the more likely by the precedents and parallels for such conduct among his contemporaries at the Inns of Court. A tongue as fetterless as an emperor's was common there, although none could rival Marston's. One feels that what was alleged about Hoskins was even truer of Marston: no obligation could bind his wit. Indeed, what appears to have energized his wit was a feeling of anger at or disdain for anything which enslaved or inhibited. His plays are filled with creatures whom philosophical codes, or passions, or fashions in clothing, manners, or language have blocked from acting naturally and freely. Thus it was consistent with his natural impulses for Marston to enlist his wit during the Jacobean period in the same political struggle that was occupying some of his most prominent colleagues.

His political interest was only one indication, and that not the strongest, that Marston would have been considered by his colleagues at the Inns as "one of us." His subjects, his language, his tones and attitudes, his aesthetic preferences all show that he was bound and preoccupied by the problems of his immediate environment. Ben Jonson's famous quip about Marston refers to another, apparently contradictory feature of his work: "Marston wrott his Father-in-lawes preachings & his Father-in-Law his Commedies." [9] Whatever this says about his father-in-law's sermons, I take it to be Jonson's way of describing and deriding Marston's strong, occasionally obtrusive didactic streak. But it is as colleague and spokesman that he delivers his "preachings." Clearly his robes are not immaculate; he knows what happens inside bordellos and lascivious palaces. The language of a disabused participant in the world validates and authenticates his images of what man is and can be; they are not the product of a "stoycall sower vertue." [10] Nor do his "preachings" ignore the intellectual challenges to the old or-

[9] "Notes of Ben Jonson's Conversations with William Drummond of Hawthornden," *Ben Jonson*, ed. C. H. Herford and Percy and Evelyn Simpson (Oxford, 1925), I, 138.
[10] *Plays*, II, 159.

thodoxies posed by such writers as Machiavelli and Montaigne. He attempts to accommodate them and assimilate them into the structure of his plays.

After the unmitigated gloom of the *Antonio* plays and the unrelieved irony of *What You Will* come a series of plays which suggest that virtue, though embattled, can at least survive. In *The Malcontent* we see the triumph of a disguised and guileful virtue, and in his last two comedies the preacher-spokesman offers images of a "generous" virtue which has a "free pleasant buxom qualitie." [11] This is a concept precisely attuned to an audience of gallants; it suggests a way for the gentry to be truly worthy of their "generosus" status. True "generosity" displays an open, candid, unpretentious acceptance of what is natural: "Ther's nothing free but it is generous." [12]

Superficially, Marston's linking of virtue and generosity is reminiscent of Viola's reproof of Malvolio in *Twelfth Night* for lacking a "generous, guiltless, . . . free disposition." [13] But the dramatic actions which support Marston's conception lack the depth and resonance of Shakespeare's; they differ as much as the Middle Temple's revels differ from the mummings and morris dances of rural England. Literally and figuratively, Marston's was an indoor drama which shut out much of the world; compared with Shakespeare's, it was abstract, intellectually conceived, the product of traditions which were comparatively impoverished or artificial. Against this standard no author could survive; I invoked Shakespeare merely to say in another way that Marston's plays were of an age and a place, not for all time. Nevertheless, at the Blackfriars in my mind (the only theater where it is possible to see these plays), Marston's visions of the dark but comic battle between a corrupt world and the integrity of the individual still convey an urgent power.

[11] Ibid., 99.
[12] Ibid., 148.
[13] I.v.98–99.

Appendix A Some Important Figures at the Inns of Court (1590–1610)

I. Winchester School Group

	Admitted to Winchester	Admitted to New College, Oxford	Member-ship at Inn[1]	Admitted to Bar
John Owen (1560–1622)	1577	1582	IT(1593–?)	—
John Hoskins (1566–1638)	1579	1585	MT(1593–1638)	1600
Henry Wotton (1568–1639)	ca. 1580	1584	MT(1595)	—
Thomas Bastard (1566–1618)	1581	1586	—	—
John Davies (1569–1626)	1580	1585 (Queen's)	MT(1588–1626)	1595

II. Members of Middle Temple Known to Be in "Prince d'Amour" Revels of 1597–98 (in addition to those in Winchester School Group)

	Admitted to College	Member-ship in MT[1]	Admitted to Bar
Richard Martin (1570–1618)	1585, Broadgates, Oxford	1587–1618	1602
Benjamin Rudyerd (1572–1658)	1587–88, St. John's, Oxford	1590–1658	1600
Charles Best (?–1631)[2]	—	1592–1631	1600

III. Some Well-known Middle Temple Writers

Edward Sharpham (1576–1608)	—	1594–1607[3]	—
John Marston (1576–1632)	1592, Brasenose, Oxford	ca. 1594–1606	
Thomas Overbury (1581–1613)	1595, Queen's, Oxford	1597–ca. 1604	
John Webster(?) (1580?–1625?)	—	1598[4]	—
John Ford (1586?–1639?)	1601, Exeter, Oxford	1602–1617[5]	—

[1] Membership of barristers is for life unless otherwise indicated.

[2] Date of death (not previously noted) given in F. A. Inderwick, ed., *Calendar of the Inner Temple Records* (London, n.d.), II, 355.

[3] Listed as "of the Middle Temple "on the title page of *The Fleir* (1607).

[4] Identity of the "John Webster of London" much in dispute.

[5] This may not be the terminal date of his residence at the Middle Temple.

IV. Other Middle Temple Writers or Men of Letters

	Admitted to College	Member-ship in MT	Admit-ted to Bar	Remarks
John Manningham (d. 1622)	1592, Magdalen, Cambridge	1598–1622	1605	Diarist
John Salisbury (1567–1613)	1581, Jesus, Oxford	1595	—	Courtier, versifier, patron of Chester
Robert Chester (of Royston, d. 1640)	1586, Trinity, Cambridge	1600	—	Possible author of *Love's Martyr*
George Sandys (1577–1643)	1589, St. Mary's Hall, Oxford	1596	—	Traveler, translator of Ovid
George Salterne (1568–1625?)	1582, Christ Church, Oxford	1584–1625	1590	Author of Latin play, *Tomumbeius*
Thomas Kedgwin	1594, Emmanuel, Cambridge	1598–1607	—	Poet and wit
Dabridgcourt Belchier (d. 1621)	1598, Corpus Christi, Cambridge, B.A. 1600, Christ Church, Oxford	1601–1605	—	Author of *Hans Beerpot* (STC 1803)

V. Other Prominent Members of the Middle Temple (ca. 1590–1610)

	Admitted to College	Member-ship in MT	Admit-ted to Bar	Remarks
John Pym (1584–1643)	1599, Broadgates, Oxford	1602–1605	—	Parliament leader
Edwin Sandy (1561–1629)	1577, Corpus Christi, Oxford	1590–1602 (intermittently)	—	Important MP
Bartholomew Gosnell (d. 1607)	1587, Jesus, Cambridge	1592–1593	—	Explorer

	Admitted to College	Member-ship in MT	Admit-ted to Bar	Remarks
Peter Maunsell	1587, Brasenose, Oxford	1594–1598	—	Gresham Professor of Physics, 1607–1615
William Lower (1570–1615)	1586, Exeter, Oxford	1589–1591	—	Astrono-mer

VI. Miscellaneous Writers in Residence at Other Inns of Court (ca. 1590–1610)

	Admitted to College	Member-ship at Inn	Admit-ted to Bar	Remarks
John Donne (1572–1631)	1584, Hart Hall, Oxford	LI (1591–1594),[6] (1616–1622)	—	Preacher at LI (1616–1622)
Francis Beaumont (1584–1616)	1597, Broadgates, Oxford	IT (1600–1602?)	—	Partici-pated in revels, ca. 1601
Francis Davison (ca. 1575–1619)	1586, Emmanuel, Cambridge	GI (1593–1595)		Antholo-gist of *Poetical Rhapsody*
Francis Bacon (1561–1626)	1573, Trinity, Cambridge	GI (1576–1626)	1583	Partici-pated in and composed revels
Thomas Campion (1567–1620)	1581, Peterhouse, Cambridge	GI (1586–1595)		Partici-pated in and contributed to revels
Thomas Lodge (ca. 1557–1625)	1573, Trinity, Oxford	LI (1578, 1595)[7]	—	Poet

[6] Including period of membership in Thavies Inn.
[7] Title page of *A Fig for Momus* designates Lodge as "of Lincoln's Inn."

	Admitted to College	Membership in MT	Admitted to Bar	Remarks
Everard Guilpin	1588, Emmanuel, Cambridge	GI (1591– 1598, at least)	—	Author of *Skialetheia*, 1598
John Harrington (ca. 1561– 1612)	1576, King's, Cambridge	LI (1581)	—	Poet, courtier, wit

Appendix B   Chronological Table of Events in Marston's Life and Related Events at the Middle Temple

Marston	Events at MT and Elsewhere
1570 John Marston Sr. admitted to MT	
1575 J. M. Sr. marries Maria Guarsi, Sept. 19	
1576 John Marston born, probably at Coventry; christened at Wardington, Oxford, Oct. 7	
1577 J. M. Sr. built chambers at MT	
1580 J. M. Sr. temporarily expelled from MT for violating a Privy Council rule	
1585	Travers-Hooker controversy
1587	Richard Martin admitted MT
1588	John Davies admitted MT
1590	Benjamin Rudyerd admitted MT
1592 J. M. matriculates Brasenose, Oxford, Feb. 4; J. M. Sr., Fall Reader at MT, using the privilege of his office, admits J. M. Jr. to MT on Aug. 2 "specially"	
1593	John Hoskins admitted MT
1594 J. M. Jr. takes B.A. in Feb.; possibly begins residence at MT then, but certainly by 1595	Edward Sharpham admitted MT John Davies' *Orchestra* (SR, June 25, 1594) Revels at GI
1595	Davies and Marlowe, *Elegies & Epigrams*
1597	Joseph Hall's *Virgidemiarum*, I–III (SR, March 31, 1597) Thomas Overbury admitted MT
1597–1599 J. M. shares rooms with father at MT	Prince d'Amour (Christmas season, 1597–98)
1598	J. Davies' attack on Martin, Feb. 9 John Manningham admitted MT Hall's *Virgidemiarum*, IV–VI (SR, Mar. 30, 1598)
J. M.'s *PI* and *CS* (SR, May 27)	
J. M.'s *SV* (SR, Sept. 8)	Ev. Guilpin's *Skialetheia* (SR, Sept. 15)
1598–1599 **J. M.'s** *Histriomastix* at MT (my conjecture) (SR, Oct. 31, 1610)	Hoskins' *Directions* (?)
1599 2d and 3d ed. of *SV*	John Davies' *Nosce Teipsum* (SR, Apr. 14) Bishops burn satires, including work by Marston, Davies and Guilpin (June 4)

Marston	*Events at MT and Elsewhere*
Marston receives payment from Henslowe for his portion of a play (Sept. 28)	
J. M. Sr. dies (Nov. 29)	John Davies' *Astraea* (SR, Nov. 17)
1600 Marston's *JDE* produced by Paul's boys (SR, Sept. 8)	
1600–1606 J. M. shares his father's old rooms at MT with Henry Hall, Reader, Bencher, and Treasurer of MT	
1600–1601 *Antonio* plays (SR, Oct. 24, 1601) for Paul's boys	Jonson's *Cynthia's Revels* (1600–01) (SR, May 23, 1601)
1601 *WYW* (my conjecture) (SR, Aug. 6, 1607) for Paul's boys; verses for Robt. Chester's *Love's Martyr*	Jonson's *Poetaster* (SR, Dec. 21, 1601) Dekker's *Satiromastix* (SR, Nov. 11, 1601)
1602	*Twelfth Night* produced at MT, (Feb. 2, 1602) John Ford admitted to MT
1603 Commendatory verses to Jonson's *Sejanus*	Jonson's *Sejanus* (SR, Nov. 2, 1604)
1604 *Malcontent* for Children of Queen's Revels and with additions for King's Men (SR, July 5, 1604)	
1604–1608 Shareholder in Children of Queen's Revels, for whom he wrote rest of plays	
1604 *Eastward Hoe!* with Chapman and Jonson (SR, Sept. 4, 1605); in trouble with authorities, possibly imprisoned for satire on Scots	
1605 *DC* (SR, June 26, 1605)	Gunpowder Plot (Nov. 5, 1605)
ca. 1605 Married Mary Wilkes, daughter of William, one of James I's preachers	
1606 *Fawne* (SR, Mar. 12, 1606); *Sophonisba* (SR, Mar. 17, 1606); *City Spectacle* for James and King of Denmark (July)	*The Fleir* by Sharpham (SR, May 13, 1606)
1607 "Ashby Entertainment" (Aug.)	Sharpham's *Cupid's Whirligig* (SR, June 29, 1607)
1608 Imprisoned in Newgate (June 8); sells share in acting company	

Marston	*Events at MT and Elsewhere*
1609 Ordained Deacon (Sept. 24); supplication to use Bodleian, Oxford; ordained Priest (Dec. 24)	
1610 Apparently living with father-in-law in Barford, Wilts.	
1616 Attacked and robbed in Knightsbridge, Essex, by Sir George Sandes (Aug.)	
1616 Incumbent of Christchurch, Hants.	
1617–18	Gray's Inns revels, including "Mountebanks Masque" (Christmas season, 1617–18)
1621 Mother dies	
1624 Son John dies	
1631 Resigns living at Christchurch, Hants.; apparently returns to London	
1633 Collected Plays printed by Sheares	
1634 Marston's will (June 17); dies in London (June 25); buried in Temple Church alongside father	
1657 Wife dies; buried beside husband	

Appendix C The Date of the *Antonio* Plays and Their Chronological Relationship to *Hamlet*

It would be useful to know the approximate dates of Marston's *Antonio* plays in order to speak more certainly about his artistic development. But the more important question of the priority of *Hamlet* or *Antonio's Revenge* is also involved. As G. K. Hunter observed in his recent edition of *Antonio's Revenge*, "The likenesses between *Antonio's Revenge* and *Hamlet* are too strong to be merely coincidental." [1] Four theories are possible about this relationship, and each has had some adherents. (1) Until recently it was generally held that both *Antonio* plays were written in 1599 and before *Hamlet* (generally dated ca. 1600–1601). Chambers, among others, accepted a passage in *Antonio and Mellida* (I, 52) as evidence for the early date:

> whose picture is this? *Anno Domini 1599*. Beleeve me, master *Anno Domini* was of a good settled age when you lymn'd him. 1599. yeares old? Lets see the other. *Etatis suae 24*. Bir Ladie he is somewhat younger. Belike master *Etatis suae* was *Anno Dominies* sonne.

Chambers comments, "I agree with Small, 92, that these are probably real dates and that the second indicates Marston's own age. As he must have completed his twenty-fourth year by 3 Feb. 1600 at latest, Part i was probably produced in 1599. The Prologue of Part ii speaks of winter as replacing summer, and probably therefore Part i is to be dated in the summer, and Part ii in the early winter of 1599." [2]

When R. E. Brettle discovered that Marston was actually born in 1576, Chambers' argument tended to be discounted, but it was revived when someone suggested that *"Etatis suae 24"* might mean "in his twenty-fourth year." Hunter has expressed a preference for this date for *Antonio and Mellida* in his edition of the play (p. x). He makes a further point which places him in some disagreement with Chambers concerning the chronological relationship of the two parts: "I cannot accept the common view that the reference to summer in the prologue to *Antonio and Mellida* and to winter in the prologue to *Antonio's Revenge* means that these plays were written for production in summer and winter. The Paul's theater was enclosed and lit by artificial light; the references are in fact to the climates of the two plays, to the masks of comedy and tragedy" (p. x).

Even if *Antonio and Mellida* had been produced in 1599, it does not necessarily follow that *Antonio's Revenge* must be so early. The Induction makes it clear that the sequel was planned but not yet written. Thus another possibility is (2) that *Antonio and Mellida* may have been written in 1599 and that *Antonio's Revenge* was written after *Hamlet*. [3] (3) Hunter raises the possibility (p. xx) that both *Antonio's Revenge* and *Hamlet* were influenced by the *ur-Hamlet*. [4] As he says, this would explain the close resemblances and (as he feels) the lack of telling verbal parallels

---

[1] Regents Renaissance Drama Series (Lincoln, Neb., 1965), p. xviii.

[2] *The Elizabethan Stage* (Oxford, 1923), III, 429–430.

[3] See Donald J. McGinn, *Shakespeare's Influence on the Drama of His Age Studied in "Hamlet"* (New Brunswick, N.J., 1938), pp. 15–24.

[4] See also J. H. Smith, L. D. Pizer, and E. K. Kaufman, *"Hamlet, Antonio's Revenge,* and the *Ur-Hamlet,"* *Shakespeare Quarterly,* 9 (1958), 495–498.

between the two revenge plays. (4) The final possibility is that *Hamlet* preceded both *Antonio* plays; it is for this view that I wish to argue.

There are several important objections to dating *Antonio and Mellida* before 1600. Chambers offers very strong evidence for placing *Jack Drum's Entertainment* in 1600. On stylistic grounds, *Antonio and Mellida* looks like a later work which refines material and techniques used in *Jack Drum*. But Caputi offers a further argument for the precedence of *Jack Drum*: "It is particularly unlikely that Marston would have apologized for the 'mustie Fictions' mentioned in *Jack Drum* after he had produced *Antonio and Mellida*." [5] To have done so would have meant publicly denigrating his first major effort and describing it in terms which are clearly inapplicable. Moreover there is a passage in the Induction to *Antonio and Mellida* (apparently hitherto unnoticed) which suggests a date late in 1600. The actors have been discussing crude acting and its spreading popularity:

> Truth: such ranke custome is growne popular;
> And now the vulgar fashion strides as wide,
> And stalkes as proud upon the weakest stilts
> Of the slight'st fortunes, as if *Hercules*
> Or burly *Atlas* shouldred up their state. (I, 5)

In the fall of 1600, the Admiral's Men opened their new playhouse, the Fortune, to rival the Chamberlain's Men's new Globe, whose sign, as we know from *Hamlet* (II.ii.378–379), showed Hercules carrying the globe on his shoulders. Thus this passage is saying that the vulgar, broad style of histrionics is "now" being as proudly practiced by the "weakest" company in its new accommodations at the Fortune as it is by the more firmly established company at the Globe.

This passage may also be specifically retorting to the one in *Hamlet*, cited above, with Marston saying that contrary to what Shakespeare claims, the public companies, regrettably, are thriving. Such an allusion is possible, but I believe that there are several far more likely references to *Hamlet* in *Antonio and Mellida*. The most telling of these occurs early in the play when the disguised Antonio appears before Mellida:

> What meanes these scattred looks? why tremble you?
> Why quake your thoughts, in your distracted eyes?
> Collect your spirits, Madam; what doe you see?
> Dost not beholde a ghost?
> Look, look where he stalks, wrapt up in clouds of grief,
> Darting his sowle, upon thy wondring eyes.
> Looke, he comes towards thee; see, he stretcheth out

[5] *John Marston, Satirist* (Ithaca, 1961), p. 261. On p. 260, Caputi is equally cogent in disputing Marston's alleged reference to himself as the "Poet Mellidus" in *Jack Drum, Plays of John Marston*, ed. H. Harvey Wood (3 vols., Edinburgh, 1934–1939), III, 221 — a reference which, if valid, would place *Antonio and Mellida* before 1600: "It is seldom pointed out that in the subsequent dialogue, a 'Musus' and a 'Decius' are also alluded to and that clearly these names were not derived from the titles of works." I would add that it would have been a most curious tactic for Marston to refer to himself by adopting a male form of his heroine's name. It is far more likely that he is referring to a poet who writes in a "sweet" style.

> His wretched armes to girt thy loved waste,
> With a most wisht embrace. (I, 28–29)

J. LeGay Brereton first noted the resemblance of this passage to the closet scene.[6] His persuasive emendation, by assigning parts of the speech to Mellida, makes its resemblance that much closer, but even as it stands a connection appears evident. Mellida's response is strikingly similar to the Queen's (III.iv.133): "Alas, I can not heare, nor see him [that is, the ghost]" (I, 29).

Marston's editor, H. Harvey Wood, suggested another allusion to *Hamlet*. After a page registers grief at his own sad song, Andrugio delivers a speech which resembles a famous moment in Hamlet's "rogue and peasant slave" soliloquy:

> Tis a good boy, & by my troth, well sung.
> O, and thou felt'st my griefe, I warrant thee,
> Thou would'st have strook division to the height;
> And made the life of musicke breath: hold, boy: why so? (I, 34)

(The last words indicate that the boy is crying.)

In one other possible allusion, Piero speaks to Mellida:

> Where's *Antonio*?
> Thou traitresse to my hate, what is he shipt
> For England now? well, whimpering harlot, hence. (I, 50)

A Claudius-like villain speaks to an Ophelia-figure in language reminiscent of the nunnery scene while referring to a Hamlet-figure on a ship to England.

If we include the "Hercules" passage from the Induction, there are then four passages in *Antonio and Mellida* which may allude to *Hamlet*. These cannot be explained away on the grounds of derivation from the *ur-Hamlet*. Such an argument has weight for a revenge play, but it does not make much sense for a play which is not related to the *Hamlet* story. On the other hand, literary allusions by the "apes" at Paul's to the latest hit at the Globe are precisely what we would expect. "Aping" was especially likely for Marston who imitated Shakespeare at least as much as any other Elizabethan dramatist; and there is no definite evidence that Shakespeare ever imitated him. Thus I favor a date for these plays which brings them close to the Stationers' Register entry of October 24, 1601. According to Chambers (II, 22), the policy of Paul's in its early days was to publish plays soon after production. All available evidence, internal and external, points to late 1600 as the earliest likely production date for the *Antonio* plays.

As an appendage to this argument, I want to suggest another way of reading the passage in *Antonio and Mellida*, quoted above, which mentions the year 1599 and the age of twenty-four. My notion is merely a tempting guess, but it stays closer to the text than does Chambers' theory. Although the speaker of the passage does not comprehend the figures, he is clearly looking at portraits of two men, one of whom is older. He concludes, "Belike master *Etatis suae* was *Anno Dominies* sonne" (I, 52). Late

---

[6] See "Notes on the Text of Marston," *Englische Studien*, 33 (1904), 225.

in 1599 Marston's father died. His will was proved on November 29, 1599; after October 7, 1599, Marston would have been in his twenty-fourth year. I suggest that this is what Marston is memorializing. It is not irrelevant to Antonio, who must cope with the problems of the world after the death of his father; and both Marston and Antonio were left with mothers named Maria.

Index